Selfless

Selfless

The Story of Sr. Theophane's Missionary Life in the Jungles of Papua New Guinea

Sr. Immolata Reida, SSpS

SAINT BENEDICT PRESS
Charlotte, North Carolina

Cover design by Caroline Kiser.

Cataloging-in-Publication data on file with the Library of Congress.

ISBN: 978-1-61890-120-0

Published in the United States by Saint Benedict Press, LLC
PO Box 410487
Charlotte, NC 28241
www.saintbenedictpress.com

Printed and bound in the United States of America.

To the Holy Spirit,
Who in His infinite wisdom,
has chosen to withdraw this work from
obscurity in the 21st century,
and to William and Louise Maier,
who raised their children to love
Christ and His Holy Catholic Church
such that their love would pass on
to future generations.

Table of Contents

INTRODUCTION

SISTER THEOPHANE, Inez Maier, was my aunt. I never met her because she had been sent to Papua New Guinea years before I was born, and died when I was barely eight months old. Yet her story was so amazing, and so far beyond the adventure of any other family member, that we all became very familiar with her exploits. This was seen to by my other aunt in the Maier family, Sister Rosalie SSJ, who was beloved by all and had an abiding interest in keeping the memory of her sister alive. Consequently, she collected and edited the fine narrative letters sent by Sister Theophane from the missions in Papua New Guinea to her mother (her father died in 1929) and to her brothers and sister. This collection of letters was published in limited edition by the Sisters of St. Joseph under the title "New Guinea Adventures." All the Maier children and grandchildren were encouraged to read this work in order to familiarize themselves with Sister Theophane's amazing life.

I was very familiar with this work, and in re-reading it again last year, I felt that the letters did not fully bring the story to life. It seemed to me that a biography of Sister Theophane was really needed to fully explain her life, and so I began to look for resources to begin this new work. After some internet searching I was amazed to find that someone had the same idea seven decades earlier, and had written an unpublished manuscript of the biography I had planned. I obtained access to this manuscript and was amazed to find not only a well written work, but an extensive bibliography showing at least two years of research that could never be duplicated because all of the witnesses were long dead. The author, Sister Immolata Reida S.Sp.S, who, although her contemporary did not know Inez personally, did an impressive amount of research. She interviewed the members of Inez's family who knew her best and obtained detailed monographs from them. She contacted priests, Sisters, friends, teachers, and fellow missionaries who knew Inez well and who could give detailed accounts of her life. The collective research is incredible, and was a remarkable find for me. It was clear that much of the work I had envisioned had already been done. My task became editing, some rewording, adding photographs, and preparing for publication, as well as preserving the priceless research that had been done.

The story is unforgettable and, at times so remarkable it is difficult to believe that this is the true story of a young woman who, from childhood, demonstrated an unwavering commitment to the ideal of missionary life. It is a story of understated suffering and total, passionate, self-giving love and devotion to the well-being of others. It contains humor, excitement, endurance and compassion; all driven by an unwavering faith in God, in a religious order, and in a timeless idea. This project was an inspiration for me and I hope it will be the same for its readers.

Gregory J. Maier
Potomac, Maryland

Preface to Original Manuscript

"SISTER, what virtue shall we say you practiced most?" Sister Milreda Zeller, pad and pencil in hand, was again teasing Sister Theophane about her future biography.

Sister Theophane eyed her inquisitor mischievously and replied: "Write that I loved animals!" Then, as though to confirm her statement, she hurried from the kitchen with leftovers from the meal for the dogs, cats, and chickens.

Sister Theophane did not know then that one day someone would reach across the Pacific to the South Seas in order to gather material about her. Neither did she dream that her passionate cry, "I want hardship!" would flash before the world as the summary of a missionary life heroic in the service of people in a remote land.

In these pages that life of missionary zeal, which burst into flame in the child of six and was quenched only when an intrepid Sister lay dead on the deck of a prison ship, is simply told. Sister Theophane's direction, "Write that I loved animals" has not been neglected—but there was more than that to tell.

Extensive use has been made of Sister Theophane's letters from the missions and of her diary notes. The diary itself fell into the hands of the Japanese and, though once recovered, was again taken and burned. No notes from it appear in the account of the last three years of Sister Theophane's life. When it is cited in the text, Sister Theophane herself states in the letter that she is taking notes from it. Letters cited, unless otherwise indicated, are personal letters addressed to the author. All other material about Papua New Guinea is taken from accounts of Sister Theophane's fellow missionaries.

I hope that deficiencies in style may be lost in the grandeur of the message held out to the world in the life of an American girl whose burning love led her over jungle trail and threatening sea in search of souls.

My sincere gratitude is extended to Sister Rosalie, S.S.J., elder sister of Sister Theophane, for invaluable aid in gathering material for the biography. Heartfelt thanks is also due to Sister Theophane's teachers, friends, and advisors in Rochester, New York; to the Holy Spirit Missionary Sisters who furnished material about Sister Theophane's postulancy, novitiate, and early religious life in the U.S.A.; and especially to Sister Ottonia, S.Sp.S., companion of Sister Theophane's Papua New Guinea labors. I further acknowledge my indebtedness to all who read the manuscript and especially to Dr. Cecil B. Williams, for suggestions and revisions of the text.

Sister Immolata Reida, S.Sp.S.
Holy Ghost Convent
Techny, Illinois
April 8, 1946

CHAPTER 1

Sacrifice of the Lambs

THE SUN rose with stunning beauty in the misty skies over the South Pacific. It was Sunday morning, February 6, 1944 and the people around the world were preparing to go to their churches to pray that the Almighty would spare them, and especially their loved ones serving in remote theaters, from the scourge of a brutal war that had enveloped the earth. Even the peacefulness of beautiful islands in the South Pacific had been shattered by the sound of exploding bombs as the relentlessly advancing forces of Imperial Japan ran into determined allied resistance.

The ever mysterious land, now called Papua New Guinea, had become the final extremity of Japanese advance. And it was here that the allied forces, particularly the American Air Force, began implementing General Arnold's strategy relying on air superiority to halt the battle hardened-Japanese military juggernaut. A key element of this strategy was the systematic destruction of Japanese coastal shipping, the principal means of military transportation in Papua New Guinea and the surrounding islands due to mountainous interiors and few reliable roads.

The Americans had recently supplied their forces with a new aircraft, the twin-engine Douglas A20G, often mistaken for the better known B25 Mitchell of similar size, but specifically designed for low level, direct attacks on surface targets. This bomb carrying aircraft was rugged, powerful, and especially equipped to strafe surface targets with a battery of six nose-mounted .50 caliber machine guns designed to enable the pilot to deliver withering, concentrated fire power on any selected target.

Pursuing the American strategy of destroying coastal shipping, twenty-nine A20G aircraft of the U.S. Fifth Air Force had attacked Japanese cargo barges at Kairiru and Muschu Islands near Wewak early on that Sunday morning, sending columns of thick black smoke billowing into the clear sky. The attack had been successful with a large number of barges and coastal craft sunk, and so the attacking aircraft, led by 90th Squadron's Major Michael Ellis, turned to begin the return flight to their home base. Just after the squadron formed up for the flight home, Major Ellis spotted a lone Japanese troop transport about six miles from Wewak churning through the blue waters a few miles off the Papua New Guinea coast. To Major Ellis, the transport, plainly visible at the head of a zig-zag wake, was an irresistible target of opportunity.

Brimming with confidence after the successful mission against the unarmed barges at Kairiru and Muschu Islands, Ellis decided to add to the success of the mission by making a pass at the transport, and if nothing else, expend his remaining ammunition. He radioed for his wingman to get out of the way, saying "I'll take it," advising that he would lead the attack on the transport.

Ellis banked the powerful A20G, pushing the yoke forward to begin a shallow dive and pointing the six machine guns in the nose of his aircraft directly at the transport. Pushing his throttles forward he accelerated the aircraft, now emptied of bombs, until he was approaching the ship at over 250 mph. He dropped to an altitude of barely 300 feet above the sea as he commenced his attack. Unlike the unarmed barges he had just finished bombing, this transport was armed with a pair of 25mm anti-aircraft guns, one located at each the bow and stern, both operated by veteran Japanese gun crews who had experienced numerous air attacks, including an attack on the previous day in which they had succeeded in shooting down an American plane. The Japanese gunner accurately tracked the fast approaching A20G and opened fire slightly before Major Ellis's smaller caliber machine guns were within range. Flying through the 25mm anti-aircraft fire, as well as a hail of mostly ineffective small-arms fire from a cluster of troops standing on the deck of the ship, Major Ellis triggered his six nose guns. The recoil of the six machine guns firing simultaneously shook the big plane and their staccato blast was clearly audible even over the roar of the twin 1700hp engines driving it through the air just above the transport. The short but lethal burst from Ellis' guns sent a storm of .50 caliber slugs into the lumbering ship and into the blur of humanity shrouding its deck. Within seconds the frantic action of the attack was over, and Ellis pushed his throttles forward to full power in order to pull away from the transport and its lethal air-craft guns as fast as possible. At this point he noticed the oil pressure in his right engine dropping and a wisp of smoke streaming behind that engine. His aircraft was seriously damaged and, although having lost one engine, was still flying. Ellis, employing his superior piloting skills, was able to keep the aircraft under sufficient control to make it to a nearby air strip where he managed to land, albeit with significant damage. In spite of the close call, Ellis had landed without killing himself or his crewman. He had not made it back to his home base, but was alive and no doubt quite satisfied that he had successfully completed his mission of delivering a serious blow to Japanese coastal shipping.

Back off the coast, within several minutes, more U.S. planes followed through in attacking the armed transport, each sending thousands more .50 caliber rounds slamming into the ship and its pitiful human cargo. Other planes were damaged by anti-aircraft fire before the 25mm guns were silenced. One A20G lost an engine cowling and bomb bay doors as it pursued such an aggressive attack, grazing the mast of the transport and streaking over the ship at the lowest possible altitude.

The transport, the *Dorish Maru*, although left smoking from two fires started by the strafing and with significant surface damage from the hail of American bullets, was still under power after the attack, and pressed on toward Kairiru and Wewak at a speed of about eight knots.

Below deck in the hold of the transport was a contingent of about one hundred veteran Japanese troops in addition to those that had been on the main deck. The surprising circumstance, certainly unknown to the American airmen, and initially unobserved in the furious exchange of fire, was that, in addition to the Japanese combat soldiers, the transport was crowded with civilian prisoners. The number was nearly one-hundred and fifty and was comprised mostly of missionaries of American and European origin, as well as some native New Guinean mission workers and their families, all of whom the Japanese were moving to prevent them from gaining access to advancing allied forces. Of the missionaries, most were Catholic and included priests and Brothers of the Society of the Divine Word, as well as the single largest contingent made up of Missionary Sisters Servants of the Holy Spirit, today referred to as the Holy Spirit Missionary Sisters or by the initials SSpS. It was this group of Sisters who experienced the largest number of casualties from the American strafing, suffering twenty-seven killed outright, and numerous others mortally wounded. As a result, the strafing of the *Dorish Maru*, while a minor loss for Japanese Imperial forces, was a disaster of monumental proportions for the SSpS—far and away the greatest single disaster ever to befall this order of faithful and committed Sisters, assigned to Papua New Guinea to announce the gospel of Christ, to educate, and to provide medical care. Innocent as they were, the cruel scourge of the world war had fallen violently upon their backs.

One of the many devoted missionary Sisters killed outright that Sunday in 1944 was a thirty-eight-year-old American born in Rochester, New York, named Sister Theophane Maier. Her family had named her Inez, but upon entering the SSpS, she selected as her religious name "Theophane" in honor of a French missionary priest, Fr. Theophane Venard who in the nineteenth Century was sent as a missionary to the Far East, and ultimately gave his life there.

Even as a youngster, Venard had dreamed of the crown of martyrdom in the service of the Church. Ordained a priest on June 5, 1852, he was sent to Hong Kong for language study, and subsequently to Tonkin, Vietnam, where he preached the gospel of Christ, an activity that was then a crime subject to penalty of death. Father Venard practiced his priestly ministry in secret for a number of years, but was eventually betrayed, captured by authorities, and held in a cage for two months, during which time he wrote to his family beautiful and consoling letters, joyful in anticipation of receiving his martyr's crown. He was executed by beheading on February 2, 1861.

In light of this history, "Theophane" was a very appropriate namesake for Inez Maier, no doubt the result of careful study and recognition of a kindred spirit. Also as a child, she had dreamed of missionary service in China leading to martyrdom. Rather than China, she was sent to Papua New Guinea, certainly as remote and mysterious as any place on earth, particularly in the 1930s. When Inez arrived there in 1935 as Sister Theophane, many of the locals had never experienced any form of civilization beyond the boundary of a few neighboring villages. Sister Theophane grew to love these people, and gave her life to the service of educating them in faith and bringing medical care to their remote villages. Often, by long rides on horseback, at night through driving rain, or by canoe voyages on wind swept-seas—sometimes by combination of both—she brought loving care and the message of the gospel to these people who lived mostly isolated from the outside world. Her story is one of passionate, self-giving love that is absolutely remarkable, especially in the context of a self-centered twenty-first century world. While it can be said that Sister Theophane lost her life in February of 1944, it cannot be said that the life of Inez Maier was taken at that time, because the truth is that Inez Maier had already given her life years earlier to service in the name of Christ, and the events of 1944 were not at all inconsistent with her deepest desires.

CHAPTER 2

First Steps to God

THERE WAS no scraping of feet, no restless moving or squirming. Forty eager faces were fixed on the young girl who had communicated to them some of the enthusiasm that flamed within her.

Sister Rosalie, who had known of her little sister's missionary zeal for the past nine years, hardly expected such an outburst of oratory, such pressing appeals, such demands for generosity in sacrifice. She had invited her little sister to speak to her class of fifth and sixth grade youngsters at St. Stephen's School, Geneva, New York. Sister Rosalie knew that it would do Inez good to give vent to the passion that was burning in her young heart and called for an outlet.

For a full half hour the young girl had kept this class captivated by stirring mission topics which she had gleaned from various reports and periodicals. Now she climaxed her mission talk with a call to arms.

> Christ didn't say, "If some of you would like to help, you could go to teach." No! His words are a command. GO TEACH! And don't think He was talking to the apostles alone. They heard, and went. They are long since dead; their share of the work is done. But there

> are still millions of people to convert. WE must go. Christ is commanding YOU and me—"Go, teach all nations!"[1]

Fire flashed from her eyes and earnestness glowed in her flushed face as Inez stepped from the platform, nodded to the children, and turned to the door. Sister Rosalie followed the young apostle into the hall.

"That was fine, Inez. Just listen to the buzz of excitement in there." She motioned to her room. "You surely got them started."

"You'll have to keep up the enthusiasm, Rosalie." Inez always forgot to add the "Sister" now that Rosalie was a nun. "Keep them interested in the mission banks, too, and let me know as soon as you need more."

Sister Rosalie smiled at the instructions. "I'll see you after school about three-thirty. See how you can entertain yourself till then."

"That gives me an hour and a half," mused Inez. "Okay. I'll see you later."

She left the school, and headed for the parish church. It would take but a few minutes to get home; so she could easily visit with Sister Rosalie for an hour and still have plenty of time for preparing the next day's lessons. Sensing that the church would be quite empty at this hour, she stopped in to talk things over with God.

Glancing out the window, Sister Rosalie caught sight of Inez's figure as it disappeared through the heavy oak doors. "Little missionary," she commented to herself, and her thoughts raced back nine years to Inez's first encounter with the foreign mission idea. She remembered well the day Inez had declared that she would go to China. But then, everything connected with her little sister was stamped indelibly on Sister Rosalie's mind. Her thoughts continued their flight now as she stood there in the hall. The years had rolled back to 1906 when she, Rosalie, was just a mite of seven. Once again she was living over a beautiful scene.

St. Michael's Church in Rochester, New York had been quiet and empty that Sunday afternoon in June. The sole occupant was the pastor, dressed in black and kneeling in the front pew. Occasionally he pulled out a big handkerchief and mopped the perspiration from his face, then reached into his vest to look reprovingly at an old silver watch. With a bit of an impatient shrug he replaced the watch for the third time. It was hot in the big church, and the glaring sun that streamed through the high windows offered no relief. As it came down in shafts of purple, red, and green, the spell of beauty that it threw over the empty pew was lost on the pastor, who plainly was waiting for someone.

As though it were a signal for action, Father Horgather rose instantly when the heavy side door creaked. He flipped open his ritual on the Sacraments to a page that was yellow and a bit ragged. Four pairs of little hands helped to push open the huge door and there on the step stood Mr. Maier with a white bundle in his arms and a gleam of fatherly pride in his eyes. The priest stepped out, and his face reflected the joy that beamed from that of the happy parent. A hearty handshake, a word of congratulation, and Father Horgather led the family and relatives into the church.

"And you'll call her?" he queried as they entered the sacristy.

"Inez," piped a shrill, thin voice. Rosalie was not going to have anybody make a mistake about that name.

Mr. Maier put his hand on his little girl's head and confirmed her statement. "Rosalie likes the name, and we thought St. Agnes would make a fine patron.[2] We'd like Louise, too, for her mother."

"Inez Louise," Father Horgather repeated the name as he adjusted his purple stole. "The sixth Maier baby to be baptized," he commented and smiled into the curious eyes that watched his movements with unfeigned interest.

"Yes," agreed Mr. Maier, "and one is already safely home."

"Richard was just a baby when he died," explained Rosalie. "And he's an angel now."

"And you remember all that?" There was more of a tease than a question in the priest's face.

Five year old Rufus gazed in wondering admiration at Rosalie, but Ray's and Gerard's glances, fixed on their little sister of seven summers, were not entirely approving. After all they were older than she—one and three years respectively—and they should be the ones to supply such information from the family chronicle.

Having finished vesting, the priest led the group to the baptismal font. With rapt attention the four little Maiers watched the ceremony. They almost giggled when the baby showed her disapproval of the salt put on her tongue, but Mr. Maier's quick glance in their direction had immediate effect.

The exorcisms were over. "Inez Louise. . . ." The children pricked their ears and nudged each other when they caught the words. "Inez Louise, I baptize thee in the name of the Father and of . . ."

Inez screamed her protest as the cold water trickled over her forehead and down her face. Silently and invisibly the Triune God took his abode and made his indwelling within the infant's bosom the life of the Trinity throbbed—deep and strong and free. Another Maier baby had become a Child of God and was duly registered as the latest parishioner of St. Michael's.

The Maiers were a comparatively new family in the parish, though they were one of the oldest families in Rochester, New York. With pride Mr. Maier pointed to his ancestors among the founding families of the city. After his marriage to Louise Michels in 1895, William Maier had settled down with his young wife in St. Joseph's parish, where the funeral establishment, begun by his father in 1872, was flourishing. William Maier and his brother Edward took over the work.[3] Their home was pretty, but small. Yet, it was the best thing to be found at the time.

Before long the patter of little feet was heard in the house, and William responded with a thrilling heart to the call of "Papa!"

When Gerard was three and Ray was looking to his first birthday, a baby girl arrived. Rosalie was just two when the doctor came again to the Maier home. After he left, the tiny girl poked her thumb curiously into her baby brother's cheek until the new arrival voiced his protest. Rosalie found that little Rufus had quite a voice!

After the birth of the fourth child, William Maier had seen the need of a larger home to accommodate his growing family. He found a beautiful site on Clinton Avenue opposite St. Michael's Church. There he had erected a large white house and the necessary buildings for his funeral establishment. With pride, William Maier brought his wife and family to the new house on Clinton Avenue in the early spring of 1903.[4]

Mrs. Maier took to the neighborhood at once for it promised to be a scene of constant activity, and there was nothing Louise loved so much as people. While William preferred retirement from the noise and bustle, his pretty Swiss wife yearned for company, laughter, and joyous socializing. Long after he was settled in his funeral home, William still dreamed of one day taking his family to a farm on the outskirts of the city. But while he dreamed of fields and wide open spaces, Louise gloried in her home here in the very heart of the bustling eastern city. From her front window she had a full view of St. Michael's school and rectory just across the street. Over to the left, partly hidden by the stone wall of the church, was the Sisters' Convent. The Sisters used the back entrance, but Louise occasionally caught sight of their white wimples as they crossed behind the church to the schoolyard.

From triple windows of the living room, even while busy at work, the young wife could see her husband in his office at the Maier Funeral Home adjacent to the lawn. Behind the funeral establishment was a lot used for the horses and carriage barns. The stables with their big black and white teams were to give intense joy to Inez until they reluctantly gave way to modern invention.

Hardly had Rufus completed his second year when little Richard came to rob him of his honor as baby of the family. But when Richard neared his second birthday, he did not prove to be the herald of new offspring. Instead heaven claimed its own. Death visited the Maier family, and the young Father went sadly to his funeral home to select the smallest coffin for his baby of twenty-one months. The next day a pair of snow-white horses walked slowly down Clinton Avenue.

Sorrow was but a year old in the Maier home when God blessed the family with another baby girl. Little did the fond father dream that the mite whose lusty cries he tried to soothe would raise her voice until it should reach to the end of the earth, proclaiming the truth of Christ to the farthest nations. When she came quietly on the twenty-sixth of June in 1906 to begin her short earthly sojourn, no one suspected what great things God had planned for the last of the Maier children. Born on Tuesday, Inez was christened the following Sunday and received Agnes, the virgin martyr of Rome, as her patron.

An addition at the dinner table meant another mouth to feed, but the new baby had a surprise in store for the family. Indeed, her coming was the opening of a new episode in the life of the Maiers. When Mrs. Maier nursed her youngest, Inez was content. But the day came when Mother filled a bottle with milk and carefully closed the diminutive hands around it. Rufus and Rosalie stretched over the side of the cradle to see Baby take her first meal alone. Inez fingered the awkward thing curiously, then began to suck. Her little face screwed up in disappointment, and she promptly removed the deceitful nipple. With vigor and perseverance, she tugged at the rubber stopper until it yielded and the cradle was deluged in milk. Surprised and chagrined Inez wailed her indignation.

Though the first performance was amusing, when Inez repeated the act each time she was given her milk, Mrs. Maier became worried. The only solution was to fill the bottle with water—this alone seemed to satisfy. "But babies don't live on water," argued Mrs. Maier, and off she went with her problem child to the family doctor.

"Give her air and sunshine and don't worry about her," advised the doctor; and he smiled at the determined blue eyes which searched his face with distrust. Baby thrived on her strange diet, and though never chubby, she was a veritable powerhouse of energy. Swift of movement and ever on the lookout for excitement, she proved a constant source of concern to her mother as she toddled through the room pulling things down and climbing up to those that wouldn't come down to her. She was a quaint little human—with glossy silver white hair and dark eye lashes shading liquid blue eyes that glowed with excitement. Her skin was tanned by long hours in the sun, for a great part of her day was now spent tramping outdoors among the flowers, poking her fingers into the blossoms as she confided her secrets to them.

To her grandmother's pained surprise Inez appeared one day at the kitchen door with a fist full of lily buds which she presented guilelessly to her astonished Mother. Grandmother's prized fuchsia met with the same disaster when it dared open its flaming blossom to the sun. Nature called to this eager, inquiring child, and she roamed for hours around the yard chattering to the trees, flowers, butterflies, and especially to the big shepherd dog who poked his nose through the fence to lick her hand. She was not afraid of him, despite the fact that in clumsy affection he sometimes knocked her over and scratched her face.

Mrs. Maier watched Inez develop with a faint uneasiness. This child was different. How? She could not tell. Mr. Maier saw the frown on Louise's face and grinned. "She's different all right. She's my kiddo!"

Inez responded with alacrity to her father's deep affection. She loved this big, strong man who was never too busy to examine any bit of weed or flower she might bring for his inspection. When she spied him coming from the office, she scurried over the lawn for a hug and a ride on Pop's shoulder. She gurgled with delight when he tossed her high in the air, and she never evinced the slightest fear of his inability to rescue her on the downward flight. Once, however, something went wrong and Pop just managed to grasp her little arm when she came down. Inez shrieked as the arm was wrenched out of place. Tiny as she was, she saw her father's pain at having hurt her, and she placed her hand confidingly in his while Mother scolded. Though tears welled up in her eyes as the doctor jerked and pulled to adjust the arm, she managed to keep a smiling face turned toward Pop. After that unfortunate incident she was content to ride on Pop's shoulder or on his foot with her hands firmly wound around his knee.

What a delight for her when Pop perched her on his shoulder and took her to the stables. Inez reached down unafraid and patted the moist nostrils of the horses, giggling when they sniffed at her little hand. She knew she loved them, even more than she loved the big shepherd dog next door. Whishing that she too was a horse, Inez would go toddling on her hands and feet around the yard. The empty space beneath the stairs leading to the second floor became her indoor stall, where for hours she would play, often standing still as she had seen the horses do in their stalls. One day, while watching George give the horses fresh green grass, she decided to try out the horse diet on herself. Her stomach, however, refused to cooperate; after much coaxing, Inez acknowledged her strange meal of grass. Once her grass venture failed, Inez contented herself with pretending that she was driving a team, rather than being the team herself. Early each morning she would hurry to the back porch, climb on the cot there, and hold the cords from the window blinds, briskly commanding, "Giddi-up!" How disappointed she was if she found that the cot had already been folded up for the day! That meant her horses wouldn't get out to work.

Rufus and Gerard and Ray enjoyed their little sister—she was very much a tomboy. But Rosalie, a prim little lass of ten now, was puzzled. With heroic abandon she offered her little sister one of her dolls for amusement. But, after a thorough examination of the proffered toy, Inez put it aside with disgusted finality. She never condescended to examine a doll again, much less consider it a probable plaything.[5]

Inez's uniqueness puzzled Mrs. Maier as she watched her youngest opening up as a wild flower of the field—loving freedom, reaching out ever into the unknown, scorning fixed convention. Even as she wondered if Inez would ever be like Rosalie, she admitted to herself that it could never be. Pretty dresses, for one thing, were a torture to the little tot.

At this time Rosalie was attending classes in aesthetic dancing, and Mrs. Maier had hopes of influencing Inez. She informed the little adventurer that she was to accompany her big sister to class. Dressed in a dainty plaid taffeta, Inez dutifully gave her hand to Rosalie and went along to her first and last dancing lesson. Her sullen little face spoke openly of her disgust at such profitless amusement. Rather than touch the silk dress she wore, she stood with her back against the wall, her hands held far from her. Rosalie, deeply embarrassed, found it hard to explain to her teacher and classmates that her little sister abhorred pretty dresses and dainty dances. No amount of coaxing succeeded in bringing the sullen victim into the dance. Inez never attended that class again.

Mrs. Maier wisely acknowledged that Inez was different. Henceforth she dressed her ugly duckling in a plain gingham frock and fastened her hair with a plain ribbon, letting it fall over her shoulders. Content, Inez ran out to play with her toys—her toy house was the enchanting world of nature.

Rosalie had not given up, however, and to Inez's horror, she cornered her little sister. After much patience and many threats, Rosalie succeeded in getting Inez into a snowy white frock. A delicate bow of pink gathered the silken locks atop the youngster's head, but beneath the pink bow a pair of blue eyes shot out their disgust and revulsion. "Now just sit here on the front step and watch the people go by," instructed Rosalie. Inez was not born to watch life go by, and the front step was deserted as soon as Rosalie was in the house.

Soon the yard became too small. There were no more things to discover. Inez's desire for adventure stretched beyond the gate where the world seemed to be moving so quickly. Aware by now of Inez's wanderlust, Mrs. Maier had instructed the milkman and grocery man to be careful about fastening the gate. But one day a new grocer came and Inez didn't miss her opportunity. The gate swung open, and—Nabiscos under her arm—she trotted off down Clinton Avenue in search of adventure. It did not take more than an hour to bring the wanderer back home, but in that time Inez had bartered her Nabiscos for a "baloney" sausage and met most of the neighborhood dogs.

A world of new adventure opened up to Inez when Mrs. Maier held her little girl of four on her lap and unfolded to her, in simple phrases, the thrilling story of God's love. Once she had learned that the Friend of children was "tabernacled" in the great stone church across the road, it beckoned mysteriously. She would stand and gaze in wonder at the great angel with the sword, high up in a niche in the gothic steeple.

And when Rosalie and the boys were off at school, Inez stole across the street to the side door of St. Michael's. She had heard Pop say that the front doors were locked during the day, and besides she could never reach the high latch. On tiptoe and with a mighty effort, she managed to pull open the heavy side door. The quiet, dim interior enchanted her. From each stained glass window the form of an angel looked down. She knew the angels, and that one was always with her. This knowledge gave her a feeling of delightful mystery. Sometimes, too, from the choir loft high above came the strains of Gregorian music. Was it here that was born that love for the chant which was to mean so much to her strong soul?

Once the supernatural world was opened to her, Inez with characteristic eagerness, gave herself entirely to her new discovery. The Prisoner of the Tabernacle drew her almost imperceptibly to Himself. She spoke little of her excursions to St. Michael's, probably because she feared her liberty might be curtailed. But the Sister who cared for the altars found the little girl there often, wandering along the aisles, examining the glowing pictures in the great stained windows, or sitting quietly listening to the organist as he rehearsed his chant for the coming Sunday Mass.

Inez was taking her first steps toward God, and she walked happily on the heavenly road.

CHAPTER 3

NEW HORIZONS

DEDICATED to the Blessed Virgin at birth[1], Inez was still wearing Mary's colors when the day came for her to start school. Mrs. Maier fastened a blue ribbon in her hair and gave Inez her last word of instruction.

"Now see that you do just what Sister tells you."

"Yes mamma," came the quick reply, and Inez skipped off to join Rosalie and her brothers.

Mrs. Maier wondered how this little vagabond of hers would ever become reconciled to the four walls of a narrow classroom and the still more cramped precincts of a seat and desk.

But anything new fascinated Inez, even if it proved painful. Several weeks before she had paid her first official visit to the dentist and then spent the afternoon swinging on her front gate proudly informing passersby, "I had an ul-cera-ted tooth, and I'm old enough to go to the dentist now!"[2] Where other young children hesitated fearfully, Inez forged ahead, eager to see what secrets lay in the unknown. With this spirit of eager anticipation, she began her days at school.

She soon discovered that, though there were only girls in her room,[3] discipline was very rigid. Yet, while her little body squirmed, her mind was eagerly venturing into new places. It was while learning her prayers that she made a startling discovery. With something akin to horror, Inez found that not all people believed the same religious truths as she. Her dismay was great when she learned that George, one of her father's grooms, was not a Catholic. It did not take Inez long to come to a decision. She at once began a systematic campaign of conversion, and every day after school she trudged to the stables in order to teach George the truth.

A pious and ardent Protestant, George was not disturbed in mind by the little zealot, but to humor her he repeated the Hail Mary after her until he could say it alone. Inez was jubilant, and when her convert refused to exhibit his newly acquired Catholicism before an audience, she merely attested, "That's because he is shy when people are listening."[4] George lived and died a staunch Protestant and, humanly speaking, Inez's first missionary venture was a failure.

Though school was proving much more interesting to Inez than Mrs. Maier had dared to hope—she knew her daughter loved her freedom and the great outdoors—Inez occasionally found it hard to sit still and do her work. One evening Mrs. Maier was disturbed when her little girl did not appear promptly for her afternoon lunch. In a deserted classroom sat the young culprit, frowning at the serene Sister who corrected papers at the desk. Pouting, Inez looked dejectedly at her own paper where, with effort, she had twice scrawled: "I must learn my lessons." Suddenly a triumphant expression came over her gloomy features. Deftly, she filled the remaining twenty-three spaces with neat ditto-marks. Inez then folded the paper, placed it on Sister's desk, and with a guileless smile bade her teacher "Goodnight."

"I finished the paper with 'bitter marks,'" she told Rufus as she recounted her unpleasant experience. There were so many things that her big brothers taught her, and she found she could utilize much of this information now that she was in school. The "bitter marks" were just one instance of useful knowledge gained from older brothers.[5]

Just when the school routine was threatening to become monotonous, Father Horgather came to the little girls' classroom with exciting news. A Missionary Sister was coming to speak to them about work among the unbelievers of China and Japan. The girls cheered, then sat back and waited for the visitor.

After what seemed an hour—but was ten minutes—Father Horgather opened the door again and brought in Sister Mary Louise. Inez sat very still and listened in rapt attention. It seemed her whole body was intent on hearing what Sister Louise had to say. Sister Louise spoke of the Chinese babies who die without Baptism, of the boys and girls who are very poor and look to the missionaries for food, clothing, and instruction. With skilled and sympathetic insight into the misery of China's destitution, the Sister portrayed for her audience drastic scenes of poverty, and of mental and moral distress. She asked the children to pray for the poor children of China and to save their pennies to help the missionaries.

When she concluded, the girls rose and applauded with perfect etiquette, and their teacher was proud of them. But one little girl did not hear the hands clapping. She hardly even saw the Sister bow deeply and leave the room. No, Inez stared fixedly before her. A startled circle of faces turned her way when her voice rang out firmly, almost defiantly, "I know what I'm going to do!"

Inez heard very little of what Sister Mary Gregory taught the rest of the afternoon. At the first sound of the bell, her books slid into her desk, darted from the classroom to the side door of St. Michael's, and squeezed through. Breathless she knelt at the communion rail and in an audible whisper confided her secret:

"Jesus, I'm going to China! I'm going to save souls for You!"

She was only six and the smallest first grader in Sister Gregory's room, but she recognized and ardently embraced her life's work—that day she became a missionary.[6]

A few minutes later Inez burst into her family's kitchen, startling her mother. "Mamma, a missionary came to school! She says there are millions of boys and girls in China who don't know a thing about God. And, Mamma, I'm going to China! I'm going to be a missionary!" She gave Mother a big hug.

Bit by bit Mrs. Maier extracted the details of Sister Louise's visit. Rosalie and the boys strolled in later and confirmed Inez's report, as the Sister had also visited their classes. They planned to save their spending money for the unbaptized babies in China, but Inez's heart alone had been lighted by a torch of zeal that was to burst into greater flame each day until it consumed her very life in the service of others.

Some weeks after Sister Louise's visit, Mrs. Maier looked out the kitchen window and dropped the beans she had been stringing. One of the big rocks bordering the drive to the funeral parlor was moving over the lawn.

"Inez," called the frantic mother, as she surmised what locomotive power was moving the rock.

From behind the rock emerged a mite of a girl, her sleeves rolled up for action.

"Baby, what on earth are you trying to do?"

"I must get strong now so I can go to China when I'm big!"[7]

Although Inez's answer was emphatic and determined, her mother thought it best for her to find new means of developing her physical strength.

Her missionary calling was duly discussed with "Moddy," one of the Miller boys who was also in the first grade and often played with Inez. Together they spun dreams of heroism among people in strange, far-off lands. There they would work and die—she, the sister; he, the priest.

"And Moddy," Inez clapped her hands in gleeful anticipation, "we'll bring millions of people to God!"

As well as she could, Inez reconstructed Sister Louise's religious garb, and in the ludicrous result she paraded through the house informing the family that she was now to be addressed as "Sister Mary Moddy." She paid high tribute to her fellow missionary by taking his name.[8]

The missions became for this child of six the sunlight of her days and a heaven of guiding stars by night. The thought of saving people in foreign lands was like a leaven that permeated every conscious act. Every penny she received for sweets, and also many nickels and dimes which she coaxed from her generous father found their way to the China Mission Box in the first-grade room at St. Michael's.

School took on new interest when Inez began her preparation for First Holy Communion. With a comprehension far beyond her seven years, she threw her energies into the task of getting ready. For her, the prospect of a beautiful white dress and dainty veil had no attraction—they were necessary evils. Rather, her eagerness and preparedness were centered on the supernatural. Solemnly Inez listened solemnly while Sister Gregory told her that she must fight against her stubbornness and not give in when she felt sulky. Having three older brothers who did not spare their sister when it came to teasing, gave Inez perhaps more opportunities than she craved to battle against her nature.

Once, when Rufus had evidently exhausted her patience, she changed her tactics and planned a neat revenge. After Mr. Maier left with the horses, Inez stealthily locked the stables and buried the keys. Then she tried to amuse herself, waiting with questionable glee for, the commotion. Mr. Maier returned and the horses stamped and neighed before the locked doors. Inez looked up from her play and with feigned matter-of-factness reported, "Rufus took the keys."[9]

With one look at Rufus's bewildered face and a glance at the clouded eyes of his little pet, and the wise father knew the truth. With indignant tears Inez finally confessed, dug up the keys and took the proper reward for her misdeed.

The story reached the ears of Inez's teacher, and the zealous Sister launched a relentless campaign against the newly discovered bad habit. "Lying lips are an abomination before God," she quoted. The words made a lasting impression on Inez's sensitive soul. Years later Inez recalled vividly what it had meant for her to conquer her tendency to lie. "I set to work," she said, "but, believe me, it wasn't easy because I had formed a habit."[10]

Thus she prepared for her beautiful First Communion Day. There was much work to be done, she knew, but did not shirk from it. Sister Gregory had sounded the child's heart and found that the love of God in that young soul was strong enough to overcome human weakness. When she found the child at fault, she had but to remind her of the Passion of Christ. Inez, docile even while humiliated, would acknowledge her fault, and after school she hurried to the "Tabernacled Friend" to pour out her contrition.

"Jesus, You suffered all that for me, and I have caused you pain."[11]

When spring blossoms opened to the sun, Inez's heart opened to welcome her Sacramental God. There were no remonstrances that morning when Mother dressed her in a delicate frock, silk stockings, and a flimsy veil. Her mind was absorbed on His coming and, for once in her life, she donned her finery without protest.

The little missionary had much to confide to the Prisoner of the Tabernacle whom she had learned to cherish. But mingled with her mission desires and plans was one deep longing. She hardly knew what it was or why she wanted it so much, but that day she asked for the grace of martyrdom. Though God was working wonders in her soul, Inez guarded her secret. Her clear blue eyes were the only window into her soul, for she offered no further information as to her life of friendship with her God. Years later she was to write to a bereaved relative: "On the altar of your heart lay quietly the offerings of pain, disappointment, and trial."[12] This reticence was always her way, and even those who thought they knew her perfectly got only a glimpse of the deep spiritual life that throbbed behind an exterior that gave no clue to the secrets it veiled.

Despite her inner growth toward holiness, Inez remained a rambunctious child. On the evening of that beautiful First Communion Day Inez deliberately raveled her silk stockings against the rough legs of a chair, Mrs. Maier sighed and admitted that Pop's kiddo was still the same clothes-hater. With admirable sweetness she had borne with the stockings all day, but now the day was over and she made certain that it would be the end of the detested silk hose.[13]

Several weeks had passed, yet Inez never spoke of approaching the Holy Table again. Mrs. Maier was puzzled and worried, but she wisely waited. The days had lengthened with late spring, and when Mother arose to get breakfast for the family, the sunbeams had long ago invaded Inez's bedroom. She was not surprised then, to see the youngster out in the yard marshaling the dogs of the neighborhood for a circus. The early riser had managed to dress herself, though not in an approved fashion. But Mother did not protest, because after breakfast Rosalie would help her make Inez presentable for school.

Then one day Mrs. Maier was accosted by the parish Sisters. After a few remarks, one Sister said delightfully, "Oh, how we do enjoy your little girl at Mass and Communion each morning!" Amazed, Mrs. Maier gasped, "You don't mean Inez is appearing like that at the communion rail?"

The Sisters said they just waited for Inez to come marching up to the front, her button-down-the-back dress in reverse to facilitate fastening, her hair ribbons serving as improvised garters below her knees, her tousled hair topped with her hat askew.[14] Though that marked the end of Inez's unique costume, the morning visits with her Divine Friend were not interrupted, and Inez's mother sighed in relief and bewilderment.

Inez was always glad when vacation days came, because then she could give undivided attention to her pets and her botany collection. In one corner of the backyard she had set up a rabbit coop of orange crates. Nearby was an old tub with a number of turtles and, skimming among them, Juniper, her black water-snake. Inez's rabbit and turtle families were prospering and multiplying until an unforeseen setback impeded further development. Mr. Maier had to keep his grounds neat and trim, yet his love for both Inez and her pets made him look benignly at the miniature slum district in the corner.

One day tragedy struck the establishment. More interested in her turtles than her toys, Inez had left shovel, balls, and blocks strewn over the lawn while she busied herself constructing a merry-go-round for her turtles. On the end of a string each turtle paraded around an old broomstick stuck in the ground. Entirely absorbed in her new invention, Inez came running when Mother called somewhat impatiently and scolded her for the disorder on the lawn.

"Now put all your playthings in the lowest drawer in the pantry. The long things you can leave on the shelf of the basement stairs."

"Yes, Mamma," Inez rejoined meekly and hastened to carry out the order before dark.

The next morning when Mrs. Maier screamed on meeting Inez's hungry turtles as they emerged from the lower pantry drawer, Inez was bewildered. In the wake of the turtles came Juniper, slithering in from his shelf on the basement stairs. In tears the little girl protested that she had simply followed directions and put all her play things in the pantry and the cellar.[15] Nevertheless, the unfortunate outcome of the misunderstanding changed her mother's attitude toward Inez's pets, and restrictions were laid down. But Inez's love for animals suffered no diminution, and any stray cat that fortunately attracted the girl's attention found a home and staunch defender.

As long as her mothering instinct was restricted to insects and small tetrapods of the animal kingdom, no violent protests were made. One day, however, Inez spied a bedraggled horse at the corner of Clinton Avenue. For an undecided moment, the horse-lover gazed awestruck at the emaciated beast hitched to a dilapidated fruit cart. Then she stepped up, took his halter, and turned determined steps toward the big white house.

"Mamma," she called, "look what I found. Can I keep him if I feed him up good?"

A gasp of horror escaped Mrs. Maier when she beheld Inez dragging the old horse and cart into the back yard. Before the astonished mother could find her voice, loud shouts reached her. From the street came rushing an irate vendor, headed for a confused little girl. Mrs. Maier snatched Inez into the kitchen and closed the door. The child stood, perplexed by the strange turn of events.

When the excitement subsided, Inez had learned a lesson from her mother, namely, that horses were not found like bugs and birds and caterpillars. Wide-eyed but docile Inez listened and formed her concept of mine-and-thine.[16]

Throughout her life, horses always fascinated Inez. One day, a frightened coal dealer rushed toward her when he saw the child with her arms around the neck of one of his heavy work horses.

"For Gods sake, little girl, get away from there," he yelled. "That horse stamped a man to death last week!"

Inez turned reluctantly. "Oh, all right. But I like him just the same," and she patted the man-killer's nose in farewell.[17]

It was a big day for Inez when Mr. Maier brought home a sleek, graceful mount for Rosalie. With patience, Pop tried to convince his kiddo that she was too small to have a horse of her own. Wistfully she watched him help Rosalie into the saddle. When she saw her big sister gingerly take hold of the reins, Inez's heart almost broke with longing. After many lessons, Rosalie learned to ride well, but Inez persisted in her efforts till she finally persuaded Pop to let her try. Her legs closed over the horse's quivering flanks and she leaned over and patted his neck. A quick tremor of joy crept over the horse; he tossed his head. These two were friends.

Yet Inez never got a horse of her own. One day, to her dismay, she saw her father examine a large black limousine. No one had to tell her what that meant. Usually vivacious, Inez began to mope about the house. She evaded the stables, as if that might help her to forget that her father's horses were offered for sale.

How often as a tiny girl she had pilfered dried apricots and had stolen away to give Daisy and Molly a treat. Inez loved this team—milk-white, alert, and proud. Others dared not come near the stalls, but she crawled, unafraid, between the dangerous hoofs to deliver her tidbit or to retrieve the baseball which had rolled into the danger spot. Now the horses were to be sold. Inez's grief was profound.

When one afternoon a prospective buyer appeared in Mr. Maiers absence, Inez stepped forward.

"I'll show you the team," she stated, "but I hope you won't buy it!"

While Mrs. Maier and the older children stood by, the young horse dealer brought Daisy and Molly from the stables, exhibited them with pride, led them quickly back to their stalls, and hoped they had not made too fine an impression.[18]

But the horses had to go, and when they did, Inez spent more time on Clinton Avenue watching for the farmers who came in to the city for groceries. While the farmers did their shopping, Inez petted their horses at the hitching posts along the curb. Should any driver have a check rein on his horse, Inez would promptly loosen it and wait for the offender to return. Then she fearlessly delivered her instructions:

"You shouldn't use a check rein on your horse. It hurts him to pull a load if he can't bend his neck."[19]

It was hard to escape the pleading of those innocent blue eyes filled with sympathy for the horses she loved. Her concern in this line was just one of the many phases of her zeal for reform. Wherever she noticed disorder under any aspect she strove to better conditions.

One day while shopping with her mother, Inez noticed the grocer give a heavy load to a delivery boy. She stepped up and told the grocer in firm language that such a load was far too heavy for a young boy to carry. He was not acting rightly in asking so much of his help. The grocer winked at the embarrassed mother and accepted Inez's rebuke.[20]

This reforming spirit continued in church where Inez insisted on absolute silence and reverence. Young and old might expect a reproving glance or a word from the ardent reformer if they whispered or talked in her vicinity. Nothing that Mrs. Maier could say made Inez see that sometimes it is best to keep silent, though reform might be needed. Strangely enough, few took offense at the young girl's reproof because there was so much sincerity in the correction and such guilelessness in the child who gave it.

Inez's love for the truth gave her mother great satisfaction, and she thanked God for the graces God was giving her child. Yet time and again Mother and Father discussed this youngest child with some apprehension. Mother exclaimed:

"I tell her again and again what a refined young girl Rosalie was at her age, but it makes no impression. She does not want to be a refined young lady."

"Never mind," soothed Father. "She likes to help me line coffins and she needn't be a refined young lady for that."

Sister Gemma, too, noticed Inez's boyish ways, and reminded her that a growing girl should cultivate gentle, refined manners. "But I've always been with my brothers," Inez defended herself. Nevertheless, she tried to placate her mother and teacher, but her efforts met with little success. It was hard to change the quick, almost hasty step, the swinging arms, and the boyish toss of her head.

Everyday life seemed to hold out more to her, and her soul sang as she saw her grammar school days coming to a close, daily bringing her nearer to the fulfillment of her dreams. Ransoming foreign mission babies in China was woven like a golden thread through each day. Inez had not allowed herself sweets or gum for years because a greater cause claimed her spending money. When the New York State Regent Examinations in Geography came around in spring, Inez saw a chance to give China the profit. Under her leadership, Sister Gemma suggested that they have a drive for foreign mission babies and by their sacrifices obtain the blessing of God for the coming examinations. Knowing that a prize always supports generous giving, Inez obtained a box of candy to be offered in a raffle. The raffle brought in a neat sum for the Chinese babies, and strangely enough, Inez won the candy. Did she pass it around? No, she hurried to Sister Gemma and asked if it could not be put up for raffle once more. The next winner followed suit, and the Chinese children benefited much from that year's Regent Examinations at St. Michael's.[21]

Sister Gemma was not surprised when Inez lingered in the classroom one afternoon after the others had gone. She toyed with the pencil on Sister's desk and then said abruptly, "Sister, do you think

I'd make a religious?" As was her fashion, Sister Gemma encouraged the girl to pray for guidance especially during the precious moments after her daily Holy Communion. Inez was satisfied for the time, but when she found herself alone with Sister Gemma the topic of her vocation often came into conversation frequently.

"I want to be a missionary Sister and go to the foreign fields," she said.

Sister Gemma was happy to have Inez's aspirations tending in that direction, and she pointed out that her Sisters were laboring in Puerto Rico. But, though Inez thanked her for the information, she said she never felt she would like to go there. Her thoughts were all centered on China. On learning of these desires, Sister Gemma offered to help Inez find an order that conducted missions in the land of her dreams.[22]

It was Inez's turn to be surprised when she learned that Rosalie was preparing to enter the novitiate of the Sisters of St. Joseph. For some reason, Inez had not connected a religious vocation with her older sister, and now she often sat and gazed at Rosalie with mingled awe and respect. One day, after observing Rosalie for some time, Inez exclaimed: "Rosalie, I want all your dresses when you go!"

Mrs. Maier was speechless when the request was relayed to her. What had come over her younger daughter to change so suddenly her disgust for clothes?

There was a reason behind the peculiar request. Inez hoped, in her childish reasoning, that wearing Rosalie's clothes might communicate to her Rosalie's precious vocation. To make certain of the vocation was worth any torture that the dainty frocks might occasion. After weeks of coaxing, Mrs. Maier gave in to the plan and worked over several of Rosalie's prettiest dresses which Inez wore with unusual fervor.[23]

Though for Inez her big sister's entrance was an exciting and interesting event, Mrs. Maier felt keenly the parting from Rosalie. Rosalie had graduated from Nazareth Academy High School the previous year, and the year she had spent with her mother had especially drawn the two closer together. Hence on the first night when Rosalie no longer joined them at the supper table, Mrs. Maier felt very lonely.

Before retiring she came to the bedroom her two girls had shared, to see if Inez too felt lonesome. Inez looked quite content with her book and her mother questioned softly: "Inez, won't you miss Rosalie very much?"

Inez was surprised at the query. "No," she answered laconically, "now I can have the whole bed for myself!"[24]

Mrs. Maier regarded her young daughter in puzzled silence. Then she left the room, her thoughts in turmoil. Rosalie was gone, but she was safe now. Inez had always been different though. To the worried mother this young girl seemed like a rushing mountain stream, frolicking past the attractions of life in a consuming desire to reach a goal. A goal that appeared to the mother as strange and vast and limitless as the very sea in which the mountain stream is lost! The distressed mother saw only the restless waters, the disregard for things others cherished, the constant urge to reach a faraway dream! It was Pop, rather, who, watching that young life race on its way, listened and heard the song of the brook—and he knew the song was true, and deep, and beautiful.

CHAPTER 4

At Nazareth

THERE WAS music in Inez's heart that September morning in 1920 as she turned in at the drive to Nazareth Academy.

"Four years here," she mused, "and then—" She was conscious of timid steps close behind her. She turned to the stranger and asked, "H'lo. Freshman?"

"Yes," came the answer. "I—I feel scared. I've never—"

Inez cut short the remark. "Neither have I. Let's see what it's like." And she transferred her books to her other arm as the slight Italian girl joined her. "My sister, Rosalie, went through here, and she thinks it's pretty classy. We'll find out soon."

When they reached the entrance the two girls indulged in a hearty laugh; they had just discovered that both were named "Inez." It was the beginning of a warm friendship.

After her graduation from St. Michael's the previous June, Inez had spent no time searching for a suitable high school. She took it for granted that she would follow her sister to Nazareth Academy. So she said goodbye to the Notre Dame Sisters and to the school where her zeal had lit a glow of missionary enterprise. However, more than once she returned to St. Michael's and spoke to the children, encouraging them to install a Mite Box for the missions in each classroom.[1] She feared lest their enthusiasm should wane, and while she could, she would keep the fire burning full flame.

She was at Nazareth now—a freshman in a dark uniform neatly set off with a white collar. Her uniform pleased her because it took away the constant torture of frills and ruffles.[2]

The change from grammar to high school was considerable, but Inez gradually adjusted to the new schedule. She was certain that she preferred this new arrangement with its greater freedom and independence in her work to her former way of life.

Inez had not been at Nazareth many weeks before upper classmen were pointing out the new student. Though not shy, Inez shrank from honors because they had no place in her plans. Yet, her individuality would attract others and a certain amount of popularity invaded her school-life. If she was conscious of it, she never allowed it to influence her actions. Her intimate friends were the few who succeeded in recognizing a precious jewel behind a boyish exterior.

Neither did the unusual freshman long escape the notice of Sister Marcella, the tall, dignified, polished Sister who filled the office of principal. Exquisite in manner, Sister Marcella's great aim was to train Nazareth girls both interiorly and exteriorly, so that anyone might recognize a Nazarite student by her refinement and culture. When Inez swished past her door, Sister Marcella raised her eyebrows and mentally resolved to make a lady of this new student. Had she only known that for fourteen years Mrs. Maier had been laboring in vain for the same ends!

Though she would not admit defeat, after some months that Sister Marcella realized that she had met her match. Unbiased in her judgment, she saw in Inez a girl of high principles; of an unusually keen appreciation for the simple things in life; and of an almost reckless disregard for established convention. After some unlooked for incident the puzzled principal would try to imagine what unpredictable idea might next occur to Inez.

One day Sister Marcella stepped outside to catch her breath. Whistling, Inez came up the stone stairs, one hand filled with books, the other affectionately rubbing the head of a big collie which kept pace with her.

"Good morning, Sister," Inez broke off her tune.

"Good morning, Inez. You don't mean to take that dog into the building?"

Inez had reached for the door and the collie pressed close to her, avoiding the black habit of the Sister. "Why not?" queried the girl in evident surprise.

"Because it just isn't done here!" The Sister's voice became severe, but the icy tone was lost on Inez.

"I can't see what harm he'll do just sitting beside me," she countered.

In an unmistakable imperative the principal laid down the law and left Inez mournfully stroking an equally mournful collie who realized he wasn't wanted.[3]

From the corner of the yard, Inez Poericca, ("Little Inez" they called her in, contrast to "Big Inez") watched the struggle. "Inez," her tone was affectionately impatient, "Won't you ever learn? Why do you do those things? You irritate Sister Marcella by staying around the biology lab after school. Now you irritate her with this dog. No wonder she is always scolding you!"

Her hand still on the collie's head, Inez gave her friend a long, level look. Then she spoke with deliberateness:

> If you think you are doing the right thing, you ought always to go ahead. It doesn't make any difference whether you make a few enemies. If you have no enemies you have no character. Anybody that has character makes some enemies. You just mustn't be afraid to make them.[4]

"Little Inez" patted the collie in farewell; then gently pushed him down the stairs. Linking her arm in her friend's, she pivoted her into the building. Once in the corridor, they cut their conversation short because silence was enforced in the halls.

Despite her precociousness, Inez gave herself unstintingly to her studies because she had decided that they were important for her future work. However, she found no such incentive when it was a question of social activities. So the dances and parties received the same scorn she had meted once out to her first lesson in aesthetic dancing. Sports, however, were a different matter. Sports helper her develop the physical strength she would need for mission work. A single criterion was applied to the varied aspects of these four years: "Will this be of help to me as a missionary?"[5]

This singleness of purpose had made the young girl serious, yet—almost paradoxically—a witty humor leavened her conversation in and outside of class.

Though as a freshman she did not take biology, Inez's interest in animal and plant life soon attracted the notice of Sister Agnes Patricia, and the teacher gladly accepted the girl's eager assistance in keeping the laboratory in order.

"Once Inez took over," asserted Sister Agnes Patricia, "I could leave the room in any state. I knew it would be in perfect order before she left for home."[6]

During the term that Inez studied biology, countless new specimens of flora and fauna appeared in the laboratory as witness of her enthusiasm for that subject. Sister Agnes Patricia recalled: "I had to be very careful not to mention what would be nice to have in the room. If a remark slipped, the object would be there—a plant, a picture, a new specimen."[7] At Christmas a canary and cage came as a gift for the laboratory. Inez had taken up a collection for the bird, but had supplied most of the cost herself.[8]

Even after her own course in biology was finished, she still hurried to the laboratory daily after dismissal to supervise the cleaning. But it was not only the plants, turtles, and fish that attracted Inez to the biology room. She had discovered in Sister Agnes Patricia her ideal of a religious.

High school days were slipping by quickly, and along the road were scattered happy memories. Among them was Inez's first retreat at Nazareth. A Jesuit, Reverend J. Johnson, conducted the exercises, basing them on "the love of God portrayed in the Passion of Christ."[9] It was an echo of Sister Gregory's admonitions, and once more Inez's heart yearned to requite the abundant love of the Son of God.

Visiting with her sister, now Sister Mary Rosalie of the Sisters of St. Joseph, Inez discussed the retreat. Then with rare openness she revealed her inmost yearning. "Rosalie, do you think that the graces of God which I have squandered in my past might already have lost for me the grace of martyrdom which I covet?" There was pleading in the questioning eyes turned toward the young Sister.

"God grants the grace of martyrdom to whomever He chooses, Inez. One cannot actually merit it." Then the shadow of mischief crept into Sister Rosalie's voice as she added, "Besides, I don't think your past shows up as a very dark picture."[10]

Other retreats followed, and each left the young girl reaching higher, straining after the fullness and richness of the Christian life. There was about her now a sense of constant, almost impatient, waiting. It was as if she were listening backstage for her cue and could not hide her eagerness to be playing her part.

One thing cast a shadow over her high school days. She found no organized mission work at the Academy. But then, by this time she had become accustomed to finding people more or less indifferent to the great cause which burned like fire in her soul.

In touch with every center of missionary activity, Inez contacted two seminarians from St. Andrew's Seminary in Rochester where the senior class had a flourishing unit of the Catholic Students' Mission Crusade. She invited two enthusiastic seminarians to come to Nazareth and have a talk with Sister Teresa Marie, who, Inez thought, would be best able to influence the principal.

Sister Teresa Marie was won over and quite enthusiastically presented the idea to Sister Marcella. But the principal was conservative, slow to begin something new which she was not sure was going to be a success. She feared lest new activities overburden the already full curriculum. The project was unusual and unexplored. Sister Teresa Marie understood the principal's hesitancy in such a matter and relayed the news to Inez. "Inez, I think the idea is a bit premature here at Nazareth." Her voice was sympathetic, for she knew how much the venture meant to this lover of the missions. "Sister Marcella has not given her approval."

Inez thought for a moment, and then muttered almost to herself, "We're not beaten yet." She threw back her head and with a voice weighted with determination, resolved: "I'm going to try once more. I'm going to Sister Marcella!"

Before Sister Teresa Marie could restrain this impetuous resolve, Inez had turned the corner and—in a manner Sister Marcella would never have approved—bounded up the stairs to the principal's office.

Disappointed but unconquered, the young missioner met Sister Teresa Marie a few minutes later.

"We can't make a go of it now," she admitted, "but we will when the time is ripe!"[11]

That time was not to come while Inez was at Nazareth. With no definite organization it was difficult to systematize work for the missions, but Inez had an eagle-eye for every opportunity to further the cause. In English class she based her speech on needy missions; in Assembly the missions were chosen for her address. But only after she left Rochester did the seeds of mission zeal, which she had planted with so much enthusiasm, almost suddenly spring to life and develop into a mission activity that would have startled Inez herself had she foreseen it as she stood in the Principal's office.

Sister Marcella relinquished her dream of making Inez a "lady," but the principal's joy was evident when the student government claimed Inez as president. There would be order; of that the faculty was confident. With a sense of deep satisfaction the teachers noted a striking improvement in discipline after Inez had organized her workers. At class intermissions she herself supervised in the main hall, and students filed past with military exactness when they sighted the president on duty.[12]

One day Beatrice McGrath, an intimate friend of Inez, stepped out of rank, presuming on the strength of her friendship as an excuse for disregard of the rule. Inez turned to her pal and in cold, even tones let her understand regulations. Beatrice winced beneath her friend's reproof and a surge of hurt feeling liquidated her smile. However, before she reached the end of the hall, her lips parted and she said to no one in particular, "What a brick! That's a character!"[13]

But Beatrice was one of the few who understood. To most of the students Inez seemed odd. She gave as little of her time as possible to a simple toilet. She wore her hair severely drawn back, cosmetics were entirely ignored, and beautiful clothes meant nothing to her.

Though to Beatrice, Inez's ascetical appearance made no difference, she thought it might be well if her friend catered just a bit to popular taste. "Why don't you curl your hair?" she suggested.

"I couldn't make myself look better," retorted Inez carelessly. "The Lord made me homely and that's the way I'll stay."

The next day, however, Inez came with her hair curled. She admitted that there was some room for improvement, but that it was "not worth the fuss!" So she never "fussed" again.[14] There were more important things in Inez's life than hair, clothes, and frivolous vanities. Her interests during those four years reached far beyond Nazareth's halls—missionary dreams embrace the world!

Unable to organize a mission unit at school, Inez worked all the more energetically at home. To the China Mission Bank was added the Brick-for-Bengal venture, designed to aid missions in India. Visitors to the Maier home seldom left without contributing to either of the banks. Rufus jokingly complained that he could not enter his own home without paying a fee, and his friends submitted graciously when Robin Hood waylaid them at the entrance, robbing the rich to help the poor.[15]

However, Inez's father was her surest aid in the financial troubles that his kiddo encountered. Forced to remain in his office late into the evening, he had invited a number of his friends to spend these hours with him. Gathered around the office table the men played poker and refreshed themselves with beer. From this group sprang the Mission Poker Club which devoted the entire proceeds of its "pot" to the cause of the missions and to poor parishes in Rochester. When Inez was in need of special assistance, she offered to serve refreshments to her father's friends, and at the close of the evening triumphantly carried off the "pot" to send to her poor missioner.[16]

Knowing that the teaching of religion would play a major role in her future life in foreign fields, Inez eagerly took over a catechism class in a nearby parish. Every Saturday she was on duty to instruct the class, and on Sunday morning she saw to it that they were at Mass and behaved as little Christians should. Her duly registered pupils knew better than to try to skip class. They would rather forfeit two hours of play than face Inez later and try to manufacture a plausible excuse for missing class.

But because Inez's zeal was not satisfied with "well enough", she was always on the lookout for new recruits. Alone or accompanied by one of her friends, she canvassed the neighborhood of the parish, ferreting out delinquents who should be attending instructions.

One afternoon Arlene Oster, a classmate, was picking her way through a filthy alley, trying to keep up with Inez who didn't seem to have any trouble making her way through tin cans and mud puddles. Indiscriminately Inez visited each family and inquired about children for Sunday School. The two girls traveled from tottering shack to crowded tenement.

Then in response to Inez's knock, a door flung open and a dark haired, gleaming eyed Italian, brandishing a long knife over his head bravado style, invited them in.

Arlene gasped and drew back. Inez bowed graciously and began to step forward. This was too much for Arlene, and she frantically clutched her friend's arm drawing her to the porch.

"Oh, Inez, don't go in there!"

Inez turned to her with an amused smile, and then stepped confidently into the house and stated the purpose of her call. The fierce-looking host grinned at her courage, and before she left Inez had enrolled four more pupils for religious instructions.[17]

The class was progressing admirably until the cold weather set in. Coming from poor families the children were scantily clad and shivered in the unheated classroom. Inez went to see the pastor, but he was not willing to heat the building on Saturdays. She pleaded, but to no avail, and the weather continued to grow colder.

When Sister Marcella announced in the morning assembly that the bishop would come to Nazareth in the afternoon, Inez's eyes lit up. The day dragged on until the signal finally came and the students, under Inez's supervision, filed noiselessly into the hall to form a guard of honor for their guest. Inez stood with her classmates and waited.

After a few minutes, Bishop Hickey came down the hall with his councilor. He smiled at the students as he passed. When he neared her, Inez breathed a prayer and then stepped out of rank into his path. Sister Marcella gasped. The girl dropped to her knee, kissed the prelates ring, and then told him, of her problem with the cold classroom. "I know that you can help me," she said.

The bishop smiled into the earnest eyes, assured her that she would have her heat, and raised his hand in blessing as she slipped back into rank. Turning to his councilor the bishop commented, "If Rochester only had more of her kind!"[18]

During her senior year Inez found a new outlet for her zeal. A city-wide organization known as the Big Sister Movement—modeled on the Big Brother Movement—had been started by a Jewish community, but, by 1925 several new groups were invited to pool their efforts with the first organizers. The Catholic Women's Club of Rochester joined the organization under the leadership of Mrs. Keough, who acted as chairperson for this division. Each division worked among members of its own denomination, and workers were usually over twenty-two years of age.

The project won over Inez as soon as she heard of it, and though but sixteen, she approached Miss E. Mertz, secretary of the Movement, and requested membership. Miss Mertz, conscious of Inez's age, was reluctant to accept so young a worker, but the eager desire to serve and the pleading earnestness of the young girl tipped the scales in her favor.

After due consideration Inez was given a "Little Sister." The unfortunate girl came from a family whose lifestyle was far below that of the average working man. Both parents came from Europe and had low standards of living. Inez's charge was the eldest of six children.

Mrs. Keough watched her new worker to see how she would meet the challenge. A few general instructions were given, but personal initiative was paramount to her success.

Utterly disregarding personal comfort and taste, Inez tackled her job. Frankly, yet tactfully, she pointed out to her "Little Sister" the advantages of cleanliness, order, and regular habits. A friendship, made possible only at the price of complete self-giving on the part of the "Big Sister", was established. As though she had nothing else to do with her spare time, Inez gave herself to her friend. After a time, she began instructing her in Catholic doctrine because she saw that the young girl's lack of appreciation for the faith sprang primarily from ignorance of its beauty.

Mrs. Maier gave Father a worried glance when Inez brought other friends similar to her "Little Sister" to the house. But Mr. Maier reassured Louise as he knew his kiddo and never feared for her strong character.

Since Inez's mind was always focused on the missions, her "Little Sister" soon shared her interest. When Inez revealed her plans, the "Little Sister" suddenly resolved that she too would be a Sister. Miss Mertz, however, demurred when Inez told her of her charge's aspirations. "Isn't she too young to know what she wants to do?" questioned the director.

"I knew what I wanted to do years ago and I've never changed my mind," observed Inez.

"But don't you think," continued Miss Mertz, "that it would be wise to help her for a number of years in her own home so that she can gradually elevate the standards of living and help her younger brothers and sister?"

Inez thought for a moment. The argument was sensible. Miss Mertz studied the girl's eyes as they looked off into space. Suddenly their blue glowed with an inner fire, and Inez's voice was soft and beautiful as she breathed: "When God calls, our plans mean nothing. Neither I nor you have a right to question further."[19]

Christmas brought more activity into already crowded schedule. The Nazareth girls packed baskets of food for the poor of the city, and Inez was chosen to care for Annunciation Parish, a poor Italian district in which she had been interested for some time. She piled the baskets into her Father's big limousine, and, with Rufus to the wheel, and started off. The car sloshed through muddy streets, cut with deep dangerous grooves. What had at first been distasteful to Rufus soon intrigued him, and he gallantly accompanied his sister to the tumble-down shacks. Late in the evening, bespattered with mud, the two giggling charity workers recounted their experiences to the family, not omitting the hour they spent getting Father's car out of a mud hole.[20]

In spite of all these interests, Inez found time for daily Mass and Communion, and for a private hour of adoration on Saturday. For several years she met her classmate, Arlene Olster, every Saturday afternoon at the cathedral where they prayed together, went to Confession, and then rented horses at the stables on Culver Road. The rest of the afternoon was spent in the country. In Inez's mind there always lurked the thought, "You might need this in the missions! Learn it well!" And thus she became an excellent rider.

There in the free open country the girls sang as they rode because their hearts were full of melody. Inez unfolded her dreams of strange lands, uncivilized peoples, and death for Christ on the mission field. Arlene understood her friend's glowing zeal and she loved the fire that flashed from Inez's eyes. She herself had her own aspirations to become a Carmelite in service to the Master.

These two friends, so radically different, were one in their passionate love for Christ. It was about this time that Inez secured permission from her confessor, Father Keenan of the Cathedral, to make a private vow of chastity.[21] Her mind was made up; she knew what she wanted.

She spoke to very few about the blue habit that had won her heart. Her mother and father were by now accustomed to the stream of mission literature that came for her, but lately they noted that regular letters were coming postmarked "Techny."

Brothers from the Society of the Divine Word often visited

at the Maier home when they were on business in the East. Inez knew that they worked with the Holy Spirit Missionary Sisters in the missions. One day she came upon Brother Homobonus sitting alone in the library. "Brother," she broke in on his reading, "Do you think they could use somebody like me in Techny?"

Brother Homobonus affected a business like attitude and surveyed the girl from head to toe, then asserted, "I'm sure they could!"

"Then, I'm going to Techny," decided Inez. "But," she added, "I'm not telling anybody yet."

Brother Homobonus chuckled. "Um-hm—well, I'll be looking for. . . ."

He broke off as Mr. Maier strode into the room. Inez greeted him with, "I've just been entertaining your company, Pop."[22]

CHAPTER 5

GRADUATION AND THE LAST YEAR AT HOME

EXCITEMENT reigned at Nazareth; it was the first week of June, 1924, just seven days before commencement. The days before graduation were filled with plans for the future. Inez's scholastic record had been excellent, but her thoughts were far from college. To her surprise and chagrin she found herself the recipient of a New York State Scholarship.[1] From the Catholic Charities Organization came a still more alluring proposition. The organization offered to finance her studies at the Catholic University of America if she would major in the social sciences and after her graduation take up social service in Rochester.[2] Inez thanked them warmly, but in the same breath refused their offer.

"It is not according to my plans," she stated simply.

She then explained her purpose in taking up work with the Big Sisters. She felt that such experience would be of great value in her missionary career, and she wanted to be the best missionary possible.

Shortly before graduation Inez approached her father. "Pop, would you have enough money to pay for my dowry if I should join the Holy Spirit Missionary Sisters?"

Mr. Maier wheeled toward her, and in his face Inez saw surprise, affection, pain, and resistance struggling for mastery. "What? What?" His voice was hoarse.

Inez felt herself weaken before this unexpected reaction from one she idolized. Yet she continued quickly, "They are the oldest and most firmly established missionary order in America. I graduate in June and the next entrance day is in October. That would give me . . ."

"Nothing!" her father broke in angrily.

"But, Pop," pleaded Inez, "you let Rosalie go!"

"Rosalie didn't have any crack-brained ideas about running off to nowhere to live with primitive people. Rosalie is here in Rochester. Rosalie stayed at home one whole year after graduation."

Inez's courage broke and she burst into tears. By turns she tried pleading, coaxing, and even storming about lack of mission zeal, but Mr. Maier was adamant.[3] The struggle was trying on both father and daughter; so he put an end to it.

"You stay here at home for one year. Then you may go. Don't ask me again till next June. Spend the year as you like!"

The answer chilled Inez's heart, but her practical nature soon gained control. A year at home? What would she do? She shied away from the scholarships, for that would mean a delay of four years.

Sister Gemma talked the problem over with Inez, and the latter finally decided to put in a year of nurse's training. She had no special liking for the profession, but she knew that medical training would be an invaluable asset in her future missionary work.[4]

St. Mary's was the only Catholic hospital in Rochester, and Inez made arrangements without delay to begin her training the following September. But what of the months between graduation and fall? Father George Weimann, Inez's friend and confessor, suggested that she take charge of the annual summer school at his new parish. She would have five or six young ladies to help her, he said.

So when the caps and gowns were packed away, Inez lost no time in getting on with her new project. During the first weeks of June, Inez finished up a class, and by the last week of the month she faced 125 youngsters in the basement of Annunciation Church. She had spent days cleaning the room, and on the opening day it looked quite cheerful, despite the poor furnishings and the lack of sunlight. Coming from extremely poor homes, the children did not mind sitting at the old tables that had been pushed together to form a square in the middle of the room.

For Inez, this experience held the thrill of mission life. Mixed with the Italians were some thirty-two Ukrainians and a smattering of other children of foreign parentage.[5] In the classes, held from nine till eleven-thirty in the morning, the children were taught catechism and learned their prayers in preparation for receiving their First Holy Communion, although they were not admitted to the sacrament until they had further instructions from the pastor.

Inez's zeal and success were recorded when the annual statistics for the parish were compiled. These records show that the number of Confessions and Communions went from six-hundred and fifty in the year of Inez's term in summer school. The following year the number rose to one-thousand two-hundred and fifty, pointing to the enduring influence of the youthful missioner.[6]

When the five weeks were up Inez approached the pastor with a problem: she had nothing to do for a month before courses began at the hospital. Father Weimann was just then a very busy man. He found himself pastor of this once-mission church, and he had no idea who his parishioners were, or where they lived. And here was a young girl, fired with energy, looking for something to do.

"I can't hang around the house," complained Inez. "I've got to be doing something to make the time go."

Father Weimann studied the eager face and, seeing firmness of mind, he broached his problem. "This parish—if there is one—is not organized. I have no idea who belongs to me. There are no records here, nothing." Inez listened intently. "If you wish you can spend that month taking up the census, rounding up the flock. But I'm warning you, it'll be a hard job, and maybe an unpleasant one sometimes."

"Just what I want," exclaimed Inez with eyes alight! "When can I start, and how do I go about it?"

The next day Inez was "on the road." Pad and pencil in hand, she went down one street and up the next. Some people were courteous and friendly; others were not. Men who had lived without the Church for many years were jolted by this firebrand who denounced their careless, sinful ways. With the accuracy of a businessman Inez tabulated her findings: Marriages, Baptisms, Holy Communion, Confirmation, Attendance at Mass, Frequenting of the Sacraments. With the courage of a Priscilla she lashed away at lazy habits, drunkenness, and neglect of duty.

With unusual insight Inez understood the handicaps of foreigners becoming acclimated to a new country. She realized that sordid living often sprang from poverty and not idleness. Her genuine love for the unfortunate parishioners was so evident to them that they soon received her with complete confidence.

However, Inez was fearful to go into detail about her "parish work" with the family at home. The neighborhood of the "parish" did not have an enviable reputation and more than one parishioner carried a gun—a fact that did not intimidate Inez but would have greatly disturbed her father and mother.

The days were hot, the dirt roads dusty, the fields high with weeds. At the end of eight hours of walking, Inez was tired. Toward evening one day Rufus was horrified when he spied his sister on a corner in the precincts of the parish, thumbing a ride. He drove up with the big car and gave her a lift, but that ride was costly to Inez.

When the family was together that evening, Rufus told of the incident and voiced his concern for his sister's safety in such surroundings. Mrs. Maier was aroused, and the next half hour a heated debate ensued. Inez pleaded. There were souls to be saved, marriages to be rectified, men and women to be reclaimed for the Church, and the sick, the hungry, and the poor to be helped.

The opposition was great but Inez held her own against it, but she finally chose to compromise. Since her father would no longer allow her to go alone to the parish, Rufus, now Mr. Maier's assistant at the funeral home, was to accompany his sister on her rounds. What at first struck Inez as a curtailment proved an unlooked-for advantage; because Rufus brought the car, they made good time. Besides, food and clothing for the poor were conveniently packed in the back seat, which was much easier than carrying the cumbersome packages. Once again Rufus was soon attuned to adventure and helped Inez raid the family larder and wardrobe to feed and clothe the unfortunate poor.

Inez's desire to help others was not limited to her assigned job. In the little mission church the priest was using a badly worn chair for a celebrant's bench. Inez took the problem to St. Joseph. On the fourth day of the novena to the Saint, she confided to her mother, "St. Joseph has five more days to round up a celebrant's bench. I'm sure he won't let us down!"

That night Mr. and Mrs. Maier were sitting in the library. "The child has such faith," urged Mrs. Maier, "Can't you do something?" Mr. Maier smiled. "I guess the poker club can take care of it!" Before the novena was finished, a big box came to Annunciation Parish, and a beaming pastor used a new celebrant's bench on the following Sunday while a young girl thanked St. Joseph.[7]

The Saint's success made Inez more observant of needed articles at the parish. Soon there was a new gold chalice on the list for St. Joseph. It came![8] If Inez suspected where St. Joseph kept his bank account, she gave no indication of it when she beamingly told Pop of her powerful patron.

Inez finished her census work in four full weeks and happily presented her report to the pastor. Now, it was finally time to get ready for St. Mary's Hospital. From the busy delightful summer the missioner had one lasting keepsake—hay fever![9]

In early September of 1924, Inez was a freshman once more, this time in the uniform of a student nurse. However, she made no secret of the fact that she would stay at St. Mary's only one year and had no intention of completing her training there. For this reason perhaps, Inez never felt quite at home among her classmates. There were other differences too. Some of the young girls were quite frivolous and did not take their studies seriously enough, at least so it seemed to Inez.

During those first months there was little ward duty for the new recruits and much of their time was spent in class. Inez dug earnestly into her *Materia Medica* because she knew that this was something that would be of value to her one day in the missions.

When Inez was given floor duty, her usual eagerness for activity became more evident. She was never as happy as when the lights flashed on and off in her hall and she could be on the go. She did notice that some lights, not in her part of the hall, remained unanswered. Something within her could not let her rest as long as a single light flashed, so she answered many more calls than were really hers. Never before had she complained of tiredness and she would not do so now. However, one day her strength gave out and she collapsed while attending a patient. The head nurse realized then that Inez had been doing far more than her share of the work.[10]

After some weeks on the floor, Inez was transferred as an aid to the surgical department. She enjoyed her new work and walked into the operating room eagerly to help Doctor Simpson. Intently she followed the procedure, anxious to learn all she could for the future. But when something went wrong, the doctor indulged in strong language, and Inez looked up surprised and hurt. When the lurid language continued, she walked to the doctor and looked at him seriously. "Such language," she said without fear, "is not proper for a doctor and in this place."[11] Doctor Simpson grinned a bit sheepishly and continued his work in unusual silence.

No matter where she was, Inez could not help being the missionary. Like so many before them, her classmates, too, were impacted by her example. Though the hospital regulations made attendance at Holy Mass obligatory on only Sundays and Holydays, Inez saw to it that her group was at Mass each morning. She did not preach religion, but it was so much a part of her that one could not associate with her without catching some of her enthusiasm.

When she was not in class or on duty, Inez could be found in the chapel. Because she was often up to mischief, her companions would tease her and say she went there to think up new tricks. Though she constantly spoke of the missions, she was careful to keep the topic rather impersonal and many of her classmates were surprised when they heard of her plans. Her great ideal of being a missionary ruled her life, but she was quick to see that others might not share her inclinations, and she wisely refrained from trying to shape others according to her pattern. Even though she saw that most of her companions were not meant for religious life, she did not on this account lose an active interest in them. Instead, her one thought was to help them meet good, Catholic boys.

Inez knew that her mother loved parties. She therefore took advantage of this for carrying out her matchmaking scheme among the nurses. Mother heartily agreed to entertain Inez's fellow nurses over the weekends. So whenever permission was granted, Inez got busy. While Mother prepared refreshments, Inez's brothers were charged to round up young men for the party at the Maier home, Inez herself brought a bevy of young nurses. She was always there to see that everything went well. Humorous incidents abounded.

Inez had her eye on a young doctor, Elmer O'Brien, whom, she thought, would make a fine priest. She was jubilant when he came regularly to the weekend parties because she had a good chance to give him some advice on how to go about entering a seminary. The young enthusiast did not know that it was a rather vivacious little student nurse named Lizette that drew Elmer to the parties. She found that out when the two were married![12]

At times suitors came to see Inez, but she dismissed them with little ceremony, or, if they looked promising, she delivered her pocket sermon on the merits of the priesthood.[13]

The year passed quickly—more quickly than Inez had dared to hope it would. She had learned much, and she was grateful for that. But the all-important thing was that the long months of waiting were over. Pop always kept his word; she knew he would keep it now.

She found him in the library and came up quietly behind him and placed her arm around his shoulder. "Pop—it's June," she whispered softly.

The eyes that looked up to her were filled with pain, but in them Inez read consent. She stooped and kissed his upturned face.

CHAPTER 6

NOVITIATE

INEZ LEANED her head against the seat and stared into the inky blackness outside. "We must be out of Rochester by now," she surmised. There were no lights flickering in the distance.

She closed her eyes. How quickly the last months at home had fled. She could hardly believe that it was October and she was on the train, bound for Techny, Illinois. With a twelve-hour ride ahead of her, she had time to think, and her thoughts raced from one hectic day to another.

She would never forget the strange shopping she had done with Mother that week. Articles of clothing she had never seen before were neatly packed now in the big trunk traveling west with her.

She thought of those last visits with the Sisters. Sister Gemma had been so happy the day they said good-bye, as if she herself were starting out on this grand adventure with Inez. The visit with Sister Agnes Patricia would remain a treasured memory. Inez smiled when she recalled the Sisters's delight on receiving as a parting gift the beautiful crucifix for her rosary.[1] Inez felt a deep gratitude toward Sister Agnes Patricia. When opposition to her missionary calling waxed strong at home, the troubled girl wondered if she was doing right in causing her parents so much grief and creating such unrest in the happy family. "Do you think I should really go ahead with it," she had questioned, tears glistening in eyes that betrayed her painful struggle.

Sister Agnes Patricia had said nothing for awhile, but when she spoke her words were unequivocal: "Yes, Inez. Go ahead! God's call comes first."[2]

Inez smiled as the words came back to her, but the smile was faint. How she had needed those words these last days. It all seemed so unreal.

For years she had dreamed of this. Then when the trunk was packed and her preparations almost finished, a strange dullness gripped her soul. What was all this? Why was she packing? Techny? What of Techny? Suddenly she realized that it meant nothing to her. How had she ever imagined that she wanted to go there?

Frightened, Inez had fled to the feet of the Lord. But the glistening doors that held her hidden God were dull, cold, forbidding. A sense of complete desolation closed in and she groped blindly for reassurance. Her spiritual guide listened sympathetically to her broken sentences. It was not an indication that she had no vocation, he told her. She should go ahead with her plans calmly and resolutely, and if indeed it should be true that God was not calling her to a missionary life, he would manifest this clearly.

Inez listened to the steady voice that spoke words of consolation. The counsel she received did not relieve the strange confusion of her mind, but it did strengthen her will. "I'm going ahead," she confided to her classmate Arlene, "but I feel no desire to do so. I am only convinced that it is the will of God. If I am mistaken I will come back, but I won't give up without trying."[3]

During the last days, no one but Inez's confessor and her trusted friend suspected what was going on in the girl's heart. Outwardly she was happy, excited, and eager to be on her way; within she was cold, desolate, and listless. She distributed her belongings to her friends—a prayer book for Little Inez, friend of her high school days; two of her best dresses for Beatrice who liked pretty clothes,[4] remembrances for the Sisters.

On the evening of her departure, she slipped away from the crowded house for a last visit with Beatrice. "I can't stand having people crying all around and embracing me over and over," she complained. "Our house is full of relatives and most of the aunts are crying!"[5] She stayed with Beatrice for some time, and showed surprise, pleasure, and embarrassment when Beatrice embraced and kissed her at parting.[6]

One more visit to St. Michael's, a long, loving visit, and then she was with the family again dressing for the train. Mother and Father dressed too, but with far less evident pleasure than Inez, who fairly skipped for joy when the hour neared. For four years she had known the time her train would leave Rochester and the hour it would arrive in Chicago.[7]

Together with her parents, Inez boarded—at last!—the train to Chicago. Inez daydreamed of the new life that she had long desired and was now, finally, about to undertake. A sudden violent jerk brought Inez back to the present. The train had stopped abruptly and she rescued her hat from the floor. Mrs. Maier laughed. "Sleeping? Or was it day-dreaming?" "Both I guess," admitted Inez, and they went off to the sleeper.

In the morning, they changed trains in Chicago, and then it was another hour ride before they arrived at the rather small country station of Techny, about forty-five miles north of Chicago. The convent chauffeur was there to take them to Holy Spirit Convent. Inez watched eagerly and sighted the building of cream brick situated on a slight incline about a mile away.

"There's my home, Pop!" she exclaimed jubilantly tugging at his sleeve.

The building stood out with delightful clarity against the

spreading green fields. As they came nearer it was obscured by the tall pine and spruce trees which enclosed the gardens.

Sister Anthony met the family at the entrance and Inez took in every detail of the religious habit she hoped one day to wear: the deep blue dress with white cincture, the blue veil and white head-dress. Against the blue background shone the silver cross and emblem of the Holy Spirit, suspended on a red ribbon and resting over the breast.

There was a brief introduction to the Superior, and then all went to the chapel to thank God for the safe journey. Inez knelt once more at the feet of Christ in the tabernacle, and then—as suddenly as it had fallen—the veil lifted.

The strange confusion of mind and the cold grip of dullness that had held her spirit disappeared. Calm reassurance throbbed again in her heart, and the old fire of enthusiasm lit up the eyes that were turned toward the altar. Although many trials would come to test that heart of steel, never again would a shadow of doubt concerning her vocation trouble Inez!

Before Mrs. Maier left Holy Spirit Convent, she met the young aspirants and postulants with whom Inez was to launch on the Divine Romance which is the core of every true religious vocation. It was comforting to find fourteen other young women afire with the same ambition that consumed her daughter, and Mrs. Maier left Techny confident that her "baby" would be happy.

Nevertheless, the aging mother could not suppress her grief—she was returning to an empty house. Rufus had married, Ray was at college, and Gerard had already left to start a family of his own. Of late years the Maier home had been the hub of social gatherings because Inez, despairing of more religious vocations in her family, had tried her utmost to steer her brothers into good Catholic marriages. Suddenly it was all over, and Mrs. Maier was no longer vivacious Louise of years ago. She dreaded the silent rooms, the unbroken quiet of a home from which youth had gone. But she knew that God's claims came first. The lonely mother turned bravely homeward; jubilantly the young girl went to meet the secrets of the unknown as she began her religious life in October 1925.

During her first recreation as an aspirant, Inez (now Sister Maier), found herself working busily on something she had scorned from early childhood—dolls! Yet her eyes danced and her fingers deftly stitched at the flashy red dresses. The dolls were for China and no one less than Father King, of the Society of the Divine Word, was going to take them along on his trip to the Orient.[8] With all her enthusiasm for the Catholic Students' Mission Crusade, Inez had never dreamed that she would one day be helping the founder of the Mission Crusade pack his trunks for China. The needle went in. "China!" The needle came out. "Soon, Lord, soon!" She had dreamed of foreign fields for eleven long years. Now they had truly become part her life. China, New Guinea, India, the Philippines—all of them crowded into her day. Around her were missionaries—young, old, middle-age—alight with the same fire that burned in her soul; all of them tense racers on their marks, waiting for the signal to dash into action. Her spirit gloried in her new life!

What thrilled her more than all else was the liturgy as it was lived at the convent. From childhood she had cherished the Gregorian Chant; now she found her delight in it every Sunday at High Mass and Vespers. With something akin to envy, she listened to the Sisters chanting the Divine Office, and she counted the weeks until she could join the Office choir.

She had always yearned to live in close union with Mother Church. The wondrous mystery of the prayer life of the Church opened to her as she entered upon her early religious life. With exuberant joy the young aspirant gave herself to the transforming of the Sacred Liturgy. On strong foundations, she now began to build a spiritual structure that would weather the shock of sternest reality in the jungles of Papua New Guinea.

As she became acquainted with her religious family, new pictures began to appear in the gallery of her soul—her Founder, the Rev. Arnold Janssen, the first Mothers of the Congregation, Sister Maria Helena and Sister Josepha. They were the type of men and women that appealed to Inez—strong, fearless, yet humbly patient.

The Congregation was made up of young people, and Inez had to smile when she remembered telling Pop how it was the oldest, most firmly established missionary order in America.

Divine Providence had followed a mysterious blueprint in the founding of the Holy Spirit Missionary Sisters. The Kulturkampf in the 1870s in Germany was curtailing the work of the clergy, and the danger of exile threatened many a priest. Rev. Arnold Janssen, rector of a school at Bocholt, Westphalia, and editor of the Messenger of the Sacred Heart, sensed in the dangerous situation an opportunity for expanding the foreign mission work of the Church. Germany, despite the pronounced Catholicity in some sections, had no missionary orders of religious devoted exclusively to work in the foreign missions among nonbelievers in God. New young seminarians and priests were faced with possible exile from Germany. It was time to act. For several years Father Janssen had seen the need of missionary priests and he now proposed his plan.

Despite urgent publicity for the mission project, no one was found who would be willing to engage in such an undertaking. At the outset Father Janssen would have waved aside any suggestion that he was the one to start the society. Once he saw clearly that Divine Providence was pointing to him as the founder, he fearlessly forged ahead.

Beyond the borders of Germany in Steyl, Holland, he found the location in which he would found a mission and seminary. Fondly, he hoped that strained conditions in Germany would be an auxiliary in training prospective seminarians to take up this new work for the conversion of nonbelievers.

Mercifully, Divine Providence kept veiled the almost insurmountable opposition and hardships that were to accompany the undertaking. Lack of funds, weak health, distrust of his capabilities, and scarcity of recruits—each of these in turn and together warred against the contemplated mission institution. Nevertheless on September 8, 1875, St. Michael's Mission House was blessed.[9] The great work was on its way. Today the Society of the Divine Word, born in that little house in Steyl, Holland, numbers over six thousand priests and brothers in addition to more than three thousand professed Sisters of the SSpS active in missions on five continents.[10]

When he founded his Missionary House, Father Janssen had thoughts of establishing further foundations. Yet as his work progressed he recognized the need for Sisters in the field. He sincerely hoped that a congregation of Missionary Sisters would be formed, and he tried to encourage the project. Little did he dream that it would be Father Arnold Janssen himself who would become the spiritual Father and founder of the Holy Spirit Missionary Sisters.

About two years after the inception of the Mission House of St. Michael, Father Janssen had a visit from Bishop Comboni, Vicar Apostolic of Central Africa. They discussed problems of the mission fields, and the bishop stressed the need for Missionary Sisters. The Rector of St. Michael's heartily endorsed the Bishop's remarks, but he gaped in silent surprise when the Bishop suggested that he, Rev. Arnold Janssen, found a new community of Sisters. For the present the zealous priest had his hands full with the new Mission House, but the suggestion dropped into fertile ground.

In 1881, Father Janssen received a letter from Helena Stollenwerk of Rollesbroich, near Aachen in the Rhineland. The young lady had a great desire to become a missionary sister and asked him for advice and guidance. Father Janssen had to inform her that there was no congregation of missionary Sisters in Germany. He then wrote that perhaps later, if he recognized it to be the will of God, he would found a congregation of Missionary Sisters.

Helena Stollenwerk came immediately—in 1882—and for seven years worked at the Mission House, always with the hope that one day, when the will of God was clear, Father Janssen would found the new community. In 1884, she was joined by Hendrina Stenmanns and two other young women who shared Helena's desire to do foreign mission work.

The founder of the Mission House in Steyl, himself of deeply ascetical mold, marveled at the heroic total self-giving of the young women, when on December 8, 1889, he made them the nucleus of the Holy Spirit Missionary Sisters, he knew he had a seed of gold![11] Planted in soil that was fertile from years of heroic sacrifice, the new Congregation spread out luxuriant branches. When the Reverend Founder died in 1909 his Missionary Sisters numbered 558, of whom 283 were active in foreign fields. Their work was again blessed by an overflow of graces stemming from the sacrificial lives of their Foundresses who were destined to train hundreds of Missionary Sisters, though never to see foreign fields themselves.

Helena Stollenwerk, became Mother Maria Helena, the first Superior General of the new Congregation. Seven years after the foundation of the Missionary Sisters—in 1896—Father Janssen started the cloistered branch of the community. Recruits from the ranks of the Missionary Sisters formed the nucleus of the Missionary Sisters, Servants of the Holy Spirit of Perpetual Adoration. Whereas the Missionary Sisters wore a habit of blue and white, the Adoration Sisters were clothed in rose and white to signify their complete consecration to the Holy Spirit. Mother Maria Helena, at the suggestions of Father Janssen, joined the cloistered branch and added the title "Virgo" to her name. Upon the transfer of Mother Maria Helena, Mother Josepha took up the governance of the growing community. In heroic humility, Mother Maria Helena, now simply Sister Maria Virgo, began her novitiate as a Sister of Perpetual Adoration under the direction of Sisters she herself had trained. She walked bravely into the shadows of self-sacrifice and scaled the peaks of Divine Love. God wanted no more. Before her novitiate was completed, however, she was called to eternity.

In 1901, twelve years after its founding, the Congregation came to the United States. It had already branched out to other continents and foreign fields. In 1895 four Sisters had gone to South America to open mission schools and hospitals in Argentina. Just before the turn of the century one band of Sisters was on its way to Africa to start a mission in Togo and another sailed for New Guinea.

When Father Arnold turned his eyes to North America he had a twofold aim in view. First, he saw among the poor blacks of the southern states a fruitful field for mission endeavor. Second, hoped to draw new recruits for the growing apostolate from the youth of America.

The five Sisters selected by the zealous founder as his first missionaries to the United States came to Techny, Illinois, on May 11, 1901. Their first convent was a small frame house near the Mission Seminary of the Fathers of the Divine Word. Here the five pioneers set to work to learn the language and customs of their adopted land. They gave generously of their time and strength to help the seminary.

In September of the same year of their arrival in the USA, the Sisters took charge of a small parochial school founded by the Divine Word Missionaries in the immediate vicinity of the seminary. During the first few years, groups of Sisters from Steyl, Holland came to reinforce the young community, and in the fall of 1906 three Sisters were able to leave Techny to begin mission work among the Afro-Americans of Vicksburg, Mississippi. In the South, one mission station after another was taken over. Today the ministries of the Holy Spirit Missionary Sisters in America include education, health care, and pastoral and social work.

The history of her religious family filled the young postulant Sister Inez Maier with pride. She gloried in her nearness to the pioneer members of the Congregation. Mother Leonarda Lentrup, acting Provincial in the United States, was the foundress of the 1901 American Province and one of the five Sisters originally chosen by the Founder. In 1931 Sister Maria Heinemann, Assistant Superior at the Convent of the Holy Spirit, has been one of the first two American postulants.

Sister Inez fervently hoped that she would one day measure up to the high standards set by Father Janssen and the first two Mothers; and she set about acquiring the virtues held by her ideals.[12] But in one thing she did not want to imitate them—she prayed that she would not have to stay at home! Her heart was in the foreign missions, and she could not bear the thought of remaining in the United States to train others for the work she herself longed to do.

Due to the happiness that filled recreation periods, Inez's homesickness did not last long. Perhaps no one was teased so much as Sister Inez about her "George" and "Pat" stories. "George," she explained, was her priest friend. But, perhaps she forgot to identify "Pat." Sister Henry had been listening to the "Pat" stories for several days, and they had her puzzled. "Sister Maier," she questioned after another tale had sent the group into peals of laughter, "who is this Pat anyway? Is that your cat?"

"Cat?" Sister Inez shot a look of unbelief at the mischievous questioner. "That is my very dear and highly respected Sister Agnes Marie Patricia of St. Joseph's Convent, Rochester, New York"![13]

During those first days of formation as a postulant there were classes of instruction in the various religious exercises of the community, and favorite among them was the class in Divine Office. Sister Maier memorized several of the psalms and hymns of the Pentecost Office, and she was often heard singing while working in the kitchen or in the garden.[14]

The postulants were thrilled when their voice tests made them eligible for the choir. If a certain selection proved very difficult the new members were given special lessons. Thus, Sister Crispina Rehnen, their spiritual directress, informed them one day that the second voice singers would have an hour of practice in the postulants' refectory.

Ever on the lookout for mischief, the budding singers with Sister Maier in the lead, planned a surprise for the choir directress. Eager hands set about to prepare a fitting reception. All the pot flowers from the corridor were brought into the refectory to decorate the organ. A rag bow adorned each chair. The ash box from the cellar was put in place for the directress. A violin stand was dressed in the complete outfit of a postulant, and Sister Henry set the old alarm clock to give a few chimes during the practice hour. It had taken some time to put on the finishing touches, and the directress waited with doubtful patience for the singers to answer her knock. Eager faces fell when the choir directress, stern and forbidding, brushed aside their joke and proceeded with the practice.[15]

A few weeks after her entrance into the convent, Sister Maier was assigned to work in the kitchen. The other postulants were soon being entertained by her foibles in the culinary department. One day she accidentally broke part of the stove; the next week the stove poker just seemed to fall into two pieces in her hands. Sister Inez began to worry that she would be shipped home for excess damage. However Sister Maristella Carr—"My Boss" as Sister Inez affectionately dubbed her—laughed away the postulant's fears.[16]

Sister Maristella enjoyed her vivacious helper, and she grinned when Sister Maier marched in resolutely with a pan of onions and, with energy, set to work at them. When the Sister passed by she heard Sister Maier dedicating each onion to the cause. "This one for China, Lord. This one for India." This continued until the pan was empty and Inez had shed her last onion-tear for the missions.[17]

If her assigned tasks were finished, Sister Maier would quickly discover new work around the kitchen, but it would always be the most menial tasks that drew her attention. In the morning she would hurry to the kitchen, and before the novice who had charge of the percolator had a chance to arrive, Inez would quickly do the dirty part of the work. When the novice came, the postulant was busy with her own work. She also delighted in cleaning the big range, carrying out the ashes, and scouring the top of the stove with ashes. "Mom always wanted to make a lady out of me," she laughed as she surveyed her soiled apron and grimy hands. She had just finished cleaning out the soot. "I wish she could see me now![18]

One day the novices had to leave before they had a chance to scrub the kitchen floor. When Sister Maristella returned, she found Sister Maier with a pail and scrub brush, happily singing a psalm. How early did this young missioner learn that prayer and work are not separate items in the life of a religious?

"Sister," protested Sister Maristella, "that is too hard for you. You must not do that alone!"

"But Sister," there was a little astonished wonder in the voice, "what I do for the Lord in behalf of the missions is never too hard!"[19]

Once, after the convent had put on the penitential spirit of Lent, Sister Maier was called to the parlor: "What," exclaimed Sister Inez on seeing her mother and father," you are breaking all the rules of the institute by coming here during Lent!"[20] Her strange welcome was supplemented by a loving embrace for Mom and Pop, and a worried Mother was convinced that her "baby" was happy.

"And how is the fare?" queried Pop.

"Grand! Don't I look it?" and she stood proudly before him, glowing as much with joy as with health.[21]

* * * * *

How the days of her postulancy passed quickly. Sister Maier could never quite understand. Before she was aware of it, the day of Investment was upon her. Recreations were filled with conjectures as to possible names, and though Sister Maier favored "George" in memory of her old Confessor, she finally settled on "Theophane." She hoped that the young martyr of Vietnam, beatified in 1909, would use his intercession in heaven to procure for her a speedy transfer to the foreign missions.[22]

On the Feast of Pentecost in 1926, the Congregation celebrated the silver jubilee of the American Province with a Tridium of Thanksgiving. Sister Maier invited Father George Weimann, her former advisor, for the celebration, and was overjoyed when he came with Father Kunz of Rochester, New York. The silver jubilee celebration terminated with a Mission Departure ceremony for Sister Ottonia Ruhol (Sister Mary Elise) and Sister Hermengardis Rossa who were leaving for Papua New Guinea. The joy that radiated from the two departing missionaries thrilled Sister Maier as she stood in breathless excitement waving good-bye.[23]

On June 29, 1926, the postulants began their retreat. After ten days of silence and prayer they were invested as novices and received the habit of the Missionary Sisters. The blue habit and scapular were to be constant reminders of the humility of Mary, while the veil and head-dress of white recalled the immaculate purity of the Heavenly Queen. The habit of the novices differed from that of the professed members only in the color of the veil and the absence of the crucifix and symbol of the Holy Spirit.

After a delightful Investment visit with her parents, during which both Mother and Father found great consolation in Inez's contentment, Sister Theophane gave herself entirely to the work of the novitiate.

During the nine months of her postulancy, Sister Maier had been gradually introduced into the special devotion to the Holy Spirit, which is the very breath of the spiritual life of the Holy Spirit Missionary Sisters. Now in the novitiate she learned that complete surrender to and whole-hearted collaboration with the Holy Spirit, the Sanctifier, was to be the prime endeavor of her life.

Sister Tiburtia Broicher faced her new novices who were gathered for their first class to study the Holy Rule. She looked over her glasses at them and smiled. They settled back in their chairs, at ease with the kindly directress who was to lead them along the way of religious observance.

"And what," began the directress, "was the main purpose of your coming to Holy Spirit Convent? Why did you want to be a blue Sister?"

The five new Sisters thought for a moment and then confidently raised their hands. The eighteen older novices seated behind them grinned, but remained silent. "I came to go to the missions," stated Sister Theophane with conviction.

"Oh, you did," smiled Sister Tiburtia and then nodded gravely at another novice. "And why did you come?"

"I guess I came for the same reason," admitted Sister Florence Henry with far less assurance than Sister Theophane.

In about ten minutes they had run the gamut of possible motives for entering the Missionary Sisters. "Now I will tell you why we, all of us, are here," said Sister Tiburtia. They leaned forward eagerly. "We are here to become saints!"

Yes, this was to take precedence over all else, over even the missionary ideal; because according to their Holy Rule, the foremost aim of a Holy Spirit Missionary Sister must be that of self-surrender to the life-giving Spirit. Their missionary vocation draws vitality from their faith in the holy, Triune God who dwells in their hearts. Individually, and as a community, they give honor and glory to God, One and Triune, by doing all they can to make God known, loved, and glorified by all people. They are to give witness to God's presence in the world.

"That's going to be a tough job," confided Sister Theophane to a fellow novice after the first lesson. "But it makes our missionary calling so much greater than I ever imagined it to be!"

Consequently, Holy Rule classes became Sister Theophane's delight, and when, during the second year of novitiate, she was employed outside the Provincial House, she was always happier on Wednesday because she said, "Tonight we go home to see Mother Tiburtia and have Holy Rule!"[24]

One Wednesday afternoon Sister Theophane and Sister Florence waited at St. Mary's Mission House for the chauffeur to take them to the convent for class. The rain was coming down in blinding sheets, and no driver appeared. "Sister Tiburtia won't expect us on a night like this," decided Sister Florence and she started back to the kitchen.

"But we can't miss class just because of a little shower," urged Sister Theophane. "Come on, we'll hike it home!"

Sister Florence bewailed the plight of her starched white veil, but there was no resisting Sister Theophane once her mind was made up. Drenched and panting, the novices were met at the convent entrance by their directress.

"What on earth are you doing here on a night like this?"

Classes were over by the time the two arrived, but they did have a visit with Sister Tiburtia. It was worth the drenching.[25]

One hour a week the novices attended the class in Holy Rule; the rest of the time was devoted to living the lessons they were being taught. The Holy Rule, Sister Theophane soon found, sketched in bold strokes the outline of her life, and it reached into the finest details of her daily work and prayer. It was at once both wide and free and also minutely exacting. Under its influence, Sister Theophane's inner life was expanding. Blended with her mission zeal there was now a full-time endeavor at unflinching self-mastery for the love of Christ. Her day had become one round of generous self-giving love. No one ever hesitated to ask Sister Theophane for help because she never refused, but rather she beamed her joy when performing the kindness.

When one evening Sister Alice Berghoff found that a novice had forgotten to turn off the liquid soap in the basement, she just turned to Sister Theophane and whispered a word about the probable state of the basement floor. "I'll go right down," replied Sister Theophane, though it was already after night prayer.

The floor was one mess of soap and unfortunately another professed Sister had come down for something and slipped. Sister Theophane hurried to help her, cleaned her habit, and then stayed to finish up the floor.[26] Acts such as these were a part of Sister Theophane's daily life.

Sister Meline Karasz worked with her in the kitchen and remarked, "If I had not watched she would have done all the hard and dirty work that was mine to do!"[27] When the two novices were alone in the kitchen one day, Sister Theophane smiled ruefully.

"I can do all the dirty work," she said, "but neither of us knows much about cooking. Good thing my pop is an undertaker."[28]

If Sister Theophane came across a Sister doing some very heavy or tiring work, she would interpose pleadingly, "Come, Sister. Let me do that for you!"[29]

After one happy year in the novitiate at Holy Spirit Convent, Sister Theophane and Sister Florence were summoned by their directress. Both expected to take up further studies now that their canonical year was over.

Sister Theophane's face fell when she was told to be ready to leave for work at St. Ann's Home about a mile from the convent. In a few hours they were gone, but no one detected her disappointment as she joked about her first mission appointment.[30]

After six weeks the two novices were sent to work in the kitchen of St. Mary's Mission House. Their new tasks were many and lowly, but they performed them with the same cheerful energy. Sister Theophane became King of the Kitchen and Sister Florence assumed the role of Queen. Their jolly pretense amused the older Sisters working with them. Sister Theophane helped Sister Agathone Boenig in the meat department. In her letters home, the mischievous novice wrote about "tossing around those pigs and half-cows!" The "King" and "Queen" laughed merrily when Sister Rosalie wrote back, "But, Baby, don't you have a butcher?"[31]

At recreation the young novices were a source of merriment. When Sister Severina Knapp celebrated her silver jubilee, they staged their "King and Queen Pretense" for the community. At the close of the play, gifts were distributed to the audience. After an appropriate speech, Sister Theophane rolled out a thirty-seven pound cheese for Sister Agathone.[32]

* * * * *

For the most part, Sister Theophane was a private person in regard to her inner spirituality. Though her life was one continuous prayer, she shunned much outward display. In her conversations one could not detect what went on in the depths. She delighted in spiritual topics during recreations, but seldom introduced them herself and always strove to keep them impersonal.[33] Her inner life was for God alone. An inadvertent remark here and there lifted the veil and gave those about her a glance into the beautiful sanctum where a soul kept constant vigil before the Almighty, wrapped in the exultant prayer-life of the Church.

So their days passed—carefree, happy days. And yet the day of taking vows creeped ever closer.

"You don't suppose they'll slip anything new across after vows, do you?" Sister Theophane questioned Sister Genevieve Regal one day.

The latter grinned. "You've got the Holy Rule in your hands," she laughed, "That's all there is—it's enough, isn't it?"[34] Sister Theophane agreed that it was.

The last months of her novitiate were especially dear to Sister Theophane because she could return to the novitiate at the Provincial House. She had missed its quiet and seclusion. Now, for ten days before July 6, 1928, the novices began their retreat in preparation for their consecration in temporary vows.

A bit excited, but intensely happy, Sister Theophane knelt before the altar on the morning after her retreat and pronounced the Holy Vows which made her a Holy Spirit Missionary Sister.

CHAPTER 7

Facing Failure

WHEN Sister Theophane pronounced her vows, she knew her missionary career was truly beginning. The summer weeks following her profession were spent in normal courses at the Provincial House in Techny. Early in August mission appointments began to filter through the Provincial's office.

In a few days the basement became a model secondhand store where cheerful, blue Sisters, their sleeves rolled up, packed trunk after trunk of clothing and toys for their mission stations in the South. Sister Theophane sat on her trunk and eyed Sister Dorothy Fox at the far end of the basement. "Lucky fellow," she said under her breath. "Wish I had her appointment instead of mine!"

Sister Dorothy sang as she stacked piles of music books into boxes marked "Manila."

"Some people get all the breaks," the words were muttered to herself as Sister Theophane clamped down the lid of the trunk and got a label for Greenville, Mississippi.

"They surely picked out the right station for a greenhorn at teaching," she continued licking the label. "Just imagine me cooped up with a bunch of kids in a classroom! Oh, for Papua New Guinea's jungle trails!"

"Sister Theophane, would you help me pack away some . . ."

Before Sister Makaria Iten had time to finish, the young Sister was on her feet ready to help. "Sure, Sister. Let's go."

"Why so glum, Sister? Aren't you thrilled about your first mission appointment?"

"No, I'm not," came the answer in decisive tones. "I don't think I can do it. I wasn't made for a classroom."

"Everybody feels like that at first," countered the older Sister. "Besides you'll appreciate this experience when you are in the foreign missions."

Sister Theophane swung the heavy box onto the shelf above her head. "I guess I might," she conceded, and Sister Makaria smiled when she noted the attempt at a grin.[1]

Possibly it was the novelty of a first mission, or perhaps the enthusiasm of the rest of the departing missionaries was contagious; whatever the cause, Sister Theophane was delightfully excited when she and her companions left Techny early in August, 1928, for the Southern Missions.

Long before Sister alighted from the train, she knew they were in Dixie. Dry, hot air poured into the crowded coach from the open windows. To close the offending ventilators meant steaming suffocation. The Missionary Sisters preferred dry oven-heat.

A few days after the Sisters were settled in Sacred Heart Convent in Greenville, MS, the trunks arrived and Sister Theophane, unused to Southern heat, knelt on the floor alternately mopping the perspiration from her face and hands and pulling out an article of clothing. The habits were damp and crushed and Sister Superior called for volunteers to begin the pressing. Drenched as she was, Sister Theophane hurried to offer herself for the work. She ironed for hours in the scorching heat, but her heart sang because she could begin her missionary life with sacrifice.[2]

As she explored her classroom the new recruit was almost eager to see those desks occupied, but when a crowd of noisy fifth and sixth graders stampeded into the room on the first day, her old fear gripped her. Only after the prayers had been said did she notice that one of the boys had no feet. He was squeezed into a seat. How he got there she did not know. How he would get out she wondered. The sight unnerved the Sister so that her thoughts ran riot for a few seconds, but she crushed her rising panic and, with assumed matter-of-factness, plunged into the day's work. The first day is always a strain, and in the evening Sister Superior consoled the exhausted new teacher with the prediction that practiced routine would soon make the work easier.

As the weeks wore on into a chilly, damp winter, Sister Theophane found herself marking off days on the calendar. It made the return to Techny seem nearer.[3] Work in the classroom was not becoming easier. On the contrary, the young teacher was face to face with the fact that her class was below the expected standard. Well might her steps now have lagged as she crossed over to the school building each morning. Well might she have made her distress the dominant topic of conversation. But neither of these things would have been characteristic of Sister Theophane. Her troubles were her own, and she was often caught talking to herself about them. But for her Sisters she kept a sunny demeanor, and laughter often reigned when she joined a group.[4] For the community she saved the amusing incidents of her day; for herself and her God she kept the hard spots.

"This morning," related Sister Theophane, "one of my youngsters wanted to know if, by any chance, I had hair on my head. I asked him if he thought I grew feathers like a bird!"[5]

Discouraging as were her attempts in the classroom, they in no way curbed Sister Theophane's broad interests. While her Sisters might expostulate, tease, or even reprove, nothing could alter her love for animals. Any stray dog or cat that wandered onto the grounds of Sacred Heart Convent found a protector. "Just give the poor thing something to eat," Sister Theophane would plead. "Then we can let it go."[6]

"But, Sister Theophane," remonstrated the kitchen Sister, "do you really intend to start an asylum for lost dogs and cats? We are not bound to feed everything that walks to our place!"[7]

Sister Theophane was not abashed by this reception, and she continued to bring her furry friends to the kitchen door. One morning she dropped two bedraggled kittens on the back porch. When she managed to persuade Sister to give her some milk for the outcasts, she gleefully offered her first orphan a sip. The bewildered kitten spat back furiously at her benefactor. Sister Theophane thoroughly enjoyed this reaction. "Look at the spirit!" she ejaculated. "We'll call her 'Pugno.'" The other little waif was too sick to show any reaction, and he was promptly dubbed "Bonus."[8] Sister Theophane's choice of names for her pets was a perennial source of merriment. There was Juniper, a childhood pet snake, Nucleus and Nucleola, two Chinchilla rabbits at the laboratory of St. Therese's Hospital where she later studied, and there would be equally unique names for her Papua New Guinea pets.

To supply for their own needs, the Sisters kept chickens and a cow, and though Sister Theophane did not have charge of these animals, she was always there to help. "I wish Rosalie could see me," she laughed as she helped Sister Alwine lead the cow to the neighbors across the road.[9]

In spring the Sisters acquired a calf, and Sister Theophane promptly offered to go along to bring it to the convent.

> Our pet calf (animals were pets to Sister Theophane) was duly installed in its new home Saturday. It took the strength of three husky people to make it navigate along the street. People stopped to tell us that she was a pretty calf. I think in Rochester they would stop to tell us we were crazy nuns to push a calf through the city.[10]

But Greenville was not Rochester and the local folk among whom the Sisters worked saw nothing odd in the incident. The mission was poor and it was only natural that the missionaries should economize everywhere in order to help their people the more.

Nature, so luxuriant in the South, absorbed Sister's interest and time when she was not occupied with school work or visiting parishioners. Before her arrival in Greenville, a Mississippi flood had destroyed much of the beautiful park and garden around the convent which the Sisters had been cultivating since the opening of the mission in 1913. In one of her letters home, she wrote:

> We have about twenty fruit trees, but they will not yield much this year, this being the first year for most of them. The flood destroyed everything. It must have been a small paradise here before the disaster. When my poppies show up, will you please send a husky plant or two?[11]

Time and again in her letters she asked for seeds, shrubs, even trees, and every sunny day after school she was busy hoeing, planting, or weeding. Fridays found her smiling more than usual because she anticipated a full day in her garden on the morrow.[12]

She was never happier than when occupied with some manual labor, preferably a sort that proved hard or tedious. "The Man of the House," the Sisters called her, and if something broke, all knew where to turn for help. When the old sidewalk rotted away, it was Sister Theophane who dragged new boards and laid another walk.[13]

Spring comes early in the warm South and school work shrinks in importance as the locals prepare for work in the cotton fields. Sister Theophane was joyfully looking forward to the close of school at the end of May and then to a glorious vacation at the Provincial House.

But toward the close of March, an element of anxiety clouded the beautiful spring filled with promise. "Pop" was ill. He had been taken to the hospital and his illness threatened to keep him there for an indefinite number of weeks. No one was dearer to Sister Theophane than "Pop," just as he in turn cherished with a special tenderness his "kiddo." She wrote to him:

> Rosalie said you are rather sad about having to be in bed so long. That is easily understood. I had to stay in bed about three days last summer. The rest made me feel much worse than the sickness. Now when I get sick I quote your famous statement, 'It needs work.'[14]

Despite the fact that the family tried not to cause her undue anxiety, she realized that her father's illness was not slight. In the same letter to her father, she expressed her keen disappointment at her inability to be with him:

> I feel pretty bad that I am so far away, especially since I am the only one of the family not there now. But you know that even if I were with you, I could not do much. If I were a nurse at home, I would be your day and night nurse and 'not charge you a cent for my trouble.' Even this bargain is out of my reach to give you. Never mind, I was your pal all the while I was at home. It is time the rest of the family took a turn. I never felt so proud as when you called me your 'hired man' or talked to me in a businesslike way.[15]

Frequent letters had to make up for the absence, and these were filled with a joyous, lighthearted spirit which she knew her father would appreciate.

> Pop, you always knew everything—how would you prevent Southern cats from getting sick? My second cat is dying now. We have great entertainment here with our six-week-old calf. She is a cute little lady. You would like the South. Everything here grows so lovely. It makes me feel a bit like asking Pop: what he is going to put in this year? Our vegetables are all sprouted up about a week already. We moved the potted plants to a rare-looking shed that I just completed.[16]

Yet, it was she alone who—realizing his danger—frankly reminded him of death.

> Pop, one letter said you are to have a third operation and that you might not pull through. I hate to think of it, but we all must. Go bravely on, Pop, and do not be afraid. . . . Say the 'Memorare' and pray to St. Joseph often, then look straight in the face of whatever dares to come. . . . Tell the Lord to make haste to help you.[17]

During Holy Week Sister Theophane increased her prayers for her father and had her class remember him. On May 20 Sister Rosalie's letter brought news of a critical condition. Sister Theophane quickly penned a few lines of consolation and encouragement, reminding her father again of the great mercy of God. However, before she could mail the letter the next morning, a telegram arrived announcing her father's death.

Sister Theophane received the news without comment and retired to the chapel. Later in the day she sent a message of beautiful faith to her sorrowing mother:

> I hope the boys and Rosalie are calm and brave. Be brave too, Mama. We have the happy assurance that we will meet again. . . . The boys will be good to you, Mama, and Papa is in the hands of a God Who delights to be called 'Father' and Whose loveliest name is 'Divine Love.'[18]

In June one of the Sisters at Greenville became ill, and Sister Theophane's dream of a happy vacation at Techny was shattered. She was sent to Holy Spirit Convent only for retreat and a few days of rest, and after, she was appointed to stay in the South to take the place of the sick Sister.[19]

Later, when she came up for the retreat, she had a long talk with the Provincial, Mother Leonarda. The Superior realized that the difficulties Sister Theophane had encountered in her class work had made the year hard. Knowing the young Sister's capabilities, she thought that perhaps a position with high school students would be more suitable. The fault seemed to lie in her inability to come down to the level of her class. Mother Leonarda laughed heartily when Sister Theophane told her about the Latin psalm she tried to teach her youngsters for the pastor's feast.[20]

Yes, Mother Leonarda was certain that Sister Theophane belonged in high school. In September, 1929, Sister Theophane faced a class of freshman at St. Joseph's School in Meridian, Mississippi. Many of the ninth grade boys towered high over their teacher. Before long she acknowledged to herself that the class was not working with her. As a dynamo of energy, she could not understand the students' lack of initiative. Her lectures, so carefully planned, were not taking with the class. Some students nodded lazily as she spoke, others were restless, few were attentive. She worked on through a trying year, puzzled and dismayed by her inability to advance her class. Early in June, 1930, she returned to Techny, cast down by her failure. "I'm not worth the salt they give me for my soup," she told Sister Florence when the latter asked about her work.[21]

Mother Leonarda, too, was puzzled. She would try once more to place the young Sister in a position fitted for her. She had thought that Sister Theophane, so masculine in her bearing and manners, would be just the teacher for the high school boys. It had not worked.

A new mission was being opened in North Little Rock, Arkansas. Perhaps a relatively small class of primary youngsters might prove easier. When Sister Theophane heard of her transfer she remarked rather sadly, "My Superiors don't know what to do with me. Others get to stay at a station a few years, but I'm always changed because I'm just a failure."

Sister Genevieve tried to cheer her. "It's not so bad, even if you do give the youngsters a picnic oftener than is good for them. Not all the Sisters can take a change as you can and buck up under it. The Superiors know that and they bank on your good will.[22]

When school reopened in September, 1930, Sister Theophane was at her new post as the first and second grade teacher and the organist in North Little Rock. Since the mission was new, there was no home for the Sisters and no school. The Sisters stayed at an older mission in Little Rock and daily crossed the river to go to teach in North Little Rock. A former Protestant church, used for church services on Sundays, became a school house for the rest of the week. If lack of conveniences—even of necessities—make a good mission, then North Little Rock was one of the best.

Acutely conscious of her unsuccessful terms at Greenville and Meridian, Sister Theophane began her work with trepidation. In the old church the atmosphere was not congenial to quiet study, and before long she was desperately battling the problem of discipline. "I demand your decorum!" she commanded in an exasperated tone when the children had used up all her patience.[23] A few of the youngsters stopped to look wonderingly at their teacher; the rest gave no heed to this strange language.

Shortly after the opening of school, Mother Leonarda arrived in Little Rock for the yearly visitation. Saturday evening she inquired about the next day's schedule for the new mission, and expressed her desire to go with the Sisters so that she might hear Sister Theophane play the organ at Mass.

Sister Theophane received this announcement with real dismay. As she herself said, she had been "exposed to music' though never greatly affected. Thus, she desperately—yet respectfully—replied, "If you do that I'll put pepper in my handkerchief and promptly have hay fever. Then I won't be able to play."[24]

Though she seldom missed any duty or religious exercise because of it, her hay fever was always with her. An annoying case of asthma had also developed. When the two combined to make her feel miserable, she went out to "work it off."

In North Little Rock, as in her former missions, joy and interest in the garden and animals pushed other difficulties to the background. For some time a friend drove the Sisters to and from school, and Sister Theophane took her work sleeves and apron along with her in the car so that she might be ready to go to the garden as soon as they reached home.[25]

Again it was "Dear Mom" who supplied shrubs and rose bushes to beautify the convent garden. When some of the Sisters wondered if Sister was asking her mother for too much, she affirmed: "You don't know what a good Ma I have. She is a real missionary."[26]

Complete responsibility for the garden left her little free time, yet her Sisters never hesitated to seek her help. When the chickens developed a disease, Sister Bertholda Gruhn simply mentioned her difficulty to Sister Theophane. The next day after school, clad in work clothes and armed with a tub and medicinal solution, Sister Theophane appeared at the poultry run to bathe some fifty hens.[27]

Crowded as were the hours of the young missioner, even a young kitten in distress might count on her for assistance. One day, she climbed up a ladder to rescue a frightened kitten which had scampered high into an oak tree for safety from a pursuing dog. "Such trouble over a little cat," remarked one Sister, almost impatiently.

Sister Theophane smiled. "Just think if you were sitting up there, wouldn't you be glad to have someone take you down?"[28]

Though she seldom came in close contact with horses now, they were still her old favorites. One day at recreation she took out her watch, and Sister Superior noticed an odd medal dangling from the black ribbon. "Sister Theophane, what saint do you have there?"

"Oh, that's St. Equus," grinned the young Sister rather sheepishly.

"St. Equus?" queried the Superior puzzled. "Let me see." The trinket, a horse's head, disappeared from the ribbon.[29]

Because she was always working, Sister Theophane preferred a worn habit, veil, and shoes. "I can work better in that," she said[30] Her needs in food, clothing, and equipment were not many. Anything, her Sisters knew, would satisfy Sister Theophane. A missionary must not want everything she may have," she was to remark one day in far off Papua New Guinea.[31] Those who lived with her admired—though some had not the courage to imitate—her austere spirit of poverty.

Her third year in the Southern missions was almost over. Sister Milita Gans, who taught school at Little Rock, began her packing early. She was appointed for the Papua New Guinea mission and expected to leave in the summer of 1931. Sister Theophane took time to help the missionary get her things together. She could understand why Sister Milita seemed to be walking on air, but few understood what the young Sister suffered as she packed another's trunks. Papua New Guinea was Sister Theophane's land of dreams.

The Sisters in Little Rock, Arkansas cast lots to see who should accompany Sister Milita to the train. Sister Theophane was one of the chosen companions. "The cruelty of fate," she sighed, "that I should see her off instead of going myself to the inhabitants of Papua New Guinea."[32]

Back in Techny, they began to prepare for the mission departure celebration. There, Sister Theophane's former postulant directress, knowing the Sister's eager desire to be off for the missions, remarked, "Wouldn't it be fine if you would be one of the Sisters going now?"

Sister Theophane's eyes shone with inexpressible longing. "Sister, I think I should die of joy!"[33]

After the bustle of departure came the quiet days of retreat for the Sisters at the Provincial House. Shortly after, Sister Theophane was called to the office of the Provincial.

They had decided, Mother Leonarda told her, to have her go to Waukegan to finish her nurse's training and take up laboratory work. Sister Theophane received the appointment with mixed feelings. For some reason, which she never discussed, she had a strange aversion to nursing. She seems to have met with some disappointment during her year of training at St. Mary's Hospital, and this changed her attitude toward the profession. Now religious obedience was placing her back into hospital work. She knew the blessings of obedience would be hers and sustain her.

"I wouldn't be a bit surprised if this is the means of your going to the Far East," prophesied Sister Genevieve. "They need nurses as well as teachers, and how much better if you are both!"[34]

Sister Theophane was cheered, though not convinced. "I hope I take root someplace," she sighed.[35]

In August, 1931, Sister Theophane moved to St. Therese's Hospital and was assigned to work in the Clinical Pathology Department. Sister Gabriela Hausdorf met her. The newcomer's eyes were tear-filled and her look was one of utter helplessness. "I am a complete failure in school," she confessed. "See what you can do with me." Her next statement, however, was characteristic of her selflessness. "I met Sister Julianne Dickenson on my way up here and she told me to be good to you. I promised her I would. Don't spare me; tell me all you think I should do and I will do it."[36]

In the laboratory, God's creation, which was ever her delight, began to reveal new mysteries to Sister Theophane as she studied it under a microscope. Her new work captivated her and enlisted her whole-hearted energy and interest. Besides her training for a certificate as a laboratory technician, she was also finishing up her regular nursing. However, she spent most of her time under the direction of Sister Gabriela in the laboratory.

If the study of medicine fascinated her, the laboratory's experimental "menagerie" was an even greater delight. She immediately took charge of "Brummelbear" and his three baby guinea pigs which she fed with a medicine dropper, not forgetting to give them generous doses of cod liver oil. "Nucleus" and "Nucleola," the Chinchilla rabbits, were Mom's gift to the laboratory. Nucleola's oldest offspring, "Magnolia," was brought in one day to be operated on for what Sister Theophane thought was a goiter. The anesthetist was summoned and proceeded to put the bunny to sleep while Sister Theophane scrubbed her hands as carefully as if she were about to assist at a major operation. After carefully incising the fur she scaled out a caterpillar. The operation ended and a few minutes later Magnolia entertained her "surgeons" by trying to get the bandage off her supposed incision.[37]

One day a professor wanted to have the guinea pigs for class to demonstrate the procuring of blood from the heart for a Wasserman test. Ten little pigs were brought in. The first two attempts were unsuccessful. Sister Theophane became uneasy. When a third attempt failed, she stepped up, bundled the remaining seven piggies in her arms and disappeared from the room, leaving the class and professor speechless and rebuffed.[38]

But her circle of animal friends extended beyond the laboratory pets. A few days after her arrival the neighbor's cow was at the fence to eat out of her hand, and before long she had a name for each member of the adjacent farm yard.

As if the extensive gardens of the hospital were not big enough for her energy, she took the notion to have a roof garden. Off went a letter to Mom for seeds, and when the answer came Sister Theophane was busy collecting boxes for her new venture. Shortly after that the hospital chaplain and some of his friends met her energetically unloading the garden implements off the elevator on the seventh floor. She took their teasing and refused their help.

That summer, the chapel altar was decorated one morning with flowers from the roof garden.[39]

Yet, her love for nature and her love for animals were but a shadow of her love for humanity. One day she had to go to the city in connection with her studies. Her road lay through the slums of Chicago. As the elevated train passed the weather-beaten porches of the tenement houses she broke into tears, exclaiming:

> Look! What poverty! They try to raise some flowers, but there's not enough sunlight. See that wedged-in tree. All the luster is out of the leaves from dust and soot. Look at those kids there on the roof! They don't get enough to eat. I've got to do something. I can't go on like this. I have to get to work![40]

Whenever she encountered misery, poverty, or pain she was fired with this urge to "get to work!" Her work in the hospital did not bring her into frequent contact with the patients, but those whom she served have never forgotten her devotion. Anything that might cheer a patient was secured for him. She brought not only the medicines and food, but flowers, plants and even a pet canary for Sister Genevieve when the latter was ill.[41]

For Sister Theophane the call of a patient was the call of the Suffering Christ. She lived the doctrine of the Mystical Body. This lively faith would not allow her to ignore the slightest wish of a patient. While on night duty she mourned the fact that there was so little to do. Finally, she obtained permission to light a vigil lamp before the statue of St. Joseph to "get things moving." The light burned for some time, and then St. Joseph must have gotten busy. One night several accidents came in; the telephone buzzed incessantly; and the doorbell joined in the music. Sister scurried back and forth, but she could not keep up. Finally she stepped up and blew out the vigil light. "That's enough now, St. Joseph," she informed him.[42]

Sister Theophane had been working in the laboratory for two

years when her Superior met her in the hall, smiled broadly, and handed her a small blue envelope. Sister Theophane thanked her and hastened back to the room to read the letter. Sister Gabriela saw her enter, slit the envelope, and then grow pale. The paper trembled in her hand. The message seemed to have startled her. A moment later the young Sister turned to Sister Gabriela, calm and smiling.

"I'm going to Papua New Guinea," she said. Neither her voice nor her eyes betrayed the vision of her soul as it swept over the probable sacrifices that awaited her in the mission of the South Sea.

CHAPTER 8

OFF FOR PAPUA NEW GUINEA

"BE SURE you have a spirited horse ready for me, and a big dog!"[1] read Sister Theophane's reply to Sister Ottonia's letter of welcome to Alexishafen, Papua New Guinea. It had been more than eight years since she last rode a horse and her hand yearned to grip a bridle again.

She herself was busily assembling everything that promised to be of any use at the mission. Of course, all the collecting was done in spare moments between lessons in the laboratory, and her friends in the farmyard must have wondered what had happened to their faithful visitor who now never came around.

With all her eagerness to pick up material for her mission, she was always on guard, lest even in the smallest thing her spirit of poverty be endangered. Permissions were faithfully obtained for each item that went into her mission cupboard, and if she had a doubt about any article, it was put aside until she was assured that proper permission had been granted.[2] It was Mother's generosity that quickly filled Sister Theophane's mission boxes. Medicines, medical instruments, and varied hospital supplies were carefully sorted and packed for Papua New Guinea.

Because she had expected to leave soon after her appointment,

Sister Theophane was dismayed when news came of an indefinite sailing delay. Sister Ehrentrudis Schuster, Regional Superior of the Papua New Guinea Mission, was attending the General Chapter of the Congregation at the Mother House in Steyl, Holland. She wrote to Sister Theophane, informing her that at the close of the Chapter she would come to the United States and after a brief visit in America, return to Papua New Guinea taking her new mission worker along. Sister Theophane had no idea how long the Chapter would last, nor what connections her Superior would be able to make. The date of the departure was simply unsettled.[3]

During the months of waiting, the young missionary was working doubly hard to finish her training and get her certificate as a technician. Then, in July, 1933, she returned to the Provincial House at Techny for a six-month preparation for her final vows. Hay fever and asthma allied to make study difficult, but she plodded through the hot weather.[4] A Sister passing through the laundry one day saw her clutch the steaming mangle, gasping for breath. When she ran to help her, Sister Theophane just smiled and managed to sputter, "It's just . . . my . . . old hay . . . fever . . . and asthma. I'm O.K." Her spirit was indomitable![5]

Winter came and still there was no definite news about starting for the missions. The quiet, happy days of preparation for final profession were completed, and on January 6, 1934, Sister Theophane vowed her life forever to Christ as a Holy Spirit Missionary Sister.[6]

As she reverently pronounced the words of the vow formula, her soul—looking into an unknown future—embraced without flinching the privation, the loneliness, and the labor of a missionary life.

> May God wash away all the guilt of my sins and complete my offering on the altar of his love, since I am willing to accept, for God's sake, all the hardships it may entail.[7]

She was not taking a blind step. With glad freedom she was embracing the evangelical councils that would bind her forever to a life of evangelical poverty, consecrated chastity, and apostolic obedience. And because she was setting out for the jungles of Papua New Guinea, she knew that poverty would be dire and the obedience at times perhaps heroic.

She knew all this as she said:

> Therefore, I, Sister Theophane, Ines Maier, vow to Thee, Oh Holy and Triune God, to observe forever poverty, chastity, and obedience in the Mission Congregation of the Servants of the Holy Spirit.[8]

The words were spoken, and for a few silent seconds she knelt there, realizing that in that act of oblation her desire for martyrdom had a mysterious sense of promised fulfillment. Slowly she raised her hand and the officiating priest slipped on her finger the ring of Divine Espousal.

Since they were planning to visit Techny at Sister Theophane's departure for Papua New Guinea, not one of the family was present on the day of final vows. Sister Theophane felt their absence keenly, but after her first disappointment, she was bravely joyful with the other final vow Sisters who were enjoying time with their loved ones.[9]

After the celebration Sister Theophane returned immediately to the hospital. In March, 1934, she passed the Nurses' State Board Examinations. From then on she went quickly from one department to another getting an extra bit of special training wherever she could. She also took the opportunity to visit several outstanding hospitals in Chicago.

Spring came singing of new life, and still she waited. Summer drawled its welcome and brought along new hay fever attacks, and still she waited. Techny was flaming in September glory when Sister Ehrentrudis finally arrived. Sister Theophane wrote home jubilantly:

> At last the date is certain! We sail December 12. My Superior landed here September 31, and came to see me October 3. She is a nice, gentle, quiet sort of person who looks as if nothing on earth could disconcert her. She did not offer to drown me in the sea, so perhaps she is not as disappointed in me as she might have been.[10]

Though, to her, the departure was pure joy, she did not forget that her mother might not fully share her sentiments. So her letter concludes: "Write and let me know when to expect you. But don't come feeling bad, because this is about the grandest thing that can happen to a fellow."[11]

The sailing was moved up a week and, though it meant a change of plans for Mother's last visit, Sister Theophane was glad to be off as soon as possible.

She returned to Techny to prepare for the great day by spending three days in silence and prayer. In calm meditation she faced the fact that she was embarking upon a life where danger ran free. Up until now she had lived within her community, sheltered to a great extent. She had been surrounded by the beauties of the liturgy, almost cradled on the bosom of Mother Church. Now she was going to the outposts of Christianity; going where evil still held powerful sway. She might have quailed before the tremendous undertaking, but in her heart blazed a zeal to bring to people the fullness of God's love that casts out fear. She knew in Whom she believed; she knew she could always count on the love, life, and grace of God.

At the close of her three-day retreat, Sister Theophane received her mission cross in an impressive ceremony. "Sweet are the feet of those who bring the message of peace," sang the choir. She would carry Christ's message of peace and hope across thousands of miles, to a lonely isle, lost in the vast expanse of the tropical seas.

The ceremonies were over; the date was set; Sister Theophane was spending the last days with her family. Those who observed her with her relatives during that last visit would have thought that leaving them meant nothing to the departing missionary. Appearances were far from true. "I may not cry," she confided to Sister Gabriela Hausedorf. "For Ma's sake I must be brave."[12]

On November 30, 1934, the community once more assembled in the chapel. Sister Regional Ehrentrudis, Sister Theophane, and two other Sisters, Emiliana Koedel and Auxilium Reiser, who had been spending some time in the United States and were now on their way back to Papua New Guinea, knelt at the altar and received the priestly blessing for their voyage. The Sisters implored the protection of the Star of the Sea in the beautiful stanzas of the "Ave Maria Stella." It was the last farewell to the convent chapel, and within ten minutes the Sisters were at the entrance of the convent, getting in a last word before the cars left.

Sister Rosalie, who had come to see her sister off to the missions, could not restrain her tears. But Sister Theophane's glowing mission zeal would not admit of sorrow at the parting. Seeing her mother's sad glance, she embraced her and whispered, "It's great, Mom. Just think what Pop would say!"

The cars moved from the drive and the Sisters, who watched them go, broke into song. They were jubilant, because in each heart rose a prayer of gratitude that once more Holy Spirit Convent was sending forth willing hands and intrepid hearts to spread the Kingdom of Christ on earth and bring love and peace and joy to hearts that were shrouded in the night of unbelief in the gospel and the shadows of death.

The four Sisters traveled to Canada and left on the *Niagara*, which sailed from Vancouver on December 5, 1934. Sister Theophane kept her mother posted on the progress of the journey. The sea, though calm, was not finding a place in Sister Theophane's affections. "If it were not the only means to a noble end," she wrote, "I would not consider any reason strong enough to get me on the sea."[13]

Keeping this in mind, one wonders at her sea exploits in Papua New Guinea. A Brother on the Mission declared that "she would have made a splendid sea captain!"[14]

The Sisters enjoyed a day in Honolulu, visiting the Maryknoll Mission there. Sister Theophane noted with pleasure that "the Chinese, Japanese, Filipinos, and European peoples mix socially and racially in Hawaii and nobody says a word about class or race distinction."[15]

The next stop, seven days later, was at Suva, Fiji. Sister Theophane found a bit of home in the quaint store windows which displayed Heinz's 57 varieties. Because of frequent showers, most of the buildings had a roof extending over the sidewalk. Despite the rain, the missionaries took a stroll through the city.[16] A Fijian met the Sisters and offered to take them to a convent. On the way he stopped every man he saw. Probably he was so proud that he felt obliged to announce his honor to everyone he knew. After a few hours with the Sisters of St. Joseph of Cluny, who conduct a boarding school in Suva, the missionaries returned to their ship, which sailed that evening for Auckland, a seaport in Northland, New Zealand.

Two days before Christmas they reached New Zealand. On Christmas Eve they were again at sea. They had anticipated a Christmas on the ocean and were not surprised when Sister Regional, Sister Ehrentrudis, ordered them to the deck after supper. When they returned to the cabin it was decorated with evergreen and holly, and in a corner nestled the Christ Child. Sweets and sealed envelopes labeled "Open Dec. 25," completed the celebration. The Sisters had to give up having Holy Mass, as there was no Catholic priest on board.[17]

On December 27, the ship entered the harbor at Sidney, and the Sisters quickly hailed a taxi to take them to Epping, the home of the SSpS in Australia. Back with their own Congregation, the four missionaries rested from the long voyage before continuing to Papua New Guinea. The rest was short-lived, because friends of the Sisters in Epping vied with each other to show the Papua New Guinea-bound Sisters all the scenic beauty of Australia. Sister Theophane remarked in a letter that she saw more of Australia than of the U.S.A.[18] The zoo, the National Park, and institutions of various religious communities working in Australia were on the program.

It was not until February, 1935, that the four Sisters resumed their journey, boarding the *Macdhui* for the last leg of their trip.

> We had about eight stops with a nice time on land. . . . The *Macdhui* was full of gold-seekers, heading for the Papua New Guinea gold fields, and of missionaries too. We had two Masses daily, there being two Sacred Heart Fathers aboard. . . . We took about twenty-five mules aboard for the gold fields and tons of household necessities for the gold-seekers. . . . At Salamaua the gold seekers left us to fly inland to the mountains. You'd be amazed at all the airships and airlines in Papua New Guinea—all drawn here by the gold business.[19]

In Salamaua the Sisters visited the grave of Brother Eugene Frank, who had been speared by members of the mountain tribes. The news of the murders of the young Brother and the equally young priest, Father Carl Morschheuser, reached the Sisters on their voyage. Sister Theophane's heart beat fast as she heard of the tragic incident. The priest had died immediately of his wounds, but the Brother, attacked a week later, managed to escape with the help of a faithful inhabitant. Other friendly inhabitants helped to care for the wounded Brother, until eight days later a government plane found him. He was brought to the hospital at the Salamaua, but died after three days because his wounds, festering from the tropical heat, were too far along for the doctor to treat.[20]

Sister Theophane stood at Brother Eugene's grave and thought with "holy" envy of this young missioner who had given his life for the spread of the faith. "I sang the *'Te Deum,'* " she said later, "and how I lingered over the words: '*Te martyrum candidatus, laudat exercitus*!' "[21] To her the incident was not terrifying; it was glorious! Her secret longing to share in the grace accorded the Brother and Priest lies hidden between the lines of her comment: "This wild place where the martyrdom occurred is not very near to us, but there is talk of sending Sisters there. There is no chance for me—unless they want a nurse."[22]

After discussing Brother Eugene with the nurse who had cared for him, Sister Theophane inquired about the person who had accompanied Brother. The nurse answered rather laconically that he was still there. No one bothered much about him, nor thought of sending a report of his condition back to Papua New Guinea. The boy wept with joy when the missionaries came to see him, and took him back with them. He was Sister Theophane's first patient in the missions, and—because of his loyalty to Brother Eugene—was treated with special care.

The last stop before Alexishafen was at Madang, the government headquarters in Papua New Guinea. Here Sister Theophane met the doctor whose work took in the Catholic Mission. The doctor's pet cockatoo stood around wanting attention and patting. "He is all white with yellow head trimming," she noted, "and he rolls his bulging eyes like a cartoon. Such a comical pet I never saw."[23]

At about three p.m. on Saturday, February 17, 1935, the *Macdhui* dropped anchor at the harbor of Alexishafen. The Bishop, priests, Brothers, and Sisters were at the dock to welcome the new missionaries. Sister Ottonia, who was eagerly waiting to greet Sister Theophane, scanned the deck. Sister Regional, Sister Auxilium, and Sister Emiliana came sedately down the gangplank. Where was Sister Theophane? After a few minutes Sister Ottonia sighted the new missioner giving last directions to the patient for whom she had cared on the ship. When she finally came down the gangplank,

Sister Theophane seemed to be as calm as though coming to Papua New Guinea were an every-day-affair. Beneath the exterior serenity, her heart beat fast when she stepped on the shore! Papua New Guinea at last.[24]

Bishop Francis Wolf, SVD, spoke a few words of welcome to the new Sisters, and then all went to the Cathedral of Christ the King, which was under construction. After a prayer of thanksgiving, the Sisters returned to their own chapel to sing the "*Magnificat.*" After luncheon, the new missionaries laid aside their blue serge habits, and donned the cool habits worn in the tropics. "I felt quite a pang at laying aside my blue habit," wrote Sister Theophane. "It had become very dear to me after wearing it six years. We even get buried in white so that we cannot even go to heaven in our blue habits!"[25]

For the time being, Sister Theophane was stationed at Alexishafen,[26] central station of the Papua New Guinea Mission. Though now the main station, Alexishafen was not the first mission to be opened on the islands. The Fathers of the Society of the Divine Word came to Papua New Guinea in 1896 and began their work on the island of Tumleo, just off the mainland of what was then known as Kaiser Wilhemsland, North-eastern Papua New Guinea. In succeeding years other smaller stations were opened within traveling distance of Tumleo. All these stations remained dependent on the mother-station. When the mission could purchase a small sailing vessel, the missionaries established new stations along the coast, going as far down as Bogia. However, in 1904 there was a sudden change of route for the ships that had been bringing supplies to Tumleo. Under the new arrangement, no steamers stopped at Tumleo, and supplies for the mission had to be left at a port some distance down the coast. Sometimes the supplies lay at the port for months before a vessel sailed up the coast to deliver them to the missionaries. This meant both a loss of time and money.

The Superior of the mission of Tumleo went down the coast to search for a suitable sight to establish a mission station. Alexishafen attracted his attention. The harbor was good, and the land was covered with virginal forest. The next two weeks were spent surveying the land, and when it was found to be satisfactory, a contract of sale was closed with the owners, natives of Sek, an island opposite the entrance to the harbor. Within a month, a tract of the land had been cleared and the first building completed. It was a two-story house, built entirely of roughly prepared timber, having a roof of corrugated iron. Since transportation facilities played a large part in the matter, Alexishafen became the central station of the mission. The mission's main school was transferred from Tumleo to Alexishafen and new buildings appeared almost like mushrooms in the harbor station.[27]

When Sister Theophane arrived in 1935 the mission had thirty years of glorious history in its chronicle. In her first letter home from Papua New Guinea she gave a detailed description of the mission.

> Our mission is the very best looking sort I have seen on the whole trip. The cocoanut [sic] palms are planted in rows all over the place. The grass is a mean, seedy type, but looks neat. It is kept down by the cows, but in our neighborhood it is cut by the girls with long, flexible knives. They are used like sickles. All sorts of ornamental palms have been planted around here. There are flowers galore. The birds are fresh, freakish, and beautiful. They have amazing calls; most of them seem to be imitations of some animal call or of the human voice. The frogs in Australia make a noise like sawing wood; but the frogs here sound like the first "chug" of an auto on a cold day.
>
> We walked around the buildings in the missions for a few days. There is little beauty in them, since the locals know nothing about preserving order. The Sisters do wonderfully well.
>
> Our convent is a long, low house made of sheet asbestos nailed

over a wooden framework. The whole thing consists of rooms for sleeping quarters and the chapel. A wing across one end has a serving room, visitors' room and Sister Regional's room. The dining room is part of the verandah. The kitchen is a separate building, because the natives learn to cook.[28]

The laundry is separate for the same reason. The tubs in the laundry are all made of polished cement and are easy to keep clean. We have a mangle which must be turned by hand. All the soap used here is home-made. It is very nice lathery soap made of coconut oil.

This much belongs to the convent. We have good sanitation and clean well-water. Everything is plain, but neat and sanitary.

The buildings for the girls consist of a house for the half-castes [mestizos] in which are school rooms, dormitories, and quarters for the principal. The Sisters have an embroidery room here, where vestments are made, and the half-castes help. They do nice work. Another building is for the larger girls, with sleeping quarters and class rooms. A second and similar building accommodates the younger girls. There are a few small sheds around used to store wood, because on certain days the girls are allowed to cook in the local style with a camp fire.

Somewhat apart from the girls' compound is the hennery. Around the corner is the "cowery." We keep about two hundred cows here. They give a quart or so of milk each day and are milked only once a day. The best cows go almost dry unless they are given special care. The grass here has little nourishment because it grows so fast and is all water.

About ten minutes' walk from our place is the Bishop's residence and that of the priests, Brothers, and boys. We also went through the shops with Bishop Wolf. The shops are merely sheds. They have a metal workshop, a boat-building shop, a slaughter house with meat and sausage machinery and ice box, and a saw mill with a carpenter shop. I think the shops produce everything but nails and screws.

We saw hinges being made for the Cathedral doors, and stacks of arches were lying around. One Brother usually runs a shop and

> has from twenty to fifty boys working with him. It is a pity better lumber cannot be raised here. Everything made in the shops now will be used for the new Cathedral. The framework is complete, but only the front half is covered. The Blessed Sacrament is reserved in the old chapel and is brought to the Cathedral for benediction or Holy Communion. The people attend Mass daily in the Cathedral, and a surprisingly large number receive Holy Communion. . . . They kneel on low narrow benches which serve both as kneeler and seat.
>
> A little to the rear of all this is the hospital. . . . This building is for the males. . . . The female patients have a building in the girls' compound near our house. In a future letter I'll write at length about these. I am not yet well enough rooted to say or think much.[29]

Such was the main station at Alexishafen in February, 1935, when Sister Theophane came to Papua New Guinea. From this throbbing center of mission life on the island priests and Sisters had pressed up the coast, into the jungle, and to the Bismarck Mountains. It was to these small stations in the bush that Sister Theophane turned with eager longing. Here was the life she had dreamed of. Here were the mission trails—soul trails!

Sister Theophane found the Sisters at Alexishafen all clamoring for a chance to go to the mountain districts. But Bishop Wolf was wisely hesitant about allowing the Sisters to take up work in this dangerous section, though several priests were pioneering there.

For several days Sister Theophane waited to get her definite assignment. When it finally came, she swallowed hard but managed a smile. She was appointed to work at Alexishafen.

Four years old, 1910

Above: Inez at ease with horses at age 10, 1916.

Right: From left to right: Loraine Magin, Inez, Louise Magin, Alberta Magin, Rosalie Maier. The Magin and Maier girls attended St. Michael's school together. This photo was taken July 28, 1917 at the Magin's "Rifle Range" farm.

Alma Magin and Inez with the Magin's dog, Shep, on July 25, 1917. Alma married Inez' brother, Raymond on July 4, 1929. Alma and Ray Maier are the parents of Editor, Gregory Maier.

Opposite: Inez as a 17-year-old high school senior in 1923.

Right: Inez 18 years old, 1924

Below: Inez at home with cats, 1924

Opposite: Inez as a nurse with her beloved "Pop", William F. Maier in 1924 while at St. Mary's Training School for Nursing

Above: Inez as a nursing student in 1924.

Inez, now Sister Theophane, with father and mother in July 1926 after receiving habit of the Holy Spirit order

Sister Theophane with Sister Mary Rosalie of the Sisters of St. Joseph, her sister, and their mother Louise, July 1926

Opposite: Sister Theophane with Sister Gabriel at St. Therese's Hospital in Waukegan, Illinois, 1931.

Above: Sister Theophane with her sister-in-law, Alma Maier, Alma's son, Stephan, and Alma's mother, Louise Magin in Waukegan, July 1933.

Right: Sister Theophane with her mother at Holy Spirit Mother House in July 1930.

Below: Passport Photo, Fall 1934.

Above: Sister Theophane and nephew Stephan, July 1933. Stephan Maier is the editor's older brother, now deceased.

Right: Map of the north coast of Papua New Guinea in Mandang Province, showing the locations of many of the villages and small islands where Sr. Theophane was active in performing her missionary work. Over the decades some of the smallest settlements have disappeared from modern maps.

Madang Province
0 25 50 km
BISMARCK SEA
Wewak
North Coast Hwy
Angoram
SEPIK RIVER
Keram River
EAST SEPIK PROVINCE
Cape Franseski
Broken Water Bay
Awa Point
Boroi
Awa
Manam Island (1829m)
Stephan Strait
Hansa Bay
Bogia
North Coast Highway
RAMU RIVER
Rivo Island
Malala Island
Ilala
Ulingan
Bunabun
Salemben
Josephstaal
ADELBERT RANGES
Isumrud
Mugil
Cape Croisilles
Aronis
Balbe
Karkar
Karkar Island
Mom
Mt Kanangio (1831m)
Dangsal
600m
Bagabag Island
Strait
Mt Schrader (2053m)
SCHRADER RANGES
Sogeram River
1554m
MADANG PROVINCE
Sek Island
Nobanob
Alexishafen
Utu Mission
Slar Island
MADANG
Yabob
Astrolabe Bay
Erima Harbour
Cape Rigny
Pommern Bay
Cape Iris
Helmholtz Point
Saldor
Aiome
Mt Aiome (2830m)
Simbal
ENGA PROVINCE
Ramu River
Jimmi River
To Wabag & Porgera
Usino
Mt Herbert (4267m)
BISMARCK RANGES
WESTERN HIGHLANDS
Mt Hagen (3791m)
Highway
MT HAGEN
PROVINCE
Highlands
Bundi
Brahmin
Mt Wilhelm (4509m)
Kegsugi
SIMBU
KUNDIAWA
PROVINCE
Mt Otto (3546m)
EASTERN HIGHLANDS
GOROKA
PROVINCE
Mt Kubari (1865m)
FINISTERRE RANGES
3780m
Ramu
Dumpu
Mt Glendaco (3231m)
Highway
To Lae
Teptep
Mt Finisterre (3765m)
MOROBE PROVINCE
Wantoat
Kabwum
To Sialum
Sarewak Bay
VITIAZ STRAIT
609m
Crown Island
Mt Reamur (1304m)
Malala
Lake Wisdom
1112m
Bok
Long Island

Opposite: This picture is thought to show Sister Theophane (left) on her horse Caesar being guided by villagers while on a sick call.

Above: School children at Alexishaufen dressed for a mission festival.

Below: The Sisters' house at St. Michael's Mission. It was destroyed during the war.

Opposite: Nuns following a guide to a remote village from the Mission.

Above: Sister Theophane returns from a sick call in the 40 shilling canoe donated by friends and supporters in Rochester, NY.

Above: Sister Theophane arrives at the island station as swimmers are called out of the water (1940).

Below: Sister Theophane returns home with her crew after visiting island villages.

Opposite: Seeking solitude at St. Michael's Mission guided by villagers while on a sick call.

Opposite: Christmas celebration in Papua New Guinea.

Above: Sewing class at the mission.

Right: Happy mother and child at St. Michael's Mission.

Opposite: Sister Theophane using a typical bridge to cross a swift river.

Above: Several of the SSpS nuns wounded on the Dorish Maru and who died in Hollandia were transported back to the SSpS cemetery in Alexishaufen shortly after the war.

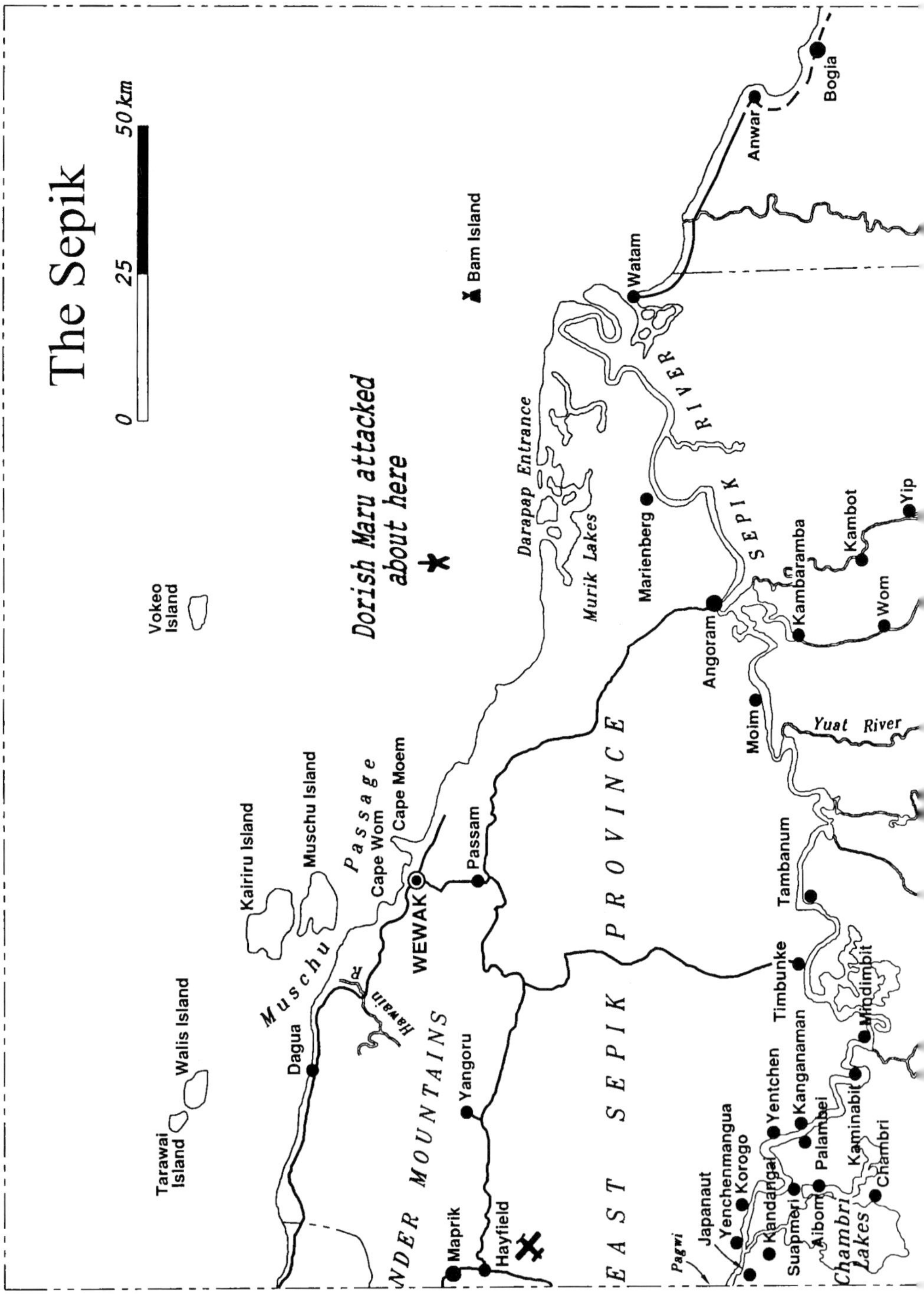

Map of the north coast of Papua New Guinea showing the coastal area of Sepik Province, located just to the north of Mandang Province. This map shows the general location of the troop/prison ship Dorish Maru during the fateful attack by aircraft of the 5th U. S. Air Force in February, 1944.

CHAPTER 9

BREAKING IN A NEW MISSIONARY

SISTER THEOPHANE watched some of the people of Papua New Guinea look in at the door of the hospital and eye her with interest. Finally one mustered enough courage to come in. "New fella Sister come. Me try him," he announced in Pidgin to his comrades, and he propped his leg on the stool before the white-clad Sister. There was no hesitancy the next day when the boy returned for treatment. "New fella Sister, she no hurt. Me go to him," his voice was full of confidence.[1]

The strange Pidgin English used by the people in their contact with the missionaries was in reality a mixture of Spanish, German, Latin, and English, an amalgamation of grammars. At first Sister Theophane felt like reminding the people that they were using the wrong case. She laughed at her teacher's instinctive lookout for grammatical errors, and decided that hearing and speaking Pidgin was to be just one of the sacrifices of mission life in Papua New Guinea.[2]

The hospital was to be her principal occupation for some time. Sister Barnaba Zirkel, a veteran of the first struggling years of Saint Michael's Mission at Alexishafen, was in charge of the hospital. Respected and trusted by whites, mestizos, and Papua New

Guineans, old Sister Barnaba was the life of the hospital. On his arrival at Saint Michael's Mission in 1926, Father William Ross intended to leave a phonograph at the hospital to entertain the patients. However, after a quarter of an hour with Sister Barnaba, he decided that the hospital had no need of a phonograph as long as this Sister was there.[3]

Having been in Papua New Guinea almost a quarter of a century, Sister Barnaba was certainly not abreast of modern methods in her medical practices. On the other hand, Sister Theophane—was a trained nurse conversant with the latest methods. But the people were shy of a newcomer and degrees or certificates were meaningless to them. To win their confidence, and also because she was an assistant, Sister Theophane had to use the old methods which the people knew and trusted.

Though it must have frustrated Sister Theophane to conform to outmoded methods, her fellow Sisters never suspected her sacrifice, since she did not allow herself to speak of it. Instead, she channeled her frustration into rich merit for the service of the gospel in Papua New Guinea to.[4]

The hospital, though small and furnished in primitive fashion, was well equipped. Not only Papua New Guinians, but also whites, patronized it. About 20,000 patients a year received treatments for tropical diseases, such as malaria, typhus, black water fever, and dysentery. Tropical ulcers, snake bites, and broken bones were also regularly treated.[5]

Besides her hospital duties, Sister Theophane was given the coveted task of caring for the chapel. The baking of altar breads, which also fell to her lot, took up a good deal of her time since she was asked to supply several of the smaller stations as well as Saint Michael's.

When Sister Theophane left for Papua New Guinea she took along a colony of bees, a gift from one of the priests at the SVD seminary. On the third day at sea, the bees seemed strangely immobile. The four Sisters watched them curiously and decided they must be asleep. When a strange odor accompanied the supposed "sleep," Sister Theophane realized that her bee family had perished.[6]

At St. Michael's, bees came into her life again when she was assigned to help Sister Ottonia in the apiary. She comments:

> The bees are a side joy of mine here. The stings don't bother me half as much now as at first. The bees are interesting animals, but the honey business here is rather poor. The honey is dark and thin with a strong flavor. Just at present the Brother who takes care of the SVD bees is in his novitiate, so we have his to look after, too. One queen escaped on me last week, and another which I tried to introduce into a colony was murdered.[7]

At one time the two Sisters collected as much as sixty pounds of honey from one colony, but the success was short-lived. The Papua New Guinea bees followed in the wake of their intended companions.[8]

Such were her regular duties, punctuated richly with what Sister Theophane called "real mission life"—trips with older missionaries to out-stations. New recruits in the mission were always intiated to the work in the villages by accompanying older missionaries.

One Sunday morning Sister Ottonia took Sister Theophane to the Island of Sek. The two Sisters set out in a rather dilapidated canoe, letting several young boys row. The sea was calm and the morning beautiful. Upon arriving, the Sisters immediately set off to tour the island, some two miles long and very narrow. Along the two-mile stretch lay several small villages, each of which the Sisters visited, tending the sick and treating wounds.

Sister Ottonia then had the catechist blow the triton shell to call everyone for catechetical instruction. As Sister Theophane watched the people leisurely stroll to the large hut she saw once again how she was learning patience. After an hour or more, enough had assembled to warrant the opening of class. Sister Theophane, not yet fluent in Pidgin, was an attentive spectator during the first part of the lesson. Her focused attention was unique in that hut—the people knew little of concentration. The class was far from homogenous. Mothers with loudly protesting infants elbowed youths and old warriors munching betel-nut, while children, dogs, and pigs ran in and out.

Sister Ottonia caught the look of despair in her young companion's eyes and smiled. "It takes time for them to settle down," she grinned.

When Sister Ottonia checked up on the progress of the class she saw that her catechist had not been idle. She handed the class over to Sister Theophane for a singing lesson. The people seemed to be immune to rhythm and quite innocent of varying tone quality. The memory of that class remained vivid as Sister Theophane's letter testifies:

> The girls and women have harsh, screechy voices which were in perfect harmony with the sentiments of the mob . . . whom they represented in the Gospel responses. The answer of the rabble, "Non hunc, sed Barabbam," was piercing, and caused a mental reaction I never had before.[9]

After what seemed an endless ordeal, the class was over.

Once the formal part of the visit was finished, the children gleefully surrounded the Sisters, ready for an hour of games. Mothers brought their babies to get the delicious doles of white bread which the Sisters never forgot to bring. After the games the children raced to the shore to give the canoe a push as the missionaries launched out for home.

However, the sea—so calm in the morning—was rich with foam and threatening waves. Sister Ottonia looked dubiously at their old craft and at the inexperienced schoolboys who had rowed them over. Perhaps the people would row them home in one of their canoes, she suggested. A show of unwillingness met this proposal. They were not eager to trust themselves and their canoe to an angry sea. Sister Theophane nudged her companion. "Let's not let them think we depend on them. Come, we can try in our own craft."

They set out, but the rough sea proved unmanageable for the young rowers, and they were caught in a strong current. Sister Theophane saw the danger and crawled to the oars. "You'd better rest a while," she explained, trying not to frighten the children.

The pulling was hard but the boat managed to break away from the swift current and then labor over the restless sea to Alexishafen.[10]

Everyone at the mission knew that these contacts with the people were Sister Theophane's delight, and older missionaries sought opportunities for her where she could quickly get the training needed to go on her own mission trails. Father Jakob Weyer, stationed at Alexishafen, had a considerable stretch of territory in his care and he often called on Sister Theophane to take the sick calls that came from his people. She rode off gleefully on the good priest's horse.[11]

One day Father Weyer came to the convent asking for two Sisters to go to his distant chapel on the peak of the mountain. He had no catechist there to care for the place, and he was certain that both the chapel and the adjacent hut, which served as rectory, were in need of a scrub brush. Sister Superior laughed at the glee in Sister Theophane's eyes when she was told to call Sister Ferdinanda Mundelein and saddle the horses. Since the Superior thought the job would require at least three days, she cautioned the Sisters to take along provisions.

The morning was cool and beautiful, and the jungle echoed with song as the two Sisters started toward the mountain chapel. Sister Theophane rode "Caesar," a favorite mount she was breaking in. Today the spirited horse acted strangely. The road was familiar to him, yet he placed each foot carefully. They passed the first of the two small churches and stopped to get the keys at the rectory for the mountain chapel. Sister Theophane returned with the keys and mounted Caesar. He reared, kicked, threw her off, and ran a few feet away. Undaunted, Sister Theophane strode to him and remounted. He liked her spirit as much as she liked his, and they rode on peacefully.

"When we came to the first river through which we had to go," she wrote later, "I let him stand, thinking he might enjoy a drink. He thanked me by plunging his front hoof vigorously into the water several times, splashing me pretty well. I like his spunk, but he is afraid of me because of my habit."[12]

As soon as they reached the mountain chapel, a cool place was found for the horses and fresh water supplied for them by a spring. Then Sister Theophane was ready for work. They began with the chapel and the little house of God rang with the happy voices of the Sisters, raised in song as they scrubbed. The poor altar seemed almost animated with gratitude when the Sisters—finished with the scrubbing—covered the crude boards with immaculate linen and surrounded the tiny tabernacle with blossoms from the mountain side. Sister Theophane's heart was filled with intense joy. This was part of her mission dream coming true. On the morrow this poor chapel would be filled with people and the great God of heaven would condescend to their lowliness—Christ would become Incarnate on this altar! And the people of this unnamed mountain village, unlettered, unknown, and poor, would become rich in the possession of Him who containeth all things.

The two Sisters spent the night in Father Weyer's bush hut. The next day they were again busy cleaning up the grounds. Their food supply ran short and Sister Theophane bargained with the locals for eatables. The cleaning finished, they made a tour of the surrounding villages and treated the sick. Evening brought a downpour.

Unmindful of her own discomfort in the leaky hut, Sister Theophane hastened to find a dry shelter for the horses, lest they fall sick from exposure. She led Sister Ferdinanda's horse to the barn, but did not take time to tether him. When she came hurrying in with Caesar, the first horse made a leap through another opening and raced off. She tied Caesar carefully and gave him some bananas.

The next morning the torrential rain still swept down from the darkened skies. The two Sisters stood there for a moment; then they laughed heartily and set to work. Both saddles were firmly fastened on Caesar's back, and all their luggage was tied to the saddles. The Sisters brushed their dripping veils back from their faces, gathered up their waterlogged habits, and started walking down the mountain, led by the horse carrying their saddles and luggage. The brown clay, soaked from the heavy rain of the night before, now gave way and they skidded back and forth, clutching the bushes to keep themselves from sliding headlong down the mountain. Caesar whined, hesitated, and balked. Sister Theophane patted the frightened beast and spoke to him. He tried again, slowly and carefully, lest a misstep send him hurling down the bank into the soggy ravine.

"It's a blessing that one horse is gone," remarked Sister Theophane. "We would surely have tried to ride if both had been here—and I'm afraid we would have had our legs or necks broken sliding down this rain-soaked clay."[13]

They slid and skidded until they sloshed into Alexishafen where a concerned Sister Superior rushed to meet them. They were safe, however, two things about them had changed: their habits of immaculate white were bespattered with a generous coating of clay, and the glow of joy in Sister Theophane's eyes was deeper and more beautiful.

* * * * *

One morning in August 1935, just after the Sisters had breakfasted, a catechist rushed breathlessly onto the verandah. Sister Superior Milita Schafer from Mugil had sent him with an urgent call for help. Going to her aid meant crossing the open sea in a canoe and then seven hours on horseback. The Superior at Alexishafen knew that the trip was dangerous and she hesitated. Sister Theophane was comparatively new in the tropics and there was danger from crocodiles in the rivers she would have to cross. Yet, once she had weighed all the possibilities, she decided that Sister Theophane should travel to Mugil. Sister Theophane noted:

> Sister Superior finally gave permission saying that if I died, it was a noble sacrifice and I should be consoled that I perished on an errand of mercy. Armed with these heroic sentiments and my medical kit, I set out on the most delightful trip I've had in Papua New Guinea.[14]

Soon after the permission was granted, Sister Theophane was ready. The catechist helped her get out a motorboat which would make better time than a canoe. After the boat ride came seven hours on a horse through rivers, bush, and mud. One river proved too deep, and Sister Theophane had to hunt up a canoe, while the catechist helped Caesar across. Arriving at the little mission completely exhausted from the glaring August sun, Sister Theophane was told that her patient was just another hour's ride further into the bush. Caesar whined; the Sister petted him and let him munch a banana. Sister Superior Milita and Sister Alexis Lederer joined her and they were off through the bush.

Twilight caught up with the "flying" missionary, and when she entered the ill-smelling hut she could hardly discern her writhing patient in the shadows. A smudgy kerosene lamp gave a little light and a considerable odor. Quickly she spread her working materials on the floor. The typical hut boasted no furniture, and the floor—with slats a few inches apart—did not make an ideal surgical table. Sister Theophane brushed aside these inconveniences and set to work. For three hours the catechist sat at the door and waited.

Exhausted from her journey, Sister Theophane was more conscious than usual of the stifling heat of the hut. The condition of her patient did not lighten her spirits. When the Sister finally crawled through the low opening into the night air she was dripping with perspiration and heavy with discouragement. "I'm afraid we came too late," she told Sister Milita. "I don't think she'll pull through, but she's resting now."

With a promise to return in the morning, the missionaries mounted their horses and started off with a quick trot to Mugil. Before midnight Sister Theophane was in her cell for a brief respite, but at nine o'clock the next morning she found herself bending over the poor woman. She saw, however, that there was little to do. Neglect and poor sanitation had done their deadly work of infection. Gently the Sister tried to warn the poor woman of impending death, but the startled woman screamed and rushed out of the hut. Amazed, Sister Theophane watched the sick woman scramble through the bushes toward the jungle. Excited relatives pursued the woman and tried to persuade her to return, but she refused. Sister Theophane explained to the group that she would not follow a patient into the bush. If the patient did not want her treatment, she could not make her accept it. The people nodded solemn assent.

Six months with the Papua New Guinean population had given the young missioner an insight into their mentality. Had she treated the woman and failed to save her life, they would have lost confidence in the Sister. As it was, they laid full blame on the woman herself, who died in the bush a week later. Not even the best treatment in a fully equipped hospital could have saved the woman, said Sister Theophane.[15]

As there was no resident nurse at Sister Milita's station, the Superior had Sister Alexishafen take Sister Theophane on a tour of the surrounding villages. Four days were spent tramping from one village to another, up one mountain and down another. On the evening of the fourth day Sister Theophane, completely exhausted, had retired to her cell and was just dropping off to sleep. She had the seven-hour ride to Alexishafen ahead of her in the morning.

> I hoped my bones could have a bit of repose before the return trip, but no. At ten P.M. came the good Father of the Station and asked if I wouldn't please return to see a woman I had visited in the morning. A man had come and had said that she was dying. My bones got out of bed, hiked an hour to the woman. We found her with a 104 temperature, lying by a roasting fire and six or seven folks sitting by looking on helplessly.[16]

Sister Theophane did not think the woman was in immediate danger of death, but since the priest was leaving for a retreat at Alexishafen, he administered the Sacrament of the Sick and then they tramped back.

> At 4:30 A.M. it was time to get moving home. . . . With the bracer of a night's rest consisting of two and a half hours, I started back to Alexishafen the next morning on my gallant steed. To save time we heard Mass and received Holy Communion at a bush Church where a priest was fortunately stopping. The riding is fairly good for the whole stretch except when the rivers are high.
>
> On the way back I promised to go up to my old place (where we had spent the three days fixing up the church) and visit some sick who a catechist had told me about. Caesar was tired and unwilling to make the trip, (an extra three hours) but he did it. When we got there the village was empty save for one old man. The people are funny. They tell you someone is dying when he only has a cold. The horse felt cheerful about the return trip, since he was four days away from home. We arrived at St. Michael's about 5:30 P.M.[17]

These frequent visits to the villages were giving the new missionary the much needed understanding of the character of the people for whom she longed to work. Her diary shows that she was acquiring a keen insight into the varied and sometimes conflicting characteristics of her people. "The Papua New Guineans are about as high in my affections now as the dear Italians I had in my summer school," she wrote to her mother. [18] She knew that each one had an immortal soul, precious in the sight of God, and she knew how little the poor people realized this.

> The people still need much Christianizing here. In some places the population is falling off amazingly, because the sin of the age has corrupted these poor folks. The Sisters tell how they have tried to raise orphaned and cast-away children, only to have them poisoned later on by the relatives.
>
> When questions of marriage arise, it is a fight to the death for the young couple to choose freely whom they will marry. A girl died here a few weeks ago, due to poisoned tobacco sent her by her father. She wanted to marry some fellow outside her tribe, and her father would rather see her dead. A few days later someone served the Father the same trick and he died of poisoning. Tobacco and betel-nut are the things mostly used to poison with. All smoke and all chew betel-nut; hence it is an act of friendship to make a gift of them to a friend. The poison in them cannot be detected until it is too late.
>
> It's only by intermarriage that tribal distrust can be killed. No person completely trusts another. When a seriously sick one comes to us, he brings a relative or a tribesman along to feed and guard him. A few weeks ago a trusty mission laborer came in very ill. His brothers and his wife accompanied him. When sickness disfigured him, her affection cooled and she looked for another man. Finding a suitable individual, she gave her husband some mild poison and then awaited results. We buried him three days later. I believe the dead man went straight to heaven. He asked for Confession a few

> hours before he died. He knew what his wife had done, but never gave her away, and even asked us to look after her because she was slightly ill.[19]

When a sick call came, Sister Theophane was never certain just what she would find. At times the Papua New Guineans seemed to try her patience willfully, just to see how she would react on finding out that they had sent her on a useless errand. She hid her impatience, because she knew that if she displayed too much annoyance, they might hesitate to call her when real need arose. It did not take the people long to realize that here was a Sister who was ready to work, and sweat, and die for them. She might scold soundly when they came to the hospital and stuck their heads in at the window calling, "Chinin I kam!" (Quinine, come here!). Like guilty children they would then come to the door and politely request an injection. But the next day they would be at the window again. Sister Theophane was far more ready to overlook their lack of courtesy toward her than to tolerate it in their relations with each other. A husband who ambled along beside his sick wife while she carried their baby, soon learned whose job it was to carry the child. After the husband took the baby, Sister Theophane carried the woman, remarking that it was a good thing the people were of small stature, otherwise she could not have managed to carry the sick.

Despite—or perhaps because of—their many unamiable traits, Sister Theophane loved the bush people and was never so happy and contented as when she could be with them ministering to their bodily needs or instructing them in the faith.

In even less time than it took her to become accustomed to the people, she became acclimated to tropical Papua New Guinea. Before she sailed, cautious confreres had given her so many warnings about poisonous snakes that when she went for her first visit to the Island of Sek her eyes were constantly on the ground. She let Sister Ottonia and others walk ahead so that she could scan the path for snakes and snake holes. "I saw holes of all descriptions," she said, "hundreds of them. And when we came to the village I noticed that near and under each hut were dozens of holes!"

Exhausted with nervousness and fear the poor Sister tugged at Sister Ottonia's sleeve. "Sister," she confided in an awed whisper, "I'm surprised there is a single human being left alive on this island. If every hole is a snake hole, and all the snakes are the size of the holes, it's a wonder everyone hasn't been eaten up by now!" Sister Ottonia doubled up with laughter. Very few of the holes were from snakes, she explained. Crabs, gophers, and various other small animals occupied most of the underground domociles.[20]

An occasional snake did show up at Alexishafen, but during the time Sister Theophane had been at St. Michael's Mission no priest or Sister had been bitten, though individuals came now and again with snake bites. The reality was nothing like the nightmare that had haunted the new missioner.

Although the waters were infested with crocodiles which often attacked the horses, the missionaries themselves were not molested to any great extent if they practiced prudence. One missionary came across a huge crocodile in the bush. The decrepit animal had lain in the swamp so long that grass was sprouting on its back. Wisely, the missionary kept his distance and let the grass grow.[21] Sister Theophane's sympathy went out to the poor horses, sometimes horribly slashed by the teeth of the swamp animal. The Brother in charge marveled at the devoted skill with which she mended the gashes.

Of other animals, Sister Theophane seldom made mention. She loved the birds with their boisterous calls; she enjoyed the occasional chatter of the monkeys; the mosquitoes were annoying, but perhaps not enough of a problem to merit comment. They were just one of the things the Sister had expected to find in a tropical mission.

When her mother inquired repeatedly about the climate, Sister Theophane assured her that the heat was bearable. The food, she admitted, was not too strange, though at times she recognized nothing on the table save the meat. As in the Southern missions, so in Papua New Guinea she was ever experimenting with new garden produce:

> We are anxious to grow everything possible, and it is only by experiment that we can find out what will take kindly to this climate. Grapevines grow, but never bear. Roses bloom profusely, but have dwarf blossoms. Tube-roses do well, and balsams, marigolds, zinnias and some others. Even dandelions must be coaxed.[22]

The experiments often had their humorous side. The Sisters had gotten a tree from Java (Indonesia) and cared for it with great solicitude. It blossomed and bore two huge fruits, something like breadfruit. Sister Superior picked one and brought it to Sister Theophane, recommending it highly. Sister Theophane took it, examined it carefully and tried to ascertain just what part of the fruit was edible.

She described the incident:

> I sawed a huge piece out. The fruit weighs about fifteen pounds. What part was edible I did not know, so I tackled one place after another. Result: a gummed mouth and lips, gummed knife and fingers, and a dreadful taste. My efforts drew a crowd and all were highly amused with the performance, but no one had pluck enough to join. At length I gave it up for a bad job and Sister Superior admitted that the thing was not ripe. The next year the tree had three or four fruits. Everyone was after me to demonstrate again. This time I baked it. In the oven three hours—tough yet. Back to the oven four hours—tough yet. Third trip to the oven six hours—black, but tough. The kernels tasted like chestnuts, but the flesh was hopeless. This year the tree had about forty fruits. We let them hang until a small spot showed a little decay. Then they are really

> ripe. Even now only half a dozen Sisters eat them. I planted about forty kernels and now have trees for the locals. The fruit emits a strange odor when it is cut, hence its unpopularity, but it is fine tasting. There is nothing at home to which I can compare it to give you an idea.[23]

* * * * *

The tropical climate had worked wonders for Sister Theophane's hayfever and asthma. These two had played their part and now were ushered off-stage, never to impede again the Sister's great missionary work.

The mission station at Alexishafen hummed with activity. Work on the new Cathedral was progressing quickly. That Cathedral in the wilds of Papua New Guinea was the pride and joy of the Bishop's heart. Daily, he came to inspect the work. The new convent for the Sisters was also under way. It was to be a two-story building, spacious enough to accommodate the Sisters who came in annually for retreats.

At the harbor, row boats, motor boats, and pinnaces were constantly coming and going as the missionaries made their regular trips to attend people on the islands. Like a queen over her subjects, the *Stella Maris* lorded it over the other smaller craft. The *Stella* had a capacity for 126 passengers, and it was her job to bring supplies to the scattered missions along the coast. She was constantly plowing the waters delivering timber, sand, and building materials to outlying missionaries. It was she, too, who quickly sailed for a missionary who was suddenly taken ill at an outpost. For smaller deliveries, the *Michael*, *Peter*, or *Maria*—all motorboats—were used.

To facilitate communications between the distant missions, St. Michael's acquired an airplane through the courtesy of the MIVA, [24] an organization established in Europe to aid missionaries in problems of transportation. The MIVA also furnished a pilot who would serve the mission until a Brother had sufficient experience to man the plane. *St. Paul*, the newly christened plane, soon made trips to all the scattered stations. The mountainous terrain made flying difficult, but by taking half its freight capacity the plane could manage to reach the stations in the hills. *Paul* was soon joined by another plane, *Peter*.

These planes, ever crossing the dark, mysterious jungle to soar over the Bismarck mountains, always kept the eyes of the Sisters stationed at Alexishafen turned to the high country. When a priest from the Bismarcks flew in for supplies he invariably visited the Bishop to plead for more Sisters to be stationed at his mountain mission. During these times, Sister Theophane found it hard to control her burning desire to be among the pioneers, to share their harsh, hard life. She found Alexishafen too full of what she called "conveniences"—there wasn't enough of hardship to satisfy her desire to spend herself in service of the people. Yet the Sisters who lived with her wondered how even her excellent physique could hold up as it did under the strenuous life she was leading. The sick of the outlying villages all looked to her for treatment, and she spent her days, and often a generous part of her nights, ministering to them. The other things she did were humorously referred to as "side jobs." But the side jobs added up—care of the bees, care of the church, baking of hosts, the garden, care of the sick and wounded animals, and any odd job that no one else seemed to have time for. It seemed like a full day to those who lived with her—but perhaps they could not fathom the consuming desire for sacrifice that was constantly urging Sister Theophane to seek out hardship, toil, and pain. These were the price of service for the redemption of souls.

Her desires are seen in the loving complaint she utters in the lines:

> Since I have been here I have not ceased to lament that I'm not a man. I am envious of the priests and Brothers who go out and rough it and blaze the trial. I am jealous of their fatigue and sweat,

> their hardships and dangers. The Lord knows that I can stand as much tough living as any man, and I long to be among the wild bush people. One has to love them in spite of their unlovableness. I half knew when I came that Alexishafen would be my post, but I never reckoned with the awful call of the wilds that burns me now. The others must labor and suffer while I sit sweetly here and grow fat and lazy. This is just another of life's little jokes![25]

Only later in life was she to realize how much this hidden sacrifice of her life's dearest longing meant for the communion in God's abundant love and salvation of those around her. Now her youthful spirit was aflame to carry the torch of truth to the farthest corner of uncivilized Papua New Guinea. But God knew the worth of Sister Theophane, and God knew how priceless were the sacrifices she made in silence.

CHAPTER 10

"PASTOR" AT LAST!

IN FEBRUARY, 1936 Saint Michael's Mission rejoiced as the first anniversary of Sister Theophane's arrival in Alexishafen drew near. The fact that the busy missionaries found time to prepare a program for the occasion is proof that St. Michael's recognized the treasure it had received in her. Sister Theophane was touched by the devotedness of her co-missionaries. She commented in her diary: "In the evening our comedian Sisters sang a wonderful home-manufactured psalm with pictorial illustrations to commemorate the event. The refrain was: *Exultabunt Kanaka, salus venit*!" In the next breath came again the impatient urge to be out roughing it: "If I didn't have to stick around this station so much, maybe more people could 'exultabunt.'"[1]

Sister Theophane's hope that there be more *exultabunt* people materialized shortly after the anniversary celebration. It was during that year, her second in Papua New Guinea, that she became a traveling missioner. Her first appointment sent her as catechist to the village of Ilala, about three hours distance from the mission at Alexishafen. The village had been among the first to receive the missionaries, but though all of the thirty or forty residents were baptized many were no more than nominal Catholics. There was a need to re-awaken fervor and the choice of Sister Theophane for the task was well made.

Father Albert Aufinger, in whose territory Ilala was situated, conferred with his new helper. She described the village in her diary:

> The good Father built a darling little school in the village. It is as poor as a church mouse, of course, but he's a tasty sort and succeeds admirably in making his little buildings attractive. He gave the people to understand that they were to appear 100% when I come up, and they do it. About fifty souls are concerned. It seems comical to be preaching at men and women old enough to be my grandparents, but they take it very respectfully. If they knew my past reputation as a professor, they might not act so deferentially. . . . The road to the place is terrible. On a good horse it can be reached in little over an hour. The hills are of treacherous, slippery clay and quite a number of boggy, dirty streams must be crossed. Many places on the road are overhung with vines and low drooping branches. One has to lie flat on the horse's neck to get by without leaving a veil or piece of it behind. Absalom would have had a hard time here.[2]

With the building of the school, Ilala's prestige took an upward climb. The sleepy village of a year ago became the pride of the inhabitants and the envy of its enemies. When young folk from surrounding villages began to filter in and settle there, resident bosses showed ill-disguised resentment. Before long they were issuing orders, supposedly from the government officials at Madang, that the Ilala residents were to move from their present site. The orders caused considerable unrest in the village but no immediate action was taken. The trouble seemed to subside, but it proved to be a lull before the storm. Sister Theophane's diary reads:

> The last time I was up to my village I was accosted by two fresh-looking young men who had been sent by the bosses with orders

for the Ilala people to come to a meeting. Nevertheless I held class. When it was over some of the men begged me to accompany them to the next village to the meeting. Such an invitation is a mark of trust, respect, and honor. I was deeply conscious of this. Mounting my gallant steed, I accompanied my upset people to the site of the meeting. I was received with extreme cordiality, and it was taken for granted that I had come for the assembly. Sitting a bit apart I took in the whole affair. It lasted about an hour and a half.

Only the men sat in council—I being the sole exception. Two "tultuls" and one "luluwai" with red-trimmed hats were the dignitaries. Betel nuts, cigarettes, and kulaus (cocoanuts) were continually served, the young boys having the duty to keep the supply replenished. In the neighborhood no child cried or played and scarcely an animal was to be seen. No woman walked around. All signs of the solemnity of the occasion. Most of the proceedings were discussed in Pidgin, so I could understand everything. There was no parliamentary procedure, but the assembly was respectfully silent when the police-hatted men spoke. The non-Catholics were quiet, but with an outward show of wrath and scorn. Every now and then a look or gesture of awe was cast in my direction. I was silent throughout the whole procedure and tried to maintain an expressionless attitude.

The conversation waxed hot! Father Weyer was "turned over the coals" and then Father Aufinger was "ripped up the back." The government was boss and not the mission, etc. etc. My catechist looked to me for moral support; then sprang to his feet and shouted, "We'll stick to Father Aufinger and the mission!" Threats of burning my village and imprisoning my locals were uttered. One must know the people to understand how serious or playful all their talk is. The dignitaries then said that my people would have stretches of roads to build into territory not belonging to them. Stubbornness was the response. After "jabbering" and chewing and arriving at no conclusion, the council ended. My people came to me with questions.

Finally it dawned on me that no *cheop* was behind the business

> and perhaps no official ever sent these police-hatted creatures. With this inspiration in mind, I told my flock to do nothing until inquiry was made in Madang. If it [could be proved] that Madang had nothing to do with the affair, those lying misbelievers would lose their beautiful hats and Ilala could peacefully increase in population from within and without. I was getting nervous about the time, but with a speed I never before achieved, I made the whole trip home in two and a quarter hours. It generally takes me three and a half hours.
>
> We have since found out definitely that Madang had nothing to do with the affair, so the miscreants will do well to hang on to their hats![3]

The unwelcome commotion had one marked effect—it tightened the bonds between the Missionary Sister and her people. Ilala loved its missionary and Sister Theophane would have given her life for her Ilala parish. Though in subsequent years she was at times far from Alexishafen her heart was always turning back to her "Philippians."[4]

Because she could not visit Ilala more than once a week for a two-hour class in religion, Sister Theophane had a catechist to help with the instructions. Michael was proud of his post and conscious of his dignity. His mental acumen did not indicate extraordinary talent, but Sister Theophane knew she could trust him. With childish pride he would laboriously perform at the chalkboard when she came. The letters he could not produce in script were simply printed. In mathematics he had achieved proficiency in addition up to twenty, but he preferred to count by hundreds. Such was Michael's scholastic record. After a few rounds of instruction, however, Sister Theophane commented in her diary: "My Michael is slightly improved." [5]

On the day of the Ilala meeting Michael sought to impress both Sister Theophane and the assembly. He had followed the Sister at some distance, but she took little note of him. When she arrived at the meeting, she spent some time chatting to her horse and then turned toward the crowd.

> I noticed a creature of importance wearing knee-length tweeds, an undershirt, and a soft slouch hat, carrying a long stick somewhat as a bishop manipulates his crosier. A person so attired appears ridiculous to the extreme. For a time I wondered who the lunatic could be. It was none other than my Michael. He had no police hat to boast of so he sought to make an impression by means of his fine clothes. . . . In a way known only locally he managed to bring the importance of his costume to my notice several times. I could scarcely refrain from laughing, but laughter would have been extremely out of place. When he spoke to me, he deferentially removed his hat. His hair, the woolly type, retained the form impressed by the hat—two hills with a valley in the middle.[6]

After years of careful training and contact with the mission, the catechists were far from efficient helpers. Regional customs and age-long disregard for the conventions of civilization held them firmly. Sometimes the training was like an outer coating—underneath the person remained untouched, as far as rules of sanitation and health were concerned.

In one of the villages that Sister Theophane occasionally visited, a catechist's wife gave birth to a baby boy on a Sunday. Neither she nor the baby was well, and by Monday both were in a critical condition. The catechist said nothing about it, but sat and looked and smoked and chewed betel-nut. Tuesday, Wednesday—still he sat and looked. On Thursday the Brother came from the mission to hold class. The catechist informed him of his ailing wife and child. The Brother rushed to the hut and saw there was nothing left to do but pray. It happened that Sister Theophane was with the Brother that day in order to give injections. He quickly called her.

> On hearing from him about the woman, I made post haste to the scene, and sent my pinnace back to get a priest. I did all I could to

> keep her alive until the priest arrived but she died in my arms after twenty minutes. The pinnace returned two hours later.[7]

Long ago Sister Theophane had learned that it was useless to become discouraged at this lack of response on the part of the people. She prayed for the dead and went on to do what she could for those who still had need of her care, toil, and prayers.

While Sister Theophane experienced great joy at the cooperation she received from her Ilala flock, the same could not be said of her other parish—the Island of Malmal. The island had been won over to the faith years before, but for some time had no catechist. The residents wanted no instruction, though they were in great need of it. Many of the adults had forgotten their prayers and evinced no desire to refresh their memory. Of the forty-five who should have been in class, not more than ten appeared. The work was disheartening. Sister Theophane was taken aback by their callous spirit. "I never expected to find that among simple, primitive people," she confessed. She tried patience and kindness and the people grew more bold and insolent; she became severe and they obeyed fearfully. At times they met her advance kindly, but such a reaction was the prelude to some impudent request. She confessed to her diary: "What course must I take to put faith and love into them? They have the sort of devil that must be driven out by prayer and fasting!"[8]

When visiting Malmal, Sister Theophane often stopped to see the residents on a neighboring island, Rivo. Some time later another Sister was given charge of Malmal and Sister Theophane took over regular work at Rivo. The new island offered meager consolation for her fiery zeal. Though children appeared for instructions, the adults showed little interest. She continued with her prayer and fasting and her heart bounded with joy when seven Protestants at Rivo asked for instructions. Two large isles nearby, entirely Protestant, had also asked for a priest. However, the mission was not immediately ready to comply with the request. Sister Theophane heard of the request and each time she passed by the Siar Isles on her way to Rivo, she resolved to risk visiting them.

One day after class at Rivo, Sister Theophane stopped the pinnace at Siar as one of her Rivo parishioners happened to be ill on the Island. This gave the Sister an excuse for her uncalled for visit. The residents gathered about her and the sick man was eager to see what she would do for him. They were duly impressed by the expert treatment he received, and they wondered at the supply of medicine left for him by the missionary. There were many visitors on the island who had come to mourn the death of a Siar woman. Those among them who knew Sister Theophane greeted her with lighthearted joy. It was a start and Sister Theophane joyfully confided to her diary:

> In a few minutes I was surrounded by residents and shown several sick people. Before I left I was assured by one fellow that my visit had been appreciated. With these people one must go slowly and carefully. Next time I tried the other Siar Island and found about forty children and the "smart young fellers" at home. They asked me to visit a sick woman. It may be a year or more before I can broach the subject of instructions, but I am not going to give up. The people are friendly to me now and wave frantically when I pass by. God help me to fish them into Peter's net.[9]

Work at Malmal and Rivo was hard and at times disheartening, but Sister Theophane's humor helped her through the difficult days. Since it was not always easy to get the use of a pinnace, she solicited money from her mission friends back in the States for a canoe. Sister Regional saw that such a gift would be ideal for the missionary, but she had her doubts as to the safety of the Sister. Past experience had shown that Sister Theophane would dare anything if a person was at stake, and the Superior wisely hesitated. The money for the canoe finally came from "Dear Mom," and in thanking her, Sister Theophane voiced her anxiety about getting the canoe.

> Thanks for the money for the canoe. Whether I'll get one is the next question. You told Sister Regional to take good care of your child, and she seems to be too conscious of the burden. She says I won't be satisfied until I'm wrecked with a horse or drowned, so she has her doubts about my prudence with a canoe. I know you won't feel sorry if I never get any—but I am not so easily pacified. Any money the mission gets will not be wasted, so don't feel bad about it. Loads of warm thanks and still more thanks. I won't beg again for at least two years![10]

When the pinnace, *Peter*, which Sister Theophane had been taking to Rivo, refused to run, the question was settled and Sister Regional gave her consent for the canoe. After much quibbling about the price, the builders finally agreed to start work on a canoe. When the boat was finished Sister Theophane spent three days trying to get it ready for the sea. She painted it and rigged up a flag. From unfinished wood she put together a shack to shield the canoe from the blazing sun. But when she took it out for a try, the boat leaked! Back to the builders it went, and new negotiations were opened with some of the people on Rivo. Again months of waiting. The Brothers appreciated her plight and offered to fix up a pinnace for her, but the Bishop thought it too hazardous. So she waited for the canoe. When the new specimen arrived it too called for finishing touches—but in the end it served its purpose. Now Sister Theophane had her own craft, and, when the call came, she could launch out without any delay in service of the gospel and her people.[11]

In the early part of December in 1936 Sister Theophane was summoned to the Superior's room. Two hours later she was aboard the *Stella Maris* with her little bundle of clothing and her medicine kit, sailing to Mugil. Four hours after she had left her Superior's room in Alexishafen , Sister Theophane knelt to receive the blessing of her new Superior in Mugil, Sister Milita Schafer.[12]

The call had come quite unexpectedly. Sister Melasia Zolch of Mugil was to return to Saint Michael's to prepare for her final profession.[13] Evidently another Sister was being considered to fill the vacancy, but for some reason a last-minute decision sent a hurried summons for Sister Theophane.

Mugil was not new to her since Sister Milita had called on Sister Theophane before to treat critical cases among the sick there. The 650 souls belonging to the main Mugil station were scattered among several coastal villages. The missionaries residing in Mugil served three other stations: Megiar, with 760 souls; Natukar with some 300; and Bargam, a mountain village with a population similar to Natukar. In Mugil and Megiar the Sisters taught in the schools, but in the smaller stations this task fell to the catechists.[14]

The Sisters' convent at Mugil formed a white cap for one of the coastal hills. It was a small wooden structure with a roof of tin. Across the valley on another hill perched a similar dwelling for the two priests and a Brother. A rather extensive coconut plantation and copra works, managed by the mission, contributed to its support. Houses for the regional workers clustered on the hillsides.

In filling Sister Melasia's office, Sister Theophane became nurse for the small hospital, overseer for the laundry, host-baker, and seamstress. Her diary preserves the record of those days at Mugil:

> To start with, the boys staged a small dysentery epidemic. As a grand display of my ability I managed to have two boys die in one week. I felt pretty ashamed, but after all, God is Lord of life and death—thus I consoled myself. After a week, Sister Melasia had a chance to go to St. Michaels's with a pinnace, and I was supposed to be broken in sufficiently to take over. A nurse in such a station means a person who looks after the sick when there are any. It does not imply that she is constantly professionally employed.

> So I had to sew, something I never did before! The first shirt I mended was a matter of 8 hours work. Gradually the business went faster, but I assure you I spent all my waking hours meditating on how to put in patches with pleasing effect. This state of affairs lasted about a month, then a feeling of capability came along and I got time to think about a few other things.[15]

The laundry too, was new to Sister Theophane, so she gave her girls full charge. They gloried in the responsibility and did their best. Both overseer and workers were greatly pleased with the results. Though she was employed a great deal of her time with these household duties, Sister Theophane noted that life in Mugil was far from dull. There were several sick calls to the villages each week.

One afternoon she was called to a woman who was reported to be in a precarious condition. The road lay up a steep mountain. After a wearisome climb the Sister found the woman's hut—but no one was ill. Two new babies lay contentedly near the mother, who was resting peacefully. One of the men who sat outside the hut felt sorry that Sister Theophane had made the laborious journey for nothing. "Sister," he counseled, "you made this long tiring journey for nothing. You baptize one baby for your trouble."

Sister Theophane recorded in her diary: "Knowing the ordinance of the Church a bit better than my sympathetic friend, I told him that that was the priest's work and he had better bring the babies to the church!"[16]

* * * * *

On one of her sick calls Sister Theophane learned something of the sorcery still practiced in Papua New Guinea. She entered a small village and asked for a guide to take her to a patient in the hills. The people hesitated, and she asked the reason for such action. Finally they produced a strangely dressed creature—short, fat, and generously besmeared with clay. The group assumed a respectful silence in the presence of this strange individual. A spokesman stepped up and, with a reverential bow toward the short man, declared, "This great Master has visited the patient and says she is all right. You need not go!"

Despite the fact that Sister Theophane said she could not accept this verdict, no one from the village would act as a guide. She was forced to return home.[17] However, the incident made her curious and when the locals lounged around the grounds in the evening she took the opportunity to question them. They grew talkative and admitted that quite a bit of sorcery was still practiced in the district. The sorcerers would invariably choose the night time for their operations. In the dark huts they could more easily fool the credulous onlookers. The sorcerer carried a stone, a strain of hair, dirt, or other objects in his mouth or concealed on his person. After weird incantations he would produce the object and the awe-stricken observers would firmly believe that the Master had massaged it out of the patient. The sorcerer would then demand an exorbitant fee and predict a quick recovery. When Sister Theophane asked why these practices continued when the people knew they were useless. They admitted that many simply enjoyed the performance and the mystery. The influence of the old surviving traditional practices was so powerful that the younger generation could not break away entirely from tribal customs.

On one of her journeys Sister Theophane passed a hut where a woman lay dying. Before the door stood a large stem of a banana tree, carved and dressed in the apparel of the dying woman. A bystander informed her that this was to fool the devil. With great ceremony the people would carry the effigy to the bush and amid shouts proclaim to the devil that this was the woman. The devil would then afflict the masked wood and the woman would recover. The bystander assured the Sister that it often helped.[18] The district had just lately embraced the teachings of the Church, and it would take patient training to wean the people from their superstitions.

As quickly as her Mugil adventure had opened, it closed. The pinnace *Michael* arrived one afternoon with orders to bring Sister Theophane back to Alexishafen. She voiced her regrets in her diary:

> Wiser and more experienced for my three months stay in Mugil, I regretfully returned to Alexishafen, April 3, on the *Michael* with two priests, four Brothers, one Sister, one white man, forty Papua New Guineans, one cat and forty chickens for companions.[19]

During the three months at Mugil, Sister Theophane's heart often slipped to Alexishafen. It was especially on Wednesdays that she longed to be with her Ilala souls who were so dear to her. As the *Michael* churned the waters, Sister Theophane's thoughts were running far ahead of the pinnace. Someone else was waiting for this meeting too!

> When I was home only a few hours communications from my parish started. What a thrill it was to hear them say they had prayed for my return, and what a heart-bouncing meeting it was when every single one came and shook hands![20]

In 1938 the Sisters in Papua New Guinea rejoiced at the prospect of having the SSpS Congregational Superior come for a visitation. Sister Theophane waited eagerly to see her again, since she had not seen her since her last visitation to the United States.

The Sisters went with the *Stella Maris* to meet the Congregational Superior, Reverend Mother Regis Fastabend, at Madang. Mother Regis was astonished to see the sisters in such a large ship, but her wonderment grew when *Paul* flew in just then, and the pilot sent the plane into curious loops to honor the arrival of the Congregational Superior. Sister Theophane marveled that Reverend Mother recognized her immediately—the meeting in Techny had been but casual and brief.

At her first opportunity Sister Theophane paraded away with Mother Regis. She hoped that Reverend Mother would understand her burning desire to be out among the mountain tribes, living the real and hard life of a missioner. Mother Regis listened sympathetically, but simply counseled her daughter to offer her desires to Christ, since she had been appointed for that station at Alexishafen and that would most probably remain her field.

Some of the sedate members of the community gasped when Sister Theophane announced that Mother Regis had agreed to accompany her to Ilala. But the young American Sister smiled at their protestations because she knew that once Reverend Mother had given her word, she would not go back on it.

On May 5, Sister Theophane saddled one of the race horses for herself and a young mare, Flora, for Reverend Mother. A little colt went along to get in the way and fall down at the wrong time. Reverend Mother was amused and delighted by the colt's antics. Flora seemed to sense that her rider was a distinguished personage and she stepped slowly and steadily. Mother Regis urged her on, and Sister Theophane gladly set a quicker pace.

Little Ilala, perched on a lofty hill and flanked by higher hills of majestic beauty, was prepared for its visitor. Reverend Mother stopped for a moment to take in the awe-inspiring grandeur. There in the hills were the little villages; below were the calm blue waters of the Pacific. The soul of the great religious, schooled in prayer and constant contact with God, was stirred by the greatness of the works of the Creator. "Ah, Sister," she whispered, "you are privileged to work here where everything sings the praise of God!"

Sister Theophane said nothing because she could not find words to express the sentiments of her heart. To her, too, nature in Papua New Guinea was ever singing a "Te Deum."

The people were all in gala dress and waiting for the Reverend Mother at the school house which they had decorated with palms and flowers. Their smiles broadened when rosaries, pictures, and medals appeared and were quickly distributed. After visiting the school, Mother Regis went to some regional homes. She was amazed at their cleanliness and their ingenuity. Sister Theophane explained that the young couples, who made up the bulk of the Ilala population, had been trained at Alexishafen. This accounted for the extraordinary progress of the village. Many of the villagers left during the morning to barter fish for yams, but each one stopped at the school to bid "Good-bye" to Reverend Mother who was leaving. A bit stiff and tired, but well-pleased with her experience, Mother Regis rode back with Sister Theophane in the afternoon. She said she would have liked to go again—but she knew that the visitation of all the out-stations would consume all her time.

After the Congregational Superior's Visitation, Sister Theophane was relieved of her hospital duties, retaining only the care of the sick in the out-lying villages. Her ardent desire to be catechizing was realized and four days a week she went out to various villages and islands for classes.

Mondays and Saturdays were now taken up entirely with the baking of altar breads. Since the demand for altar breads had greatly increased, Sister was given two girls to help her with the work. Extreme care had to be taken to keep the hosts immaculate because they were baked over an open fire. It was a tiring duty, but one that Sister Theophane discharged with intense devotedness and a deep appreciation of the sublime end for which the white round wafers were destined. For Sister Theophane, the task was a sacrament because she was helping to prepare the hosts for the altar. With loving care she packed the hosts and had them ready for the boys who called for them at Alexishafen.

The islands just off the coast of Alexishafen now became "Sister Theophane's parishes." To them she devoted every ounce of strength that she had. Despite their innate ungratefulness, the people could not but recognize in their missionary one who loved them without counting the cost—one who was ready to sacrifice herself to the very utmost to help them. They called her "Sister bilong mifelo," "Our Sister."

Every Tuesday morning, when the sun was gilding the blue of the Pacific with silver, a little canoe bobbed up and down on the waves; and the spray from the oars, brilliant with color, enveloped the boat in glory. Sister Theophane was on her way to Malmal. Two girls accompanied her. Near the island the waters swirled in a dangerous whirlpool. The girls slackened their speed as they neared the spot and they glanced fearfully toward the Sister. She smiled back reassurance and over the restless waters her voice rang out with confidence: "Oh, Lord, make haste to help me!" They prayed aloud together until the treacherous spot was passed over.

As soon as Sister arrived on the island, the catechist beat the wooden drum to call the residents together for instructions. There was no schoolhouse at Malmal. The children, as well as the adults, squatted on the ground outside a hut—this made for good ventilation and likewise for sufficient distractions. Again the old and young learned together about the wonders of the love of God! Instructions were followed by a music class so that everyone could take part in communal singing when they came to Alexishafen on Sunday for Holy Mass. Since these people could not read or write, both instructions and songs were a matter of memory work. Here the catechist came to the aid of the missionary. When Sister began her work with the islands there was no hymn book and no songs in Pidgin. She set to work translating and compiling and a small hymn book soon made its appearance.

Instructions were invariably concluded with inquires about the sick, the aged, and the new-born infants. Each was cared for and arrangements were made to have the infants brought to Alexishafen for baptism.

Shortly before noon the little canoe was on its way back to St. Michael's. In the afternoon Sister Theophane would be on hand to hold classes for the girls at Alexishafen, for the European Sisters who wished to get a better knowledge of English, and for those who wanted more instructions in the care of the sick. Of course, if an urgent sick call would come up in the afternoon, this program of classes would be dropped. It varied from day to day.[21]

Wednesday was Sister Theophane's great day—it was Ilala day. A three-hour ride on horseback brought Sister to the station. There she held catechetical instructions and then examined her students in reading, writing, and arithmetic. Her catechist Michael had charge of the school and gathered the people for morning prayer and instructions. He kept a written record of the material he was teaching in order that Sister could see what progress was made. The people of Ilala were Sister Theophane's hope and her joy. It was here that the spirit of Christianity was slowly but surely taking root. Old practices of the night of unbelief were falling away in the little community. For example, a little girl, a week old, had died of tetanus. The Christian parents quietly buried the little one and wept for her in the seclusion of the hut. There was no loud wailing, no smearing of bodies with clay or paint.[22]

On All Saint's Day in 1937, Ilala gave its missionary a pleasant surprise. It rained heavily the Sunday before the feast, and none of the villagers could come to Alexishafen for Mass. Yet, without any reminder to prod them on, they had all appeared for Holy Mass on the feast. After church services two of the girls approached Sister Theophane and asked rather shyly if she intended to hold class on the morrow. An affirmative answer caused a look of disappointment to cross over the little faces. Sister Theophane inquired jestingly, "Shouldn't I come?" The little girls shifted their feet uncomfortably.

Then they replied with hesitation, "The catechist said you

shouldn't come because tomorrow is All Soul's Day and we want to trim up the cemetery." Sister Theophane gladly agreed to drop the lesson that they might carry out their noble plan. On her next visit she went to see the cemetery and praised them for the Christian spirit they had shown.[23] "I feel mighty proud of Ilala," she confided in her diary.

It was among "her Philippians" that she first introduced the subject of altar boys. During class she carefully explained what an honor it was to assist the priest at the Holy Sacrifice. It would entail some hard study, she admitted, but it was worth the effort. Those who were interested were asked to remain after class to start learning the Latin prayers. Every man in the village stayed! Although she knew that the gray-haired warriors would never master the intricacies of the Latin pronunciations, Sister Theophane was touched by their eagerness.[24]

Attracted by the cleanliness and progressiveness of the village, new families were continually moving in to Ilala. It happened that a man with a bad reputation decided to settle there as well. The residents brought the matter to Sister Theophane's attention. She made note of the incident.

> Although this fellow is a grown, married man with a family, he took my scolding like a naughty school boy. Now he comes to my classes and to church. But he has lived too long in the company of old unreligious men to be a good Christian. His new environment is practically all Christian, so I think he will gradually come up to the standard of an ordinarily good man.[25]

It was not hard to understand that Wednesdays were Sister Theophane's "red letter days," and that the weekly visit to Ilala brought ample recompense for the many disappointments that she met with among less responsive souls. Here was a community of which St. Paul would have been justly proud.

Thursdays were now given over to work on the Island of Sek.

A few smaller islands lay between Sek and Alexishafen. Sister Theophane stopped off at these to pick up several children living there and take them along for school. The youngsters loved the boat-ride, and it was always a happy, singing crowd that landed on Sek.

Friday was reserved for the long trip to the Island of Rivo. On days when the sea was calm, Sister Theophane went by canoe. However, a canoe was too dangerous on a rough sea so Sister Superior arranged for a pinnace when the weather was bad. It was a trip of about two hours by canoe and half that time by pinnace. The time spent on the waters was never wasted. It was then that Sister Theophane wrote her delightful letters home. Her letters often began with the remark, "This is another pinnace letter. The splotches are sea spray—not tears!" Indeed, as far as tears were concerned, her life was in a perpetual drought. It was the mental, spiritual, and physical needs and miseries of Christ's brethren that forced from her noble soul tears of compassion.

The mission at Rivo required strenuous work with little visible signs of success. Slowly, very slowly, the younger generation was taking an interest in the faith. Sister did what she could in the school and sought to win the confidence of her students through the medical attention she provided. She relates that one day she was giving out typhoid shots.

> Such prophylaxis is not necessary for old folks, so we don't give it to them. One old granny perched herself in front of me and presented her arm.
>
> Nothing doing, granny, I told her. You don't need this kind of medicine.
>
> She became more insistent. Upon my further refusal she asked everybody present who she thought could influence me to try to persuade me. In order to get rid of her and of the ever growing crowd, I gave her a shot. She swaggered off like a triumphant queen

although she was skin and bones. Others can't be forced to take a shot.[26]

Ironically, when it happened to be time for school, it was the rainy days for which the missionary longed. Rain kept everyone at home, and since they could not work in their gardens, they willingly came to instructions. Of course, the rain did not make the journey any more pleasant for the traveling Sister—but that was of no account to a soul afire to spread the love of God.

Thus were the days of the week well filled, but Sister Theophane's love was untiring. Every other Sunday she rowed to an island near Madang where a few folks eagerly awaited her coming. It was a day when others rested from the week's toil, but for her there could be no thought of rest as long as there was work to do for the Lord. After instructing the residents on the island she would hurry back to St. Michaels's to spend as much of the free time as possible in the chapel. She eagerly awaited Sundays for they gave her a chance to remain longer before the altar, interceding with her God for the souls so dear to Him.

Into this regular round of teaching and nursing came the emergency sick calls from far and near. It made little difference from whom or when the call came. To Sister Theophane it was Christ calling her and she dropped what she was doing to answer without delay. Hours on horseback, through treacherous mountain torrents, tossed on an angry sea—these were the usual circumstances connected with what she called her "outings."

One day she started off on such a trip with a Sister newly arrived at the mission. A pouch with bananas fastened to the saddle to provide a meal for the horse, her medicine kit over her shoulder, she was ready to go. She noticed that her companion mounted the horse gingerly—it was her first ride. The new Sister carried a little bottle that attracted Sister Theophane's attention. "What's that you have there?" she queried.

"Why, that's the holy water to baptize the dying babies we will find," was the innocent rejoinder. Sister Theophane enjoyed a hearty laugh, and then assured the young Sister that all the babies in the vicinity were already baptized.[27]

As they rode along Sister Theophane instructed the newcomer about riding a horse in the jungle and through the rivers. A slight drizzle slowly changed into a heavy downpour. "Sister," came the timid voice of the new missionary, "won't we turn back? The rain is so heavy."

"Turn back? Indeed not! This is the ideal time to find everyone at home."

They rode on through the rain until they came to a swollen river. Seeing that the horses would have a hard time getting through, Sister Theophane alighted and gave them a refreshing meal of bananas. Then she forged ahead. When the horse refused to dare a stream, she got off and led him through. However, if time allowed, she would lead the horse back and remount him so that he would learn to take her across without fear. It was laborious training, but eminently worthwhile when the missionaries were on an errand that could not brook delay. The horses had to be trained to be fearless and it took a fearless rider to train them.

It was high noon when the two Sisters reached the village and after an hour's respite during which time Sister Theophane gave instructions, they went afoot through the jungle to the village where the sick were waiting for the nurse. The new missionary was grateful for the shade of the thick foliage, but she soon discovered that the stifling heat of the bush was harder to bear than the glaring sun. She plodded bravely after Sister Theophane, too ashamed to ask her to stop for a rest. When they arrived at the village, Sister Theophane was astonished to find her companion on the verge of collapse. A refreshing drink of coconut milk helped to revive her strength. Sister Theophane took the trek back more slowly.[28]

Now that Sister Theophane was a first class missionary on her own feet she was often given the task of introducing newcomers to the work. She took them to her regular classes, and especially for emergency calls where they would get much needed experience. What an incentive this zealous Sister was to the new recruits! The young Sisters often spoke of their lessons with Sister Theophane. They were fired by the ardor of her spirit. "I returned in the evening," said one young Sister, "dead tired and sore all over. But in my soul I felt a new zeal! I had met a missionary on whom I could model my own life in the tropics!"[29]

Had Sister Theophane heard this remark, she might have made a dry face and retorted, "Stop that nonsense, and rather say a prayer that I may do something decent for the mission!"[30]

CHAPTER 11

ULINGAN

SISTER THEOPHANE had gone to her bed. The night was hot and sultry, and she wondered vaguely how much rest it would bring. Her thoughts were cut short by a soft knock at the door.

The residents of one of the islands sent an urgent request for her to come immediately to help a young mother. She stepped out into the black night where heavy clouds blotted out the stars. Flashlight in hand, a boy led her to the shore. When they boarded the pinnace the boy took his place at the prow and carefully threw his light over the rising and falling waves. A very low ebb made sailing precarious because the sea around the Alexishafen harbor was full of dangerous reefs. Two hours of careful navigation brought them to the island.

After three hours with the patient, Sister Theophane boarded the pinnace for her return journey. Again unseen danger lurked in the dark waters, but they made their way slowly. By 3:45 in the morning the Sister was back in her bed. It was cooler now and she rested an hour before the rising bell. It made no difference to Sister Theophane that her night had been spent working instead of sleeping. At 5 a.m. she was always at her place in chapel for morning prayer, Divine Office, and meditation.

Today was June 26, 1940—Sister Theophane's thirty-fourth birthday. Before the day was over she received another unexpected appointment. This time she would have some weeks to prepare for her new mission post at Ulingan. Another Sister was scheduled to come to St. Michael's Mission to prepare for her final vows. The duration of Sister Theophane's work in Ulingan was unknown.[1]

The change meant severing ties with her precious island parishes and with her beloved Ilala. The last weeks in St. Michael's were more than busy! There was a bit of extra work at Malmal and strangely enough sick calls were more numerous than ever. Returning from catechizing, Sister Theophane would dash off on her horse to bring medical aid to the villages.

She had planned to make her last visit to Ilala a long, pleasant one, but that day someone left a gate open, and when the Sisters came for the horses the corral was empty. This meant traveling afoot, and the result was that her visit was far shorter than usual and the missionary far more tired when she arrived.

It seemed as if those last days were destined for mishaps. The pigs had broken through the fence and gone strolling. One heavyweight pig stepped on the outrigger of Sister Theophane's canoe and broke it. A little later Sister came along.

> Not noticing it, I came as usual like a marathon runner, and started to shove the canoe into the water. Some of it went and some of it remained ashore. After "blessing" the pigs for their thoughtfulness, I dashed to the boathouse and got a rowboat.[2]

It was at this time that the preparations for the Corpus Christi procession were in full swing. The procession was the most picturesque celebration of the year. While the *Stella* was out collecting the missionaries and people from the out-lying stations, the Sisters at Saint Michael's bustled about helping to build arches along the roads where the Blessed Sacrament would be carried. Several outdoor altars were erected along the line of the march. In the

Cathedral, Brother was busy practicing his music while the choir polished up for the event.

Congregational Superior, Mother Regis, who had visited numerous houses of the Congregation in Europe, America, and in the missions, admitted that the Corpus Christi Procession she had seen in Papua New Guinea in 1938 surpassed in splendor anything she had ever witnessed.

The day before the feast all was ready, but it rained during the night. Not much damage was done, however, and the next morning the Sisters were out putting the finishing touches on the altars. Then came a torrential downpour! Sister Theophane noted in her diary:

> That was the end of it. Damp and bedraggled we all repaired to the Cathedral for Mass while the rain continued to "beautify" our outdoor decorations. That was the first time in fifteen years that there was no procession.[3]

After this last disappointment, Sister Theophane quickly packed her few belongings and set sail for Ulingan. There was a peculiar joy about this appointment; it was the kind of challenge Sister had been long desiring.

Ulingan had been under Christian influence for scarcely twenty years. The Sisters had only recently come to the station. Everything was very primitive. In Sister Theophane's diary there is a description of the compound.

> All the buildings are of bush material, and they are ready to tumble down. None of them has a decent roof—grass and leaves are the roofing material. The reason the buildings are so bad is because the station was to be moved to a better situation but the desired land could not be purchased. . . . It's a load of fun to live in such a weird house. The whole thing shakes at every step you take; all sorts of insect life enjoy the hospitality of the bush material, and funny little animals fall out of the roof quite often. . . . This is the life![4]

Ulingan was not new to Sister Theophane. She had been at the station twice for rather long sick calls. During her first visit to the station, she was struck by the poverty of the House of God. A new church was under construction, but the one still in use was poorer than Bethlehem. The roof was of grass, the wall of sago palm, and the framework of poor bush wood. The rear of the roof had fallen in and was propped up with poles. Though the stations of the cross had been erected in the church, Sister Theophane never succeeded in finding all of them.

At the time, the young Sister was horrified at the poverty of the place, but it took nothing away from the sacredness of the spot. She confided to a Sister that there was nothing to distract her from the tabernacle in that poor church. She could only marvel how the Son of God had humbled Himself in making that grass hut His dwelling. The silent, living example of Christ's ardent love for all people fired the young Sister with devotion. If her God was willing to endure all this, could there be anything that she would find too hard? The tumble-down grass chapel worked a mission of love in the heart of Sister Theophane.[5] When she returned in 1940 to take up regular work in the station, the new church was completed.

The present chapel was made of local woven bamboo which presented a neat and trim appearance, but gave off an enormous amount of yellowish dust that kept the Sisters perpetually busy with a dust cloth. The floor was just plain dirt. Deep fissures zigzagged across it at irregular intervals.

Ulingan nestled in a spot of luxuriant tropical beauty. The station had a long, narrow bight in the sea and a fine harbor. Undulating hills on all sides were covered with a peculiar grass called "kunai" which was used to make roofs for the huts. It grew to a height of about two or three feet and was cut with knives similar to sickles.

Keenly alert to the wonders of nature, Sister Theophane noted that the sunrise over the hills was indescribably beautiful. The rising sun painted the entire harbor with its silver glory. Again in the evening came a moment of exultant joy as the sun sank behind the hills, leaving a path of golden beauty on the waters which scarcely had time to fade before its gold caught the light of the moon. Evening falls quickly in Papua New Guinea and the sunset and moonlight kiss. "No matter what a wild day I've had," said Sister Theophane, "this ever lovely scene never fails to create a feeling of peace."[6] And indeed she often had to turn inward to find peace and reassurance in the trying labor ahead.

The inhabitants of Ulingan were very different from those attached to Saint Michael's. Sister Theophane made comparisons between the two in her diary:

> I always called my people in St. Michael's "stone." In Ulingan they are granite, ivory, cast-iron or what have you to indicate hard-boiled in the extreme. They are of the sneering type. The are doing their best to kill themselves off. Some villages are extinct, others very much depleted. Their means to this end is diabolical. I wish there would be a penal law to deal with this business. There would be more souls in jail than out of it![7]

Though her notes indicate that she understood well the depravity of the people for whom she was working, this knowledge did not subtract in the least from her devotedness. She concludes that entry with the remark: "They are all God's children and we have to love them even if they do not understand us."[8]

Though their huts were of the poorest material and very badly made, the inhabitants of Ulingan indulged to excess in personal adornment. The men wore a broad, woven girdle that they fastened tightly. They claimed that this helped them to ignore hunger. There was very little community life in the villages, and the Sisters, who had worked in the station for some years regarded this decay of communal spirit with apprehension for it was a sure sign that they were returning to ungodly practices. Very few children came to school because no one cared enough to learn. Parents might send the youngsters but they never bothered to find out if the children had actually attended school. "Poor Jeremia would have composed twice as many lamentations if he had Ulingan to lament over," confided Sister Theophane to her mother in a letter.[9] Some months later after she had just faced another disappointment in the faithfulness of the people, she remarked in a letter to her mother:

> Mom, if you'd know the details of life here, you'd say, "Baby, that's no place for you. Come home at once!" I often think it's a good thing Mom isn't here. However, if everyone refused to associate with these poor people, how would they ever become conscious of the need for redemption?[10]

Yes, Ulingan was going to show Sister Theophane some real pioneer mission work as far as instilling the Christian spirit was concerned. She was, however, equal to the task.

Because it was a small station, Sister Theophane was again nurse, teacher, host-baker, and "jack of all trades." The school at Ulingan was assigned to her, but a mere handful of children showed up for instructions. On Tuesday she rode to Moaka and on Wednesday to another village, Amiten. Very few people in Moaka and Amiten knew Pidgin, so Sister Theophane got busy learning their language. She knew that when she had mastered the language of these two villages she could freely converse with the locals of fifteen other villages in the vicinity. Despite the language problem in Moaka and Amiten, the work there was far more encouraging than in Ulingan. About one hundred and eighty children assembled for classes.

As soon as Sister Theophane was given her out-stations and the schedule for sick calls, the question of horses came up. The Brother at the station carefully picked out the slowest horse he could for the new Sister. As he led the gentle horse to the Sister, a man visiting the station interposed. "Is that horse for the new Sister? The Brother nodded. "That will never do. Give her the wildest one and she will need no help!"

That settled the question, and Sister Theophane was given the use of "Hans," the assistant priest's runner. Her diary notes the beginning of their friendship:

> Hans has a bad name. He kicks and throws his riders and what he doesn't do isn't worth mentioning. But Theophane thinks Hans is perfect and Hans was so pleased at finding someone who loved him that he behaved like a perfect gentleman. He has a temperament like my old friend Caesar, but he's strong, willing and fast.[11]

Hans and Sister Theophane had become fast friends when something unexpected happened to cool the friendship for a time. Sister Theophane was on her way to one of the villages for school. The road led over a bridge that had been an object of fear to the horse for weeks. Over and over again the horse had balked when he came to the bridge. The rider patiently coaxed and prodded the horse.

> This Tuesday morning Hans was going to be a good boy. He bravely trod upon the bridge, all four feet on—and down went the bridge! The planks were all strong and firm, but the beam carrying them was rotten. Hans slid down into the sago swamp and Theophane slid off Hans, likewise into the swamp. The bridge gave me a mean bump on the thigh. Hans floundered several minutes in the swamp before he could get out. Then he went home. Theophane had to crawl painfully up the fallen bridge like a monkey. Of course I got out on the wrong side and had to cross over through water at a lower point. I came limping home. Navigation was slightly retarded for a few days, but nothing worse.[12]

Some of her mission journeys were water routes, and for quite some time Sister Theophane had made use of borrowed canoes. One day when she was ready to set off she found that the canoe she normally used was broken. She spied a miniature craft on the shore and deeming it large enough for two, she signaled the girl with her to get in. Some men pushed the little boat into the water. Horrors! It began to sink. The girl jumped back to the shore and Sister Theophane paddled away alone. A pinnace came along and she hitched a ride, but the helping hand was far from reassuring. The short rope with which her little boat was tied to the pinnace, caused the little canoe to ride with its prow high in the air while the stern dipped under the water. The rope was lengthened and they proceeded more safely.

When the bystanders saw the difficulties their missionary was having, they promised to have the boat they were making for her ready in a week. She was cheered at the prospect, but at that moment the ride back home was of greater importance. Her class and sick calls finished, Sister Theophane climbed into her miniature canoe. A strong, contrary wind tossed the waves and the sun was blazing with noonday fervor. For three and a half hours she paddled over the waters, and when she finally pulled the canoe ashore at Ulingan she was completely exhausted. The sun had done a good job of blistering her hands and face.[13]

Though she had her doubts about the promise of having her canoe finished in a week, she took her oars along on her next trip. The surprised boatwrights hardly expected that, and when she stated that she would go home in her own canoe that day, they set to work. Within a few hours the new canoe was out at sea. Father Lawrence Mey, the young assistant at the station, blessed the craft, and it was christened "Pat" in memory of her dear biology teacher at Nazareth High School in Rochester.[14]

Among Sister Theophane's catechetical classes there was a convert group. Just when the Sister was rejoicing over the prospect of five men in one of her convert classes, the village was shaken by the murder of several people. It seemed that the victims had been poisoned. The prospective converts forgot for the time being about their intended religious instructions. But Sister Theophane knew better than to give way to discouragement. She would wait until the village was calm again and then she would start over.[15]

As always, it was on her sick calls that Sister Theophane met with her most heartening—and sometimes disheartening—adventures.

In one of the villages the "tultul," petty officer, was hiding an illegitimate child. The Christian souls knew of it and came to Sister Theophane. She knew only too well the danger the infant was in, and she was determined to do her utmost to save it, or at least see that it was baptized. After class she persuaded two of her girls to accompany her to the village. The villagers knew the reason why she had come, but they offered no information as to the whereabouts of the child. From one hut to another she went searching. When she finally persuaded one woman to show her the baby, an angry resident interposed, screaming that the stupid woman knew nothing of the child. She came to the end of her search when she reached one of the tultul's huts where a barricaded door indicated "no admission." The tultul stood before the doorway and defied her to cross the threshold. She pleaded, scolded, and threatened the angry man, but to no avail. The tultul's surprise changed to distracted frenzy when the Sister brushed past him, removed the barricade, and went into the hut. Sister remarks in her account:

> You'd think ten maniacs had been let loose. He swore and stormed, and banged everything with a cane, and ordered me out. I had two girls and a dog with me, but in such circumstances one can count on being left completely alone. I can't deny being inwardly shaken, but I stood my ground.

Seeing Sister's outward composure, the raging tultul managed to control his anger after the first outburst—but Sister had to leave without seeing the baby.

In the meantime, Father Mey, not knowing of Sister

Theophane's visit, had sent his catechist on the same errand. The catechist arrived shortly after the Sister had left the village—her heart bleeding because she could not save the child. The tultul was surprised by the advent of the catechist. Surprised too, that the mission knew all about the infant.

As soon as she related her experience to her Superior, Sister Theophane and a companion hurried to acquaint the priest with the situation. They had not finished their account when the catechist came in to announce that the tultul was asking to see the Father.

The man that met Father at the door was not the same fiery, spiteful tultul that Sister Theophane had left scarcely two hours before. Ashamed and contrite, he now stood before the priest and begged to be forgiven for his treatment of the Sister. Father Mey called Sister Theophane at once because he knew there would be no resentment on her part. Rather, Sister felt only disappointment that the obstinate soul had refused to do his duty. The tultul begged to be pardoned and asked for a penance he could do to make up for his shameful conduct. The child was brought to the mission, baptized, and assurance was given that no harm would befall the child. After this incident, the tultul became one of Sister Theophane's staunch friends.[16]

Success, however, did not always smile like this on Sister Theophane's efforts. In Kose, another small village near Ulingan, the inhabitants were keeping an infant from baptism. They often resorted to secrecy when some unfortunate or immoral circumstance was connected with the child. They believed that if the missionaries did not know of the child, there was a better chance of doing away with the child. Word came to Sister Theophane, and she sent a message with her girls to the effect that the child be brought for baptism without delay. The frightened girls returned and told Sister that the villagers had harshly refused. The next day after school, Sister Theophane set out for the village with her two girls as guides. When they neared the settlement the girls became timid and urged Sister to turn back. Turn back? Never!

They reached the large spirit house in the center of the village and were met by the local warriors, who carried their spears. Again the girls hesitated. Sister Theophane went ahead and demanded that the villagers show her the child. They flatly refused. When she insisted, they arrayed themselves for an attack. She realized that there was but one thing for her to do—depart quickly. Sister left the village weeping while the warriors, bristling with spears, followed her to the outskirts of their compound. She admitted that her insistence had been imprudent, and her subsequent dealings with some of the villagers of Kose were marked by a certain restraint and coldness on their part thereafter.[17]

Despite such setbacks, what joy filled Sister Theophane's heart when she could note in her diary: "An evening call gave me a chance to baptize a new born baby who died in my arms after a short half hour of life."[18]

Another one of her most treasured privileges was assisting the dying. When she came for sick calls, she always inquired first about the critically ill. Sometimes she was amazed at the lack of understanding that the people showed. On one such call she was told that no one was sick, only a woman in one of the huts complained of a headache. She decided to see what might be causing the woman pain. She entered the hut and, "in two winks of an eye, the woman was dead! Her husband said she wasn't sick and he couldn't understand why she died. The truth was that she had been ill for four or five months. Such is the love in a family of some of these people!"[19]

In another place she says:

> I found a seven-year-old girl with all the skin burned off her back, hips, and thighs. She had been left at home alone one day. She had made a fire to bake a breadfruit for herself. Her grass skirt

> caught fire and she ran around in great fright. An old man who couldn't walk heard her scream. He crawled out of his house and called her. By the time he had cut the grass skirt off, she was badly burned. I gave the parents all the dressing material I had. The burns actually healed, but the badly burned cases generally develop a kidney condition. This is what happened and the poor little thing died.[20]

A call came one night when the catechist lay dying. Neither of the priests was in, so Sister Theophane started out to help the poor man. She found the catechist exhausted from spiritual struggle.

> He is the first person I ever saw die in a spiritual struggle. The others are not sufficiently informed to realize what a tremendous matter death is. This man was tempted to despair. Some good soul's prayers must have helped. It took me over an hour to get him to kiss the crucifix and be resigned and hopeful. That was the last time he was clear in mind.[21]

It was while attending to the bodily needs of some of her patients that Sister Theophane often discovered their deplorable spiritual state. At times she was baffled by their resistance to God's grace. In one of her letters to her mother she begs:

> Mom, could I dare to ask you to have a few Masses said for a very special intention? There is a poor sinner here whom I've been trying my level best to hang on to, but it seems I must stand by and see him go to ruin. Tell Sister Rose Gonzaga and her pupils to get busy. The job is too much for me. Thanks.[22]

Because she knew how much prayer meant in the conversion of the Papua New Guinians she was ever begging her correspondents to remember her work in prayer. For her part she used every spare moment to slip away for an extra visit to the Blessed Sacrament. The sicknesses and challenges she encountered, she brought to the Lord, bearing her own suffering nobly in the Lord. However, of her own illnesses only a glimpse is related in an amusing account:

> In the last six months I've had seven or eight slight attacks of malaria and one substantial siege of tonsillitis. It was very interesting. It sort of thinned me out, but no serious damage was done. On one occasion not to break my promise, I was out riding in the noonday sun with a fever of 102.6. It was very interesting—but not harmful. Now this sort of fun is over.[23]

Shortly before Christmas the Superior pricked her hand on a bougainvillia. The hand became badly infected and all the tissue sloughed off. Sister Theophane went with her Superior to Alexishafen to have the hand treated. She was grateful for the opportunity to visit the main station for a few days and renew old friendships. There were the old animal friends to visit as well.

> "Friday," my cat, still knew me and jerked her tail like an electric wire as acknowledgement. She has three golden yellow kittens who have the run of the house. But the poor little dog o' mine was gone.[24]

The infected hand took a long time to heal and it meant that the working personnel of Ulingan were reduced to three just when the preparations for Christmas came along. Sister Theophane's class was preparing a play for the feast, and she was back at the sewing machine, grateful now for her experience as seamstress at Mugil. But time flew faster than her fingers and the costumes were not quite finished when the day came. She did not fret, rather they used the costumes in whatever stage of development they happened to be. Sister Theophane was well acquainted with the ludicrous costumes worn by the people at their sing-sings, and she knew they would not find the unfinished garments odd.

Other than the play, the Christmas of 1941 at Ulingan was very quiet. No mail had come through, and the busy Sisters had not found time to decorate their poor bush house. In their hearts the three missionaries found the peace of Christ, and as they knelt with the local people at Mass they knew that they were very close to the poor, forsaken Babe of Bethlehem.[25]

However, the 1941 Easter celebrations made up for the lack of Christmas solemnities. The pastor had invited all those living within two day's distance from the main station to come for Holy Week services. Over one thousand souls received Holy Communion. "It was a real family feast," remarked Sister Theophane. She happily noted that she played the High Mass on Holy Saturday with only two mentionable blunders. It was quite an improvement on her Little Rock skills of some years before. Being sacristan at Ulingan gave her many more opportunities to play for church services, and she rejoiced at her increasing facility with the keys.

At times her sacristan's job called for an eminent spirit of inventiveness. Candles were becoming scarce and there came a day when Sister Theophane had to face the fact that she had none and could get no more. There was nothing to do but try to manufacture some from drippings. The result amused her so much that she wrote a graphic account of it to her Sisters back in Techny:

> You should have seen the result. Thirty-one of them with more angles, lines, and basreliefs than you could count. Any candle company would have blushed for shame for its own uninteresting, commonplace candles had it seen my astonishing products. They burned to three inches at the end of a twenty-five minute Mass. And miraculous though it sounds, there was nearly enough wax all over the altar to make another such work of art. This all happened about the last of January. A great worry seized me when I thought of the approaching ceremonies of February second. Nothing daunted, the good Father held the blessing and procession, a high tribute to my untutored talent as candlemaker.
>
> After the ordeal I wrote to Australia begging for candles, but none came. On high feast days I had a panic over those candles. The altar was as complete a mess as can be imagined. The missal

was spattered up, the chalice veil was a sight, and when the celebrant laid aside his chasuble during the sermon, it too suffered bad effects. Nevertheless, we were elated to have any candles![26]

The poor bush hut-convent, which Sister Theophane said shook at every step was fast giving out. Rain trickled down through the grass roof. One of the Sisters had to remain in bed because of a sore knee, and at night the rain came to give her a shower gratis. Sister Theophane got up and managed to find a dry spot for the sick Sister's bed, but when she was finished the rain was coming down on her own bed. "It's a lot of fun," she told her diary.[27]

The Sister's dilapidated kitchen was beyond repair and after Easter the catechists who had assembled for the paschal celebration remained for some time to help Brother put up a new kitchen, "house cook" they called it. An outdoor oven was also built. Heating it up involved building up a fire from inside the oven. When it was considered sufficiently hot, the fire was removed with a scoop and the bread to be baked was put in. It was in this kind of oven that Sister Theophane tried to make immaculate white hosts for the altar. Because the girls who were learning to cook used the oven during the morning and evening, Sister Theophane made the hosts in the afternoon when the rest of the community went to rest. The lilting song that accompanied her work was one born of love.[28]

After some ten months with the residents of Ulingan Sister Theophane had acquired considerable facility in their language. A new field of labor was opening up for her. She could now contact about fifteen mountain villages which previously had been a problem due to the language barrier. A young male assistant missionary rejoiced with her and set to making a plan for regular trips to the mountains. Already he had taken over two of her classes in the station to give her more time to go to the outlying districts. Now he wrote to the major Superior at Alexishafen for permission to have Sister Theophane visit some of the more distant villages. This would entail staying some place over night. She was jubilant over the prospect and studied the language every spare moment—of which there were precious few.

A government official visited the Ulingan school in the spring and advised Sister to stop the Pidgin and to introduce English. The new project was taking more planning and preparation, but the pupils were apt. She found that they had a hard time with arithmetic, but in other studies they were similar to a fourth or fifth grade child in America.

Though her preparations for the other subjects were careful, there was no subject that received more attentive planning than religion. After the fundamentals were learned, Sister Theophane was eager to have the children grasp some of the beauty and value of the Holy Sacrifice of the Mass. She begged the priest to give the children instructions in this subject during his Sunday sermon. These instructions she carefully preserved and reviewed in her lessons with the children.

The *Orate Fratres*, a liturgical magazine that she received from home, spoke constantly of lay participation in the Mass by means of the *Missa Recitata*. Sister Theophane longed to have her students share this joy, but she knew they could never master the Latin needed for it. She discussed the subject with the priest, and at her suggestion, he translated the Ordinary of the Mass into Pidgin. What was his surprise when at the next children's Mass he heard the youngsters saying the Mass prayers with him. The zealous priest recited his Latin prayers slowly in order to give the children time to say theirs in the cumbersome phrases of Pidgin.[29]

When Father Mey heard a rumor that Sister Elreda Ruiter, for whom Sister Theophane was substituting in Ulingan, was to return, he rejoiced that the added personnel would leave Sister Theophane more time for visiting the fifteen additional villages.

One morning in late April the *Stella Maris* dropped anchor at the Ulingan harbor, and Sister Elreda came happily up the path to her old convent home. But what strange message did she bring? For a moment it seemed to Sister Theophane that there must be some mistake. Despite this thought she did not hesitate, but rather she hurried to the chapel and knelt silently before the Blessed Sacrament in the tabernacle. Then she went to gather up her few belongings that she might board *Stella* on its return trip to Alexishafen.

CHAPTER 12

Love Urgeth Us!

WHILE Sister Theophane packed her belongings for the return trip to Alexishafen the *Stella* went up the coast to transact business with other stations intending to pick up the Sister on its return. In 1941, on the Tuesday before the Feast of the Ascension, hardly a year since Sister Theophane's arrival in Ulingan, the Sisters went to the harbor to bid her farewell. But just before the *Stella* reached the Ulingan harbor the motor stalled. A treacherous wind nearly dashed the helpless vessel against the rocky reefs that jutted out of the water. A motorboat, which happened to be at hand, laboriously tugged at the larger ship and succeeded in dragging it away from the reefs. The pinnace *Joseph* came later in the day to help rescue the *Stella*. A week later the *Joseph* returned to Ulingan and Sister Theophane set sail for Saint Michael's. Nine and a half hours later she was received with joy by the community in Alexishafen.[1] Without delay she took up the work she had set aside almost a year before. Her schedule was unchanged, except when a strong gale made sailing impossible, and with her usual energy she set to work.

Ilala surprised Sister Theophane again, but this time the unexpected caused Sister's missionary heart to grieve. Rumors were abroad that the youth of the village were fast gaining a scandalous reputation. On her first visit she questioned the adolescent boys and girls. Their guilty faces and shy concealment verified the reports. When the catechist had reprimanded them for their conduct he was ousted from the village. It was just another of the disappointments that dotted the rugged missionary road, and Sister Theophane's answer was to pray harder for Ilala.[2]

So passed the weeks and months, and before Sister Theophane was aware of it, seven years had passed in the service of the Lord. The account is a beautiful story of devotedness to God and neighbor, and it is imbedded with precious incidents that glitter like diamonds in a setting of gold. One such event is told with admiration by the missionaries in Papua New Guinea. It is the story of Sister's heroic journey to Ulingan to succor another Sister who was struck down with black-water fever. This story is probably one of the most courageous in the annals of missionary history.

Runners from Ulingan announced that Sister Annacrescence Wehinger was seriously ill, and her Superior requested help from Alexishafen. Sister Superior at Alexishafen demurred because there was no pinnace home at the time, the sea was rough, and an overland journey was almost out of question due to the heavy rains. Despite these difficulties, Sister Superior chose to send Sister Theophane in aid. In the afternoon the pinnace *Peter* came into harbor and within the half hour, Sister Theophane received her order to go and boarded the ship. The local runners huddled together on deck, frightened by the hazardous voyage ahead. As the wind rose higher, the locals begged Sister Theophane to turn back.

Sister wrote in her diary:

> The sea was about as peaceful as the time Jonah decided to take passage in the whale's inside cabin, and I was sicker than the whale when he decided that Jonah was an unsuitable diet.[3]

The pinnace fought its way through the waves until it reached the Mugil harbor, thereby completing only about one third of the arduous journey to Ulingan. The breakers hit the *Peter* broadside, causing it to dip dangerously. The people on board shrieked as the boat nearly capsized. "God was with us or we might have gone under," commented Sister later. Hardly had *Peter* dropped anchor when the motor stalled and would not start again. Sister Theophane looked back at the pinnace as they climbed the hill to the local Sisters' house. She knew that the engine would not be ready for more work, unless someone at Mugil could do a good engineering job.

It was 10 p.m. when Sister Theophane knocked at the door of the Superior's room at Mugil. The Sisters were alarmed, but their fright changed to surprise when they saw that the unexpected and exhausted night visitor was Sister Theophane. A volley of questions pelted Sister about why she was there and where she was going. Then she took a light refreshment, saw that her support team of six were sheltered, and turned in for a restless night.

At six in the morning they were at the shore in an effort to resume the journey to Ulingan. A bit of skill got the motor started, and the *Peter* bravely launched out into the raging sea. "A two-day-old kitten would have made better speed than our pinnace," said Sister Theophane. "We had all we could do to see that we met the breakers head on, or the pinnace would have done a somersault with each breaker. An hour of such dancing was enough!"

Unable to make headway on the seaward journey to Ulingan, the *Peter* turned back to the Mugil harbor, dodged the reefs, and dropped anchor once more. The local advisors and the Sisters of Mugil declared that an overland journey was next to impossible. Sister Theophane declared with greater conviction that she could never go back and leave the critically ill Sister at Ulingan without medical aid. The question was settled, and the boys took up Sister's luggage while a horse was saddled. The company set out at a quick pace on an epic overland journey. The road ahead led through the bush with no less than twelve rivers to cross. Heavy rains made the rivers doubly dangerous. At times the boys held back fearfully, but seeing the Sister's courage, they floundered ahead. Loyal, as only the thoroughly Christian boys can be, they risked their lives to protect Sister, who was bringing aid to a fellow missionary. As Sister Theophane later asserted, had it not been for the care of those with her, she never would have come out of the journey alive.

They pushed on through thicket and swamp and rushing rivers. Night fell and the party was miles from anywhere. Alone in the bush at night, Sister Theophane shuddered. The boys, too, seemed to feel the danger and grew very quiet. Through the stillness came the distant sound of a village drum. The boys quickened their pace and after an hour's crawling through the bush they reached the plantation of the Mangem station.

There was no resident priest or Brother at the mission, though a small bush hut had been built for the Brother's use when he made his inspection tour. The plantation workers were aroused, and the boss at the plantation came out to meet the strange group. A gracious welcome was given Sister Theophane, while the boss led her to the Brother's hut, which was unoccupied since the Brother had left a few days before. With unexpected devotedness the boss hurried about, prepared a meal for Sister and the boys, made ready her bed, and sheltered the horse. Sister Theophane was touched by so much attention. "I really thought a mother could not have been more concerned over a late home-coming child!"

Despite this affectionate care Sister slept little that night. The mosquitoes took advantage of the fact that Sister had no net, and they pestered her through the night. At the first sign of dawn she arose and in the silent morning hours made her meditation and said her Divine Office. A light breakfast and by six o'clock the little band was on its way. More rivers to cross, more swamps, more tangled bush. They pushed on for three hours and then came to the river all had dreaded. It was not too deep, and there was no swift current, but the river-banks and bed were of treacherous clay.

The horse pawed the ground and then timidly tried the banks of the river. He sank into the clay. The boys fell behind a bit, came up, and tried to find a road leading down to the river, but there was none. The frightened horse floundered in the soft clay, trying to get a foothold. Finally, Sister Theophane dismounted, and the horse, with a bit of urging, made a bold jump down the ever-breaking bank. He landed on the edge of the water and sank hip deep into the slime. The boys jumped down and led him across. They left the horse waiting in the water at the opposite side and returned for Sister Theophane. She leapt down and was caught by the boys, who then carried her across and, with much tugging, managed to pull her up on the opposite bank. The horse tried to leap up, but after several unsuccessful attempts, the distraught horse quivered with fear. He broke his bridle and raced down the river in the mud, stumbling, struggling up again, and plunging on. He was headed back to Mugil.

The loss of the horse meant that the rest of the journey must be made afoot. Three more hours through the jungle, several small streams to cross, and the party reached the shallow but wide bay, just outside the Ulingan compound. Sister Theophane was chagrined when she noted that all the missionaries were on the scene to watch her slosh through the bay. "Nobody said a word about my appearance at the time. The situation was too serious. But I heard enough about it when the anxiety passed over!"

It was four whole days since the messenger had left Ulingan to bring help. In that time the patient had grown worse and the little community of Sisters at Ulingan had lost hope.

Without stopping to refresh herself with so much as a cool drink, Sister Theophane hurried to the patient's room. For the first few moments she feared that she had come too late. However, the patient responded to a heart stimulant and gave evidence of a slight improvement. The days that followed were tense. One day the sick Sister would grow stronger, then would come a relapse. Slowly, the critical danger of death passed. However, Sister Annacrescence could not regain her strength. Sister Theophane was at her bedside full time and sent a message to Alexishafen to have the doctor from Madang come to Ulingan.

The doctor did not come, but the *Stella Maris* did. With utmost care the sick Sister was transferred to the boat and taken to Alexishafen. At the hospital, the patient fully recovered, but she would never forget how Sister Theophane risked her own life that another might live![4]

Sister Theophane's devotedness to her Sisters in religion finds a worthy parallel in her self-giving and committed devotion to her people. Where others might sometimes hesitate, Sister Theophane never did. Her exploits, often told in her self-deprecating way, conceal the great sacrifice that her work entailed.

One spring, the day after the Corpus Christi procession, Father Weyer asked Sister Theophane to make a sick call to Rempi. She took Caesar and trotted off at a brisk pace. It would take two hours to reach Rempi on an overland route. The boys led Sister to a hut, and as she neared the bush dwelling, Sister Theophane became conscious of a strong odor of decaying flesh. It gagged her, and almost overcome with nausea, she stumbled into the dark hut. Inside the air was thick with smoke, which mercifully counteracted the hideous odor of the patient's wound.

A young girl, a mere fifteen years of age, lay helplessly by the fire. Signs of neglect covered her. Unable to move, she had not been washed for weeks, and judging from her bony arms and legs, she was not getting sufficient food. Her foot, lying near the fire, was covered with pus, dirt, and shreds of decaying flesh. More than a month ago she had cut her leg with a dirty knife. Dirt and neglect of the wound lay at the bottom of her sad story.

Sister Theophane clenched her teeth and knelt next to the girl. Quickly she set to work. When she had washed away the dirt and pus she found that the gash had developed into a wound about eight inches wide which encircled the leg. After all the foul flesh was removed only the bone and the tendons remained. The girl watched her in silence and said nothing when Sister bound up the leg in clean white gauze.

Sister Theophane then looked about her for someone who could carry the child on a litter to Alexishafen. All refused, perhaps because they thought the wound too filthy to be treated by the missionaries. Nothing daunted, Sister Theophane picked up the girl and hoisted her up into her own saddle. The child was too weak to ride alone, even when Caesar walked slowly and Sister Theophane supported her, so down she came. Sister Theophane mounted and begged the bystanders to help her get the girl up on the horse with her. Caesar turned his head to watch the procedure, but he did not protest. They started off. Sister Theophane's diary gives the best description of the rest of the incident:

> Astride the noble Caesar with the girl resting in my arms, her head on my shoulder, we went down the mountains and through the rivers. She was so weak and exhausted she actually slept. When the trip was over my veil was filthy from her head and my clothing and the saddle had acquired an indescribable perfume.[5]

The next morning when Brother scolded Sister for the awful smell of the saddle, she simply rejoined, "Brother, you should talk. You're just getting one tenth of what I had yesterday![6] He said no more.

At times because of ignorance, or more commonly from sheer neglect, the relatives delayed calling for aid until the patient was beyond human help. One morning a messenger came in haste to

Alexishafen for the nurse. Sister Theophane understood that the case was urgent, but despite her speed it took three and a half hours of steep hill-climbing to reach the woman. When she entered the hut she found the mother cold and stiff, and in a corner, wrapped in dirty rags, little twins struggling for breath. The wailing villagers grouped around the dead woman, but no one thought of the newborn infants. Sister Theophane left the horrid scene and scouted around the village for a bilum, a native bag which women use to carry their infants. She found one, hastened to the hut, and carefully wrapped the babies in clean gauze. Before she tucked them away in the bilum she asked the women who would be willing to care for them. The wailing women looked at her for a second with bewildered resentment, then went on with their howling. So Sister took the unwanted babies and started off for the mission.

Any thought of taking the infants home on horseback was out of the question. The mount was too fast and too lively. So Sister Theophane packed her medical kit on the saddle and sent the horse home. She made her way slowly with the delicate twins in her arms, while two girls came along carrying an umbrella and her other supplies. Before they had gone an hour through the bush the rain came down in torrents. The girls immediately tried their best to shelter Sister from the rain, but an umbrella appears ridiculous when the water pours down from the clouds in blinding sheets. In a few minutes Sister's habit, splattered with mud and dripping with water, flapped around her legs as she tried to push through the brush. The starch in her veil diluted and the drenched veil clung to her face.

Yet her only concern was for the bits of humanity she was carrying to safety. With utmost care the umbrella was adjusted so that it would keep the infants dry. Thus she plodded on for two hours, up and down the hills, through the streams now rushing with a new influx of water from the uplands.

When they neared Alexishafen Sister Theophane quickened her pace and made for the church. In haste a priest was summoned and two babies became two precious children of God. Then Sister Theophane took little Mary Elizabeth and George to the hospital. Since the mother had been ailing for some months even before their birth, it was not surprising that the twins spent the following days in a brave struggle for life. Mary Elizabeth wearied of the fight, and after two weeks closed her eyes to this earth to look upon the face of God.

On the same day that the little girl died, Sister Theophane was out with Sister Barnaba Zirkel on another sick call. It was the eve of St. Nicholas and again a pair of struggling twins lay in the corner of a hut while the villagers crouched around the moaning woman. One look at the babies showed that they had not long to live. Sister Theophane quickly baptized the weaker of the two and gave him St. Nicholas as his heavenly patron.

The two Sisters then worked with the moaning mother, and after two hours Sister Barnaba saw that little Nick had slipped away to heaven. The remaining twin was quickly baptized, and almost immediately began his everlasting life in the bosom of God. Sister Barnaba named the mite Joseph.

The next morning a triple funeral was held in the Cathedral and the remains of Mary Elizabeth, Nick, and Joseph were interred in the mission cemetery. Perhaps George envied the happy lot of his twin sister, because a few days later he joined her in heavenly bliss.[7]

If it happened that prospective children were not wanted, the babies found more than mere neglect upon their entrance into the world. In Ulingan, especially, Sister Theophane grieved over intentional infant mortality.

One mother who developed a dislike for her twins was determined to bury them alive. Sister Theophane found that the woman could not be moved by religious principles, and it was only when Sister threatened to report her intentional murder to the government officials that the woman reluctantly allowed the twins to live. Some time later she gave birth to a sturdy baby boy. This time the woman's brother was displeased at having a nephew, and to please him, the heartless woman started starving the new baby to death. Again, Sister Theophane found out about the inhuman crime and a battle of words ensued. Cowed with fear, though unchanged in her convictions, the woman again desisted from the attempted murder.[8]

Perhaps it was the neglect that a woman knew would be her lot when she bore children, that made women look upon pregnancy as a cursed period of their lives. The villagers could not understand why Sister Theophane, the missionary, made so much fuss about the woman. At times they would purposely prevent young pregnant women from securing Sister's medical aid. Or even if they showed good will, they often waited until it was too late. The mortality rate was alarming in such cases. Knowing, as she did, that prompt attention and care would save the lives of most of these women and infants, Sister Theophane tried hard to convince expectant mothers to come to the mission where she opened a maternity ward.

Sister Theophane once related how she had rushed to aid a mother in a critical condition. The husband, a rather old man, had hurried to Alexishafen when he saw that his wife was dying. When Sister came, a circle of villagers surrounded the woman. They did nothing. The husband, distracted with grief, stood by moaning as his wife writhed in pain. Sister Theophane saw at once that she had been called too late. She did what she could to make the last moments of the dying mother less painful.

Then she turned to the infant, lying unnoticed on a heap of filthy rags. The child was in a critical condition and Sister Theophane was anxious to get him to the hospital as fast as possible. A few more words to the dying woman, and reluctantly the man left to attempt to save the infant's life. The grieving husband carried the child for some distance, but they had not gone far when the ominous sound of the wooden drum announced the woman's death. Sister could see the man was not able to proceed farther, so she took the infant on the horse. After a few paces—then she realized that riding would never do for that frail life. So she came down from the horse and walked instead. Little Robert was baptized as soon as they reached the mission, but no medical aid could prolong his earthly life.[9]

On a visit to Rempi, Sister Theophane again witnessed the results of neglect of the sick and wounded. A man was injured by a falling tree. The neighbors carried him to his hut, crudely bandaged the leg, built a fire in the hut, and left the patient alone. The accident stunned the man, and he lay half in sleep, half in a stupor, while the foot lay close to the fire. The fire spread to the bandaged leg and began to burn the foot. The injured man was not immediately conscious of his plight because the foot was anesthetized by his accident and he didn't feel the fire. Only when the fire began to creep up to the sensitive part of his leg did he realize what was happening. He screamed for help, and assistance leisurely came. By the time he was dragged to safety his foot had burned well above the ankle. Sister Theophane treated the ugly burn, but asked the villagers to bring the man to Alexishafen. She knew that if he were left in the hut, where she could not visit him daily, the foot would soon be a mass of infection and vermin. It took several days for the villagers to make up their minds, and then they brought the man to St. Michaels's on a litter. They manifested no sympathy for the man, even though they knew that he would not be able to walk again.[10]

When the catechist at Rempi saw Sister's concern for the man, he suggested that there were quite a few cases of sickness in the hills. The catechist admitted that it was quite far; some of the villages were deep in the bush. Sister Theophane gave Caesar an affectionate rub behind the ear, and mounted. However, she did not expect the road to be as difficult as it was.

> The roads were like going up and down stairs where the stairs were not. The day before there had been a deluging rain which made the going so much more lubricated. Poor Caesar was with me. He planted his feet where he could. We shoved him and he slid like a sled on the toboggan slide—down hill, naturally. The uphills were just as bad, but he managed in a way which did credit to his name. That day I visited two villages where no white person had ever been except the Brother Venantius a few days previously. On his next visit the villagers told him gleefully about the merry chase they ran me. I think it was a "frame-up" because there were so many inquiries later about how I enjoyed the Rempi mountains. There were sick to be visited but nothing serious enough to justify such a trip. However, to gain the good will of the people one must show one's willingness to please them.[11]

It was just another case of "we are made fools for Christ's sake."

Although the Missionaries of the Sacred Heart had charge of the actual leper settlement in Papua New Guinea, lepers who were only in the first stages of the disease were segregated on an island about an hour's distance from Alexishafen. These were cared for by the government in Madang, which sent a doctor for regular visits. The government gave the mission leave to send one priest and two Sisters to the island every fortnight to instruct the lepers and administer to their needs.

Leper Island was on Sister Ottonia's regular schedule, but knowing of Sister Theophane's desire to work for the lepers, the older Sister often took Sister Theophane along as a companion. Several entries in her diary reveal the joy that these visits gave her.

> On Pentecost Monday Father Weyer, Sister Ottonia and I went to see the lepers. We started out at five A.M. so that they could receive

> Holy Communion. Most of them did, and Sister and I did also. It was the thrill of a lifetime to kneel side by side with those poor dear things. I wouldn't mind much if we had a regular leper colony to care for. They smell terrible, but one can get used to that. There are about forty now on the island.[12]

As Sister Theophane grew accustomed to the lepers, she took up instructions when an opportunity presented itself. On one of her class days at Leper Island she was interrupted during the lesson. "Hey, Sister," called one of the inhabitants through the opening of the hut, "Look at that old fellow lying on the ground out there. I guess he just died now!"

Sister Theophane did not look, but rather she dashed out with her bottle of holy water. At the same moment a tropical shower came down. The poor man was not dead, but very weak, covered with leprosy, and devoid of his reason. No one offered to carry him to his hut, though they were all lepers and did not fear contact with him. He lay there, naked and helpless, and they looked to see what the Sister would do. She did just what Sister Theophane would do. She put her bottle down and picked up the poor, decaying body in which still pulsed an immortal soul. Through the rain she carried him to his hut. "Theophane's arms are young and strong," she told her diary that evening. When he was safely sheltered, she returned and finished her class.

After class the two Sisters went to the hut again. The man was failing fast. He was still unbaptized, but before his leprosy confined him to his hut, he had come to instructions regularly. "I know you'd be happy to baptize him," smiled Sister Theophane as she handed the holy water to her companion.

Sister Ottonia beamed her thanks and knelt near the man. Her hand trembled with excitement and joy as she poured the water over the leper's forehead and pronounced the words of baptism.[13]

So life went busily on in the Papua New Guinea mission.

Sisters and Brothers and priests cut through the jungle day after day searching for people in order to minister to them. What joy when a single person could be guided to the God of Love, and again what sorrow when Christians relapsed into old ungodly customs.

But apparent failure never caused the missionaries to slacken their efforts; rather it motivated them to push on into new territory. From Alexishafen the Bishop was constantly sending out his men to new districts. As the white population in the gold fields grew, a missionary was sent to them regularly, and gradually a parish of Catholics was organized. Far from the restraints of civilization these people stood in dire need of spiritual care. The missionaries knew only too well how the morals of the whites suffered in these uncivilized regions.

As more and more white people filtered into Salamaua on the coast, the Bishop sent a missionary to them. Father Franz Kirschbaum surveyed the territory for some time before he settled there and started a mission center. The venture was promising and the priest drew up plans for a church, rectory, convent, and boarding school for the white children. Full of plans, Father Kirschbaum returned to Alexishafen to get the approval of his Bishop. The Bishop shared his enthusiasm and decided that Father Weyer, a successful organizer at Alexishafen, and Father Otto Bader should go along with Father Kirschbaum to appraise his plans. Inclement weather detained the priest at St. Michael's and he waited almost impatiently for the skies to clear so that he might return to his mission.

Late Sunday morning, August 6, 1939, the pilot decided they could try flying to the station. The *Theresa* was examined by the mechanic and declared to be in perfect order. The priest and a catechist got in. Bishop Wolf and some of the priests and Brothers were on the scene to wish them Godspeed. A crowd of villagers gathered to watch the plane depart. It rose and scaled the tops of the coconut palms then, the mechanic gasped. The plane made a sharp turn as if trying to avoid the palms and land. In an instant the *Theresa* came crashing, nose down, through the palms.

The Bishop hurried to the wreck and gave general absolution. All three priests, the pilot, and the catechist lay horribly mangled beneath the wreckage. Death had immediately claimed the five men who, just a moment before, had called a merry "Au revoir." The villagers shrieked and fled from the scene. The bodies were removed with difficulty. The remains were wrapped in cloth and immediately sealed in coffins.

That afternoon St. Michael's mourned as never before. The Bishop, pale with grief but bravely tearless, officiated at the burial. God had taken from the mission three of its priceless priests, an irreplaceable pilot, and a young catechist. Father Weyer had been pastor of Rempi and his word was law with the villagers as well as with whites. Father Kirschbaum, a noted scientist, had cared for the white population in the gold fields and was just starting his new mission in Salamaua. Father Bader, a young priest of thirty-five, was principal of the boys' school and he was the spirit behind the seminary. The pilot, a whistling young man of twenty-eight, was undoubtedly the most skilled flyer in Papua New Guinea.

For five successive days Requiem High Masses were sung at the Cathedral. In twelve months the mission had buried twelve of its personnel. Europe, troubled by war, could supply no additional priests or Brothers, and the few that came from America hardly made up for the losses. Yet Sister Theophane notes that no one uttered a word of complaint. "We are in God's hands and doing His work," she noted. "If it is to succeed, He must be at the helm!"[14] On this implicit trust they staked all and pushed ahead.

Perhaps the most hazardous of ventures were those in the Bismarcks. The trail blazers to the mountains faced dangers from treacherous mountain gorges, ravines, and precipices. Added to these natural hardships were the cannibalistic mountain tribes.

The district was first explored by the missionaries around 1933. At that time the government gave little heed to the expeditions of the priests and Brothers in the mountains. However, the murder of Brother Eugene and Father Karl Morschheuser caused the district to be declared "Closed Territory." From that time on, government officials were slow in granting permits to the priests. "Hopes and disappointments come and go in Bismarck history," wrote Sister Theophane.

> The climate is very healthful, and it is a dream of the future to have a rest and recreation station there later when it is a safe place to live. A Brother had made two trips up with a small number of cattle so the missionaries can have milk. The road must be unimaginable as the Brother describes it. Up to the chin in water, then climbing steep mountains and down again, through swamps and what not—such is the road. The cows sometimes refuse to go and have to be left behind. It takes fourteen days of such going to get to the Bismarck stations. In the rainy season the water is man high and with such terrific current that both men and cattle risk their lives going there. There is no mail service to and from these stations. Everything entrusted to boy carriers—a slow and dubious method.
>
> There are a couple of planes, but the cost of air transportation is prohibitive. Our little *Paul* hasn't been flying for a few months due to an accident, but the *Peter,* a much larger plane, will be ours in a few weeks. With both *Peter* and *Paul* in service we can look out very well for the missionaries in the mountains.[15]

Despite high hopes that another plane would help to bring regular supplies to our missionaries, Sister Theophane sadly notes:

> Our planes are disabled most of the time. The companies in Europe don't understand what power is needed to scale the mountains, and our *Peter* and *Paul* are too weak. . . . Our mountain missionaries had another siege of hunger and a stretch of time without Mass because of the break of communications caused by our sick planes.[16]

But these hardships were unimportant to the priests who were working in the mountains. Father Ross, one of the trail blazers, gave a glowing account of his adventures to the Sisters at Alexishafen. He said that he found the mountain people to possess superior physical strength that was coupled with an intellectual understanding higher than that of the coastal residents. Though they practiced fewer cannibalistic customs, and had not been tainted by degrading belief in sorcery and evil spirits, they were at times very pugnacious. However, there was always a reason for their fighting; it was not mere head-hunting. While his own promising flock, he asserted, was rather peaceable, he had met up with tribes who engaged in perpetual warfare.

Yet, in his opinion, it was the practice of polygamy that would be the greatest obstacle to the spread of Christianity. One reason for this unfortunate practice may have been the fact that there was a preponderance of the female population since the men were constantly being killed off in war.

Although the tribe with which he was working showed itself well disposed toward him, Father Ross could never be certain just how far his people could be trusted. There was need of constant protection and vigilance. They were well aware of the fact that the missionary was alone, and that he had no means of communication with the coast save through runners who must be recruited from among themselves. After a time the missionary resorted to using "contract boys" who were recruited at the Alexishafen station. But these boys knew that the wild mountain people could easily overcome them, and they were not eager to be hired. On one occasion Father Ross confessed that he was afraid to start out with the group that had been assigned to him. Small of stature, the priest knew that the "contract boys" would not hesitate to attack him if they themselves were in danger.

Sister Theophane knew the truth of these mountain stories

because she had a patient at the hospital who had attacked a Brother with a knife during one of the mountain treks.

One might think that the combined dangers from the mountain men and travel would deter the missionaries from further efforts in the mountains, but the opposite was true. The Bismarcks were much more densely populated than the coast, and a rich harvest awaited the willing hands of the missionaries. Father Alfons Schaefer, working in the mountain station of Korugu, reported that 1700 souls gathered at his hut church for services on great feasts. That number was magnificent for Papua New Guinea where folks often live in small villages of only thirty to forty families.

So, while dangers persisted the missionaries persisted also, and supplies were gradually sent to the hills. Brothers made the hazardous fourteen-day trek, driving cattle, horses, pigs, and carrying poultry to the stations. Father Schaefer put in his application for Sisters and built a convent for them to hurry the transactions. Permission had been secured for the Sisters from the government, but the Bishop demurred. Father Schaefer asked his mountain men if they would harm the Sisters. One husky chief stepped up and assured the priest that he and his tribe would be the Sisters' defense. The missionary should bring them quickly. Sister Theophane remarked that this chief, a famous warrior, had killed his sister and two wives for trivial causes! "We are all afire to go up!" she concluded.[17]

After Father Schaefer's visit all the young Sisters and not a few older ones sent a written petition to the Bishop requesting an assignment to the mountains. At another time Sister Theophane persuaded Sister Regional to allow the Sisters to send the same petition to the Bishop instead of the customary greetings for his feast. Yet the wise old Bishop held back.

Five years after the first missionaries had scaled the Bismarcks, the first fruits of their labor were harvested. It was the Christmas of

1937, and the Bishop was invited to officiate at the first Baptisms among the mountain tribes. Five thousand people from the mountains assembled for the occasion.[18]

When the Bishop recounted his experience to the Sisters, again their hearts burned to go. Tales of hardships and danger only heightened their enthusiasm. "I begin to think that the martyrs of the Coliseum will have no more glory in heaven than our missionaries," wrote Sister Theophane, "and Saint Symphorosa and the mother of the Maccabees will be no prouder on judgment day than the mother of a single missionary priest!"[19] This eulogy was called forth by the recounting of an almost tragic journey Father Ross made to his station. Taken ill on the road, he had to be carried in a precarious condition to his mountain station and there slowly convalesce with only a boy to help him.

Two years later, in 1939, when all Alexishafen was preparing to celebrate the Bishop's silver jubilee, the Sisters were startled one morning by strange singing. Each tribe has its own peculiar way of chanting its monotonous chorus, but this was unlike anything they had heard. The excited Sisters hurried to the verandah, and there stood Father Schaefer with twenty of his mountain men. They had come on foot from the Bismarcks to honor the Bishop on his jubilee. The astonished Sisters could not take their eyes off the mountain men, and who in turn gazed with admiration at the strangely garbed women.

> These men were a sight to behold—men considerably stronger than our coast tribes, all besmeared black. They carried beautiful spears eight or eight and a half feet long. The men were decorated with shells and had headdresses of all sorts of feathers and wings of birds. Our coastal people looked their share at them too. These strangers had white teeth, because they have no betel nut in the mountains. . . .

> Father Schaefer said that of the whole crowd, there was not one who had not killed at least two or three persons.
>
> The mountain men looked with amazement at the buildings, ships, auto, church services etc. These fellows are truly people from the Stone Age. You can imagine their bewilderment at seeing the modern civilization of the great city, Alexishafen. They were pleased to see how we train and school our girls and promised that when the Sisters come to the mountains they would send them all their girls.
>
> The Bishop asked one fellow for his spear. The native answered, "This is a new spear. Now you cannot have it. When I have killed someone with it, it will have value. Then I shall be pleased to give it to you!"
>
> The day after their arrival the retreat in preparation for the jubilee opened, so they had to get off the scene and be retired. On all the Sundays they were here, they were in church with all their paraphernalia, spears excepted. They never wash, but rub their skins with pig grease. One smells their proximity almost before visualizing it. In church it was very loud.[20]

Again the Sisters were enthusiastic to travel to the mountains, but the Bishop decided the time had not come. The mountains still held too great a danger for the Sisters. With what resignation they could, the Sisters waited.

When Sister Theophane first came to Papua New Guinea and had perforce to endure some months getting acquainted with life in the missions, she thought she could not wait to be actively engaged. After years in the Pacific Isles she possessed an eagerness far greater, deeper, and more mature than when she first came. But with the passing of time and under the influence of the Divine Master, she also more deeply valued the little things in daily life. Not that this was anything new to her. It had simply become more vital. Because she lived this conviction, her life was an unbroken succession of heroic service. She could not always be on the trail, crossing rushing streams, braving mountain passes, or sweltering in the jungle. And yet, when these were not hers to offer in love to others, she found another mine of priceless worth. Tired from her mission trek she found she could conceal her fatigue and joyously offer her services to a Sister who had much work to do. When she would rather spend a quiet hour after an exhausting day in the bush, she could laughingly recount her experiences to the Sisters at recreation and let them enjoy the day with her. Her heroic missionary exploits were reflected against her beautiful life as a religious, just as the brilliant jungle flowers nestle in a background of cool, refreshing green. Her life with her Sisters became for her as vast a mission field as the uncharted jungle. She grew in grace in one field and in the other.[21]

Gifted with a rare natural charm, Sister Theophane unconsciously attracted others to herself. She was puzzled by this, and often remarked to Sister Ottonia that she could not understand what such or such a person saw in her. Indeed, she gave no impetus to such inclination in others, was hotly averse to any show of sentimental feeling, and wondered that many did not take offense at her openness in expressing her opinion.

Aboard the *Machdui* on the trip from Sidney, Australia, Sister Theophane met a wealthy woman traveler who inquired about Holy Mass on board the ship *Sunday*. "There will be a Holy Mass about 8:30," replied Sister.

"Eight-thirty," spouted the woman. "I can never get up at that hour. I might be able to make it by eleven o'clock."

"What!" retorted Sister Theophane. "Do you expect the priest to wait with Holy Mass and his breakfast until noon while you lie in bed?"

The woman appeared for Holy Mass at the designated time. When she visited Alexishafen sometime later, she immediately asked to see Sister Theophane and solicitously inquired if there was anything at all that Sister might desire to have.

Stationed for the greater part of the time at Alexishafen, Sister Theophane was given charge of the visitors who came to the convent. She noted with sadness that the tropics were no place for ordinary white people. They were too far from the conventions of civilization and easily gave way to a loose life. Yet in this very fact she saw a field of endeavor, and she prayed that she might prudently guide aright the straying who thus came in contact with her.

The pilot of the *Theresa*, in search of amusement, became entangled with some whites in Alexishafen who flaunted a questionable reputation. They came to the island to suck money from a land rich in gold. With apprehension Sister Theophane watched, prayed, and waited. Then one day she accosted the young pilot and plainly told him of his danger. "You don't know how they laugh at you behind your back," she concluded.

The man was struck by the courage and straightforwardness of Sister Theophane, thanked her, and dropped all connections with his unscrupulous friends. Some days later he returned to the hospital to repeat his thanks, and he offered Sister Theophane his good canoe in gratitude. Though she was just then looking for a good canoe, she firmly refused the offer. She had not aided him so as to receive a reward. The pilot, overcome by the nobility of Sister, recounted the incident to the priest at the mission. It was not long after this affair that the young pilot was killed in the tragic crash of the *Theres*a.

One of Sister Theophane's outstanding characteristics was her esteem for the priesthood. As a child she bewailed the fact that she was born a girl, since that meant she had absolutely no chance of ever becoming a priest. Her joy was unbounded when two of her childhood friends entered the Society of Jesus. In Papua New Guinea she stood in constant admiration of the heroism of the priests. More than others she realized what life in the jungle meant for these men of refined culture and often eminent learning. She remarked that her heart beat with pride whenever she saw them, dirty and tired, returning from the jungle, when she knew they might be occupying a professor's chair in a university.

Shortly after her arrival in Papua New Guinea, the Sisters received word that one of the priests in the mountains, because of an imprudent act, had become involved in political trouble. Through bribery on the part of the enemies of the mission, the priest had been sentenced to six months of imprisonment. Sister Theophane burst into tears when she heard the announcement, and after the Sisters had dispersed she hurried to her Superior and begged to be allowed to take the priest's place. He was frail, she pointed out, and six months of hard labor would bring him to his grave. On the other hand, she was strong; imprisonment would not injure her. While her Superior saw that her resolve was noble, she knew it was hardly practical.

Whenever a priest came to the hospital for treatment, her respect for the sacerdotal dignity was quickly noted. Often the missionaries from the mountains were worn out from their strenuous life, and then Sister Theophane with joy gave her own blood for transfusions. If she could not be a priest herself, at least she could give her very blood to strengthen the ministers of God. Sister Ottonia remarked that with Sister Theophane's advent in Papua New Guinea there was a noticeable change of attitude toward the priesthood which was evident to all.

The seminary was the young Sister's great concern and came in for a generous share of her prayer and sacrifice. She was sadly aware of the fact that it would take years before the Papua New Guineans could be brought to realize the tremendous import of a priestly vocation. Again and again boys would attend the seminary for a time, tire of the routine, and then run off to their former jungle haunts.

Second only to her esteem for the priesthood was Sister

Theophane's high appreciation of the religious vocation to which she was called. This esteem, however, was not characterized by any feeling of superiority. On the contrary, she once told a Sister who enjoyed her confidence and was at times given a glimpse of her inner life, that she always felt that the community had stooped to admit her. She had never deemed herself worthy of so sublime a calling.

On this guileless humility, she built her regard for fellow religious. Though her sensitive eye could not but detect obvious faults, she was never at a loss to find an excuse for the supposed imperfection. One may regard the erring with scorn or with sympathy, but to Sister Theophane the former was unknown. When occasional friction was felt, as it must be, she hastened to make the most of the opportunity to grow. "Never," remarked a priest, "have I seen her bear resentment for a single hour!" She met those who opposed her with a friendliness and sincerity that immediately disarmed them. It was only when she was dealing with herself that she was absolutely relentless. To her the motto of St. Ignatius, her ideal, was not an empty slogan. She was ever practicing his *Agere contra.*[1]

Sister Theophane's desire to work against her own concupiscence was never satiated unless it had something hard to lovingly bear. So when she was not enduring the dangers of a mission trek, she was on the lookout for what St. Therese called the "straws which keep the fire burning." A fellow missionary attested that Sister Theophane did not indulge in bodily comfort of any kind. During the first years of her religious life, her desire for mortification as a means of freeing the spirit for greater things won from her Superior permission to sleep on boards instead of a mattress. Yet it was only after her death that this came to light. In Papua New Guinea, where she occupied a little cell of her own most of the

---

1 To act against. The deliberate effort one to overcome evil tendencies by doing the opposite of that to which one is sinfully inclined.

time, she had every opportunity to keep "the secrets of the King." These she never spoke of, but despite her care to conceal her acts of self-denial, observant eyes noticed.

For a time she had charge of the Sisters' refectory, and one of the Sisters remarked that it was easy to tell where Sister Theophane sat at the table. That section of the table would never be found with any special delicacy that might have been brought to the Sisters. If it happened that fruit was on the menu and Sister Theophane knew it would not be enough for everyone, she cleverly managed to be the last one served. Yet in the matter of food, it is unknown whether Sister Theophane's desire for mortification prompted the act, or whether it was simply that she just forgot herself in preparing little joys for others. The latter seems to have been the case.

Some could not endorse her custom of going out on long mission journeys with no supply of food, save for the horses. However, since her Superiors did not object, she kept up her practice. Sister Theophane happened to accompany a missionary of like mettle on a tiresome jungle trip. In the afternoon the Sister took out a package with two pieces of dry bread. Turning to Sister Theophane she offered her one with the remark, "Sister, I wouldn't offer this as a lunch to anyone else, but I know I can give it to you!" Sister Theophane smiled her thanks, but just as she was ready to eat, her horse got a whiff of the delicious smell of the bread and sniffed pleadingly. Sister Theophane took a bite, laughed, and handed the rest to her mount. Then she enjoyed watching him munch his bread.

When a pinnace failed to pick her up at a village, she was compelled to remain while the villagers prepared their meals. She accepted an invitation to dinner with sincere joy, though the mush she received was hardly palatable to an American appetite.

This constant mortification may well have been the secret of her buoyant spirit, her outward joy, and her contagious humor.

If one were looking for her at the station, they only had to listen intently for the echo of a song. She sang when she worked, when she rode through the jungle, when she attended the sick. The birds of the jungle were roused from their sleep by bits of Gregorian chant when Sister Theophane came racing through in the early hours of the morning. Sometimes after she had finished very hard work, she would come merrily to the house chanting the "Alleluia!" Unable to contain her happiness, Sister Theophane constantly tried to make community life more pleasant, more enjoyable for her Sisters. During the time of the yearly retreat, her spirit of joy reached not only the Sisters of her own station, but all her confreres in Papua New Guinea.

The missionaries came for retreat in two groups, the *Stella* collecting one group while bringing another back. After each retreat the Sisters at Alexishafen prepared an entertainment for the visiting missionaries. A yearly "Family Feast," designed to celebrate the nameday of each of its members is observed in all houses of the Congregation. Since the Papua New Guinea community could never assemble at one time, two Family Feasts were held, one after each retreat. For weeks, and even months, before the retreats, Sister Theophane was busy working out an amusing program for the occasion.

During the entire year the Alexishafen Sisters kept reporters busy in the out-stations. At Family Feast the *Alexis Sun* compiled from these reports, was read. The Sisters then enjoyed hearing about all that had happened in the various houses during the past year.

On the Family Feast that followed Sister Theophane's arrival in Papua New Guinea, the *Alexis Sun* carried a cartoon of the American Sister and her companions making their way through the streets of Sidney with so much supplies from the U.S. that they were leaving a trail of packages in their wake.

The Sisters' new house at Alexishafen was also the cause of

much merriment during the long process of construction, and it figured again and again in the "Alexis Sun." Often the work on the house had to be interrupted because the Brothers were needed for work on churches in the stations, or because the supply of wood gave out.

One afternoon during the time for siesta, when the framework of the building had just been set up, Sister Ottonia and Sister Theophane decided to surprise the community by assigning the rooms of the new house. They printed each Sister's name on a label, and when they were sure everyone else was asleep, the two Sisters scaled the scaffold and tacked the signs on the framework of each door. Sister Superior was the first to notice, and after the community had enjoyed the plan, she sent two native girls up to get the tags down before any outsider should see them. Unfortunately, the girls missed a few, and the next morning who but his lordship, the Bishop, should come across them on his inspection tour. He did wonder how the Sisters managed to get up the scaffold, but he did not wonder who the culprits were.

When the house was at last finished, just in time for a summer retreat, Sister Theophane and Sister Ottonia were busy again. Of course, the whole building was first put in perfect order, but then the two Sisters slipped away to make some very pertinent signs. Above the front door they placed a placard that read: "Walk over the rafters—concrete not dry!" In the private rooms and dormitories appeared the notice: "Sisters are requested to turn their beds upside down during the day." At the foot of a flight of stairs "Will be pulled up with a rope on request." Finally for any puzzled retreatant this advice was given at the side entrance: "In case of doubt interview the Bishop—He knows the house!" Again the two mischief-makers looked at each other in consternation when his lordship came to see if all was well just before the *Stella* brought the retreatants.

A little fun around Christmas time was always in order. At St. Michael's Mission the German traditions of the original missionaries were followed. Therefore, like in so many other lands, St. Nicholas found his way to Papua New Guinea. Even in Sister Theophane's days, the customary German song of "Heute ist St. Nikolaus Abend da" would resound through the dining halls on St. Nick's Eve. Each Sister had a plate for gifts on the table; and next morning, sure enough, St. Nicholas had been there and left for each—three pins (for the veil) and a bar of soap. (The same as on Christmas!) The Sisters were grateful; it wasn't the gift that mattered, but the love of the giver.

Now, once again, St. Nicholas's appearance was due; and putting their heads together, Sister Theophane and Sister Ottonia decided that not only should the immediate community be involved in this festivity, but the girls as well. Accordingly, they quickly put some ideas together and with the permission of their Superior, who was always a good sport when it came to creating a good time for the community, went to work on preparations.

Sister Theophane was to dress up like a Bishop and be St. Nicolas; whereas, Sister Ottonia was to be his servant, Rupert, to lead his horse. The following was the scene at the girls' hall.

It was dark. When some of the girls, looking in the direction of the priests' compound, spied the phenomenon of a white cavalier and escort advancing up the hill, the rest of the party was quickly alerted and thrown by the sight of it into complete confusion. What could this be? Only Sister Alphonsa Reiger, who was in charge, had been informed about the visit and remained in possession of her calmness, acting as if nothing unusual was happening. There appeared a large figure and a young local boy walking toward them, with the large figuring bellowing: "Good evening!" Then turning to Sister: "Have all the girls been good?"

But by then most of the frightened little girls had scurried into corners, crawled under the tables, their faces covered with just enough open space to peep through and see what was happening. The din, the commotion and crying drowned the holy man's voice; but gradually encouraged by the composure of their leader, curiosity prevailed over erstwhile fear and one after the other emerged from hiding into the fantasy of vision. The tall figure on the horse in white robes, mitre, and golden crozier must have been a human being after all.

"Look, he's calling us to come and get something." As the local boy Rupert opened up the big bag with all sorts of goodies such as betel nuts, oranges and bread, smiles creeped across the tear-stained faces of the little ones. Holding out a dozen little 'paws' eager to receive the bounteous gifts handed out, they said: "Oh, this is wonderful—these men from space. Or, it is Bishop Wolf? No, it can't be. It's not his voice. But it's his beard! It must be Father Joseph?" After everyone became calm and happy, it was time for St. Nicholas to go.

Taking hold of the reins, Rupert turned the stallion around, and with a wave of his gloved hand St. Nicholas departed, amid the chorus of the hundred voices: "Thank you, goodbye, goodbye, thank you. Thank you, thank you!"

The next morning when Sisiter Alphonsa came to breakfast, she broke out into a hearty laugh. "Sisters," she chuckles, looking toward Sr. Theophane, "what a success last night! The kids will be talking about this all year round and telling other folks about it. You must do that again next year. You must do that again!"

* * * * *

Sister Theophane's pets were a perennial source of amusement to the community. "Friday," the big yellow China cat which she had obtained in trade for a common cat with the Rivo villagers, was the pride of the collection. When "Friday" first became a member of the Alexishafen household, she refused to eat with the rest of the cats and for some days observed a strict fast. Then, chastened by her hunger, she condescended to dine with the rest, but she still took her afternoon walks on the roofs of the houses instead of on the ground. Sister Theophane thought that perhaps her ascetical nature was due to her Chinese blood.

"Forty" was Sister Theophane's pet turtle, a birthday gift from Sister Ottonia. Since she had no time to take him out walking, Sister often took him along for a pinnace ride. On one trip he got a bad spell of seasickness, and to spare him the ride home, Sister Theophane presented him to her lepers. They enjoyed him immensely, but on her next visit, she found that the lepers thought he had tasted even better than he looked.

Rating above her cats, dogs, turtle, and ducks were always her equine friends. There is hardly a letter among the vast collection that does not relate some horse story. Each horse had a name and each new colt quickly acquired one, if not before his first lesson in riding, then surely after it. Brother Sylvester often took advantage of Sister Theophane's courage and gave her an unruly steed to break in. In only one case did she return the horse, though not before she had taken him for an hour's ride just to prove to the Brother that she could handle the horse if she wanted. Brother had walked up shyly that one morning when he offered her "Dick" for her journey. "A perfect horse, Sister," he ventured. "She is the best for jumping ditches, going through mud and rivers."

Sister Theophane's diary continues:

> She stood quietly to let me mount. She stood quietly to let me arrange myself. She stood more quietly than ever when I signaled her to go, and I'm sure she would have maintained her quietude until now, if Brother hadn't taken a hand. I won't describe in detail how she had to be treated to get the best results, but the performance was lively enough to attract the Brethren out of their workshops to

> view the impromptu theatrical. Yours truly sat upon the beast singing "Deus in adjutorium!" and Dick went down on her knees. After orders to rise had been enforced, I mounted again, proceeded with a verse or two of an appropriate psalm and Dick went down again with her hind knees too! This time I had to jump to save a leg, causing one shoe to sail as high as a coconut tree. If Brother thought he had a "lily-livered" woman to deal with, he missed his bet. That horse carried me an hour's ride away just to prove that I'd manage her, but since it was a wet day I didn't feel like risking any bones for reputation's sake. I brought her back and got another animal.[22]

Life without horses would have been very dreary for Sister Theophane, and she often remarked to her Sisters that in heaven she would have all the time in eternity to enjoy riding on the clouds.

* * * * *

Sister Nazaria had been observing the American Sister for some time, wondering how she could keep up so arduous a program. The two Sisters were cleaning up the house after the summer retreat, storing away the mattresses in the attic for the next year. After an hour of tramping up and down the stairs, Sister Nazaria slumped down on the stairs and panted, "Sister Theophane, don't you ever get tried?"

"Oh yes," admitted Sister with a laugh, "but I try not to show it, because Sister Superior would never let me go out on a journey if she knew I was so tired!"[23] She succeeded so well in not showing it that no one ever scrupled about seeking her assistance for extra work. Sister Superior admitted that when she had any specially arduous task, she invariably asked Sister Theophane for help, because the latter was never too busy to find time to help another.

All marveled at this sustained buoyancy. They realized that grace alone could be the basis of such untiring fervor, and self-giving charity. It was not the mere enthusiasm of youth. It was that, plus the strong, enduring spirit of a soul that had conquered the weakness of nature. Writing to Father Weimann, confessor of her girlhood days, Sister Theophane admitted, "Physical hardships mean nothing to me any more." Where lay the secret of this moral strength? Life in the tropics is not naturally conducive to strenuous effort. The steaming jungle and blazing trail sap the strength of the missionary, and unless the spirit is strong, the person cannot but yield to the pleadings of nature.

The fortress that protected Sister Theophane from any attack on her zeal was not built of straw! This fortress started to be built in the dim past when this wild flower, now in brilliant bloom, was yet a closed, delicate bud. She was just four when she stole away to St. Michael's Church and hid in the pews to listen to the Gregorian melodies that filled the empty church. Unconsciously she was borne away by the simple beauty of song and drawn into the pulsing life of the Holy Church. She did not understand then; she just knew that she was happy. But as the years passed, she began to see that for her, only one thing would suffice: the great, free, wide expanse of the liturgy. Pious devotions wearied her, and she dropped them one by one, to immerse herself in the life-giving waters of the great prayer of the Church. Her whole life revolved around the great Sacrifice of the Mass, the center, source, and climax of God's love and of the Church's prayer-life. The spirit of the Eucharist was and is always the spirit of exultant joy, of brimming life, and thanksgiving. It was here that this great missionary drank of the Savior's fountains.

CHAPTER 13

THEN CAME THE WAR

THROUGH the summer of 1942, the deadly octopus of war had been stretching its poisonous tentacles to entrap the isles of the Pacific. The missionaries of Papua New Guinea saw the monster crawl closer to their beloved island. Flee to safety? Leave the people to their fate? The Australian government had sent word that the priests and the Sisters could evacuate, but the choice was left entirely to them. The missionaries stayed.

Mail became scarce and news took a long time to break through the tightening lines of war. Yet life in St. Michael's Mission was proceeding on its usual way, save that now the chapel was seldom found empty.

December came and with it the always welcome rush of preparing for the great Christmas celebration. Such opportunities were never missed by the missionaries. The great feasts of the Church were always observed with the greatest solemnity.

Into this busy whirl of joyous Christmas preparations burst a runner from Ulingan. Sister Elreda had broken her arm on a mission trek. A pinnace was quickly put in order to bring the wounded Sister to the hospital, and aboard the pinnace rode Sister Theophane to take the missioner's place. She was perhaps the best fitted to replace the disabled Sister, because she had been at Ulingan and knew the nature of Sister Elreda's work.[1]

The two Sisters met after a relatively easy journey over a calm sea, and Sister Theophane laughingly remarked, "I'll do my best for you with the classes, but I hope you won't find your school in too great a disorder on your return." Then, at a wave of the hand, the pinnace was gone, and Sister Theophane was helping paddle the canoe to the bank of Ulingan. She jumped to the sandy beach and knelt to receive the blessing of the priest.

"I'm sorry you had to leave Alexishafen just now," began Father Lawrence Mey sympathetically, "Christmas celebrations must be . . ."

"Oh, I'm where God wants me to be right now," broke in Sister Theophane, "and I'll be just as happy here!" She started up the path to the sorry building that still served as the Sisters' Convent. "I'm so glad to be here again," she told Sister Superior. "There are so many conveniences at Alexishafen that are missing here. I like this!"[2]

The next day she fell into her old jobs as nurse, teacher, sacristan, and "jack of all trades." Father Mey's dreams about the mountain villages were coming back, and once again plans were beginning to form in the devoted priest's mind. Of course the regular work must not suffer, but he was certain they could find time to reach the mountain villages.

The priests and the Sisters at the station noted with anxiety that Sister Theophane was thinner, and they soon noticed that she often suffered from fever, though she was not confined to bed. However, after a few days they rejoiced to see her on the trail again, and even if her health had suffered some her dedication was as ardent as ever. And the war was creeping closer. News took a long time to filter through to Ulingan, but even before Sister Theophane had left Alexishafen, a Japanese warship had been sighted off the coast of Papua New Guinea.

A month passed and Christmas came, yet the hearts that sang, "Peace to all of good will" felt uneasy. Then, through the jungle came the news that Japanese troops had landed at Madang and Alexishafen. More definite reports were unavailable.[3] Just what turn things were taking at St. Michael's Mission was hard for the missionaries in the out-stations to conjecture. They did know that work on the islands and villages had been stopped, and they knew that the *Stella* was not coming up the coast with supplies.

To protect the Blessed Sacrament from danger, the missionaries at Ulingan no longer reserved it in the chapel. This made the mission a lonely spot, but it also made Mass more precious to the missionaries.

Sister Theophane, normally fearless, harbored an irrepressible dread of contact with the Japanese soldiers. She approached Father Mey with the proposition of fleeing over the mountains to Port Moresby. "Once the Japanese get a hold of us we won't be able to do a thing for our people," she pointed out. "If we escape we can get back as soon as the Americans come—and they will come!"

Father Mey discouraged the plan because at that time he saw that it would be impossible to cross the mountain range in safety.[4]

Sister Theophane shrank with horror when she saw the first ships of the Rising Sun, the Japanese Imperial Navy, drop anchor at Ulingan. *Deus in adjutorium meum intende*, she breathed, and she went to meet the foe. The Japanese were not slow to let the missionaries know who was to be boss at Ulingan.

The two priests, the Brother, and the four Sisters were immediately called before the "captain." Any petty officer was referred to as "captain." The missionaries were then brought individually before the Japanese officers, questioned, and accused of espionage. Immediate death was to be their lot should they deny having helped the enemies of the Rising Sun. The bewildered missionaries confessed that they did not understand how they had been helping anyone. Sister Theophane was the last to appear before the officers. Summoning up her traditional courage she walked into the hut and met the barrage of questions from her accusers with the frankness and sincerity that were an integral part of her. Espionage? Absolutely not! If they didn't believe her word, they could take her life. She would not lie to save it![5]

After the grand session was over, the Japanese led the missionaries to the chicken coop and locked them in to demonstrate their absolute authority over the station. There they lived for the next ten days. No one was allowed to leave the coop unless guarded by a Japanese officer. When the "prison term" was over, the Sisters were allowed to return to their own building and the priests took shelter with the Brother in a room built off the sacristy of the church.

Of course any thought of mission work was out of the question. The Japanese soldiers had the run of the station, and the missionaries were simply told to work in the garden, raise a good crop of vegetables, and see that there was sufficient food for all. Work never frightened Sister Theophane. It did not bother her now. What did disturb her was the Japanese's treatment of the horses. She had protested hotly when they confiscated the horses for their use, but the pastor, Father Ewald Van Barr, showed her that opposition would avail nothing. She saw his point, but it did not ease the pain of seeing her beloved horses mistreated.[6]

One afternoon she found the Japanese soldiers in the shade while the horses they had used were left tied to a stick stuck in the hot, parched ground. Sweat rolled down the flanks of the tired horses. Sister Theophane strode up to the soldiers and told them to take better care of those horses. Did they not know horses needed special care in the tropics? Those horses could not stand the blazing sun any more than could the soldiers themselves. Had they no feeling for them?

A coarse laugh was the answer. Sister Theophane saw that

they had no intention of moving a finger to relieve the horses. She brushed past the lounging soldiers, and made her way across the burning ground. The Japanese watched her with surprise as she untied horses and led them off to water. There she stayed with them, talking to them softly as she caressed their manes. Then she took them to the shade.[7]

If she was not working in the garden or in the church, Sister Theophane was usually in her room. She avoided all possible contact with the soldiers. The weeks passed slowly and the Japanese grip grew more firm and more irksome.

One day the officers came tramping angrily to the Sisters' house. They must see Sister Theophane at once! Important official papers had disappeared from the church. Sister Theophane was seen there last. Sister Theophane saw that protesting would be useless. So when the officers brushed aside her first simple statement that she knew nothing of the missing papers, she said no more. The soldiers fussed and fumed and chattered in Japanese. Then they led Sister off to solitary confinement. Sister Theophane sat for a while in the dark, sultry hut and mused on the strange course things were taking. She knew that the Japanese had resented her undisguised disdain of their threats, but she hardly expected anything like this. The guard at the door stirred when soft tunes came from the hut. This was a strange prisoner. Then all was quiet for a long, long time; the guard did not know that his prisoner was silently communing with the Great Prisoner of Love. That was a long hot day and a long dark evening, but it gave Sister Theophane just the thing for which she had waited—time to pray! At midnight soldiers from Bogia appeared with the missing papers.[8]

While the missionaries at Ulingan worked their garden for the joint benefit of the soldiers and themselves, the missionaries at Alexishafen were engaged, on a larger scale, in the same occupation. In March the community at St. Michael's Mission was definitely interned and all mission work there was at an end.

The shadow spread. In April the *Rising Sun* touched the beautiful mission on the volcano island, Manam. The first encounter was no more than an unpleasant visit. The missionaries were informed that a new party was in power and that they would come again. They did, but this time the detachment of soldiers was greater and they seemed to be in search of food. The villagers were ordered to bring all the pigs from the pens to the pinnaces manned by the Japanese. A show of reluctance on the part of one of the Sisters was answered with a blow. The priests of the mission were kept bound on the pinnace for some hours. Then, as suddenly as they had come, the soldiers left, releasing the priests and returning some of the pigs.[9]

Though their locations were so close to each other, the missionaries of the different stations were almost entirely ignorant of one another's fate. Yet, they did sense that on the heels of the *Rising Sun* advanced the mighty forces of America. Not long after the Japanese arrival, American bombers begin flying over the mission. The priests at Ulingan built an air-raid shelter behind the altar of the little mission church. Similar shelters were built at the other mission stations. The first great air raid came to Ulingan on April 10, 1943.

Sister Theophane was working in the church with a girl and paid little attention to the planes which had become quite an ordinary sight in the past weeks. Besides, the planes never frightened her; they were coming from America and something within her thrilled when she heard them come. The other Sisters were in the house this tenth day in April, and when they heard the planes, they fled for shelter. The two priests and the Brother also noticed the advancing squadron. Sister Theophane's helper saw the priests rush for the shelter and followed them. "Where is Sister Theophane?" called Father Van Barr when he saw the girl come in alone. The noise became deafening and no answer came from the church.

Twelve large aircraft swooped over the church, raining down death and destruction. The machine gun bullets pierced the corrugated iron roof; whistled through the church; and buried themselves in the supporting posts or crashed through the windows. Several Japanese soldiers who had taken cover in the nave of the church screamed as the rounds found them.

As soon as the planes passed, Father Van Barr hurried out to look for Sister Theophane. He ran to the sanctuary, but stopped. There before the altar, her face ashen, her hands folded in prayer, she knelt. Before the priest could recover from his surprise, the drone of planes came nearer once more, and again the strafing machine guns riddled the roof. Then the squadron veered off and attacked another Japanese hideout.

The priests and the Brother crawled out from the shelter. Sister Theophane still knelt immovable before the altar. Around her were numerous bullet holes and debris from the strafing, but she was untouched. When asked what she was thinking when the bullets rained through the roof, she answered simply: "I was not afraid, but I must have said 'Jesus, Mary, Joseph' at least a thousand times. How beautiful, I thought, I shall die in the service of God and in the very house of God!"[10]

As the weeks passed the American bombers came more often and the squadrons became larger. The Japanese saw that if they intended to hold their own, they must concentrate their power. So they planned to herd the missionaries together as much as they could. After the feast of Our Lady's Assumption (August 15), the Ulingan missionaries were told to pack their belongings. The Japanese would take them to "safer" surroundings.

There was not much to pack at the poor little mission station. On August 17, 1943, the Ulingan group was loaded on a truck. They were not told where they would go, but all of them knew

Papua New Guinea well enough to guess which way they were heading. It was the road north to Bogia.

As they neared the Japanese base at Bogia, the Sisters noticed that a large plot outside the mission compound was entirely enclosed with a high fence of twisted palm fronds and brush. Evidently the Imperial Army had already established a prison camp. But who was within the enclosure? Over the main gateway hung a sign, "Welcome! International Concentration Camp!" So! The inmates must have known someone was coming. To Sister Theophane's surprise and joy she was met and embraced by Sister Ottonia. Soon the rest of the internees, including all the missionaries from Manam Island off the coast near Bogia, surrounded the newcomers.

After unpacking her few belongings, Sister Ottonia told Sister Theophane about the last days of the Manam Mission. With tears she related the sad story of the final visit of the Japanese.

The Sisters and the priests of Manam were all at Mass the morning of July 6, 1943, when they heard the purr of motorboats in the distance. The noise grew louder and a babble of voices announced the landing. A few minutes later four Japanese officers marched up the center aisle of the church and halted by the Superior's pew. They demanded to see the priest who was there at the altar; at once! Sister Superior answered calmly that such a thing was not possible. The priest was celebrating Holy Mass and could not be interrupted. The officer grunted disapprovingly and strode into the sanctuary. He mumbled something to the priest and then, scowling, sat down to wait for the end of the ceremony.

After services the priests were first interviewed. Then the Sisters were lined up in the verandah of the rectory and told that within two hours they must be ready to leave Manam Island. They should not worry about their property; the Japanese would take care of it. A lamentation arose among the frightened people when the missionaries returned to the church and the priest distributed to the Sisters the Sacred Hosts remaining in the tabernacle. With sentiments of sorrow the Sisters received their Lord. They looked up at the altar and at the empty tabernacle. God could not stay there now. In silence the Sisters filed out of the church and made their way to the convent to pack. Japanese guards and other soldiers dotted the mission grounds and not a single movement was possible without observation.

Then the soldiers decided they would not leave that day. Perhaps the next morning would be better. The Sisters and the priests repacked more carefully. Sister Ottonia returned to the church, but to her horror she found that the soldiers had already taken up quarters in the House of God. Boisterous laughter filled the church as the soldiers broke up the benches and shoved them around. Sister Ottonia wept as she told Sister Theophane of the empty tabernacle. "There seemed to be no room for God on Manam," she said.

In the afternoon of the next day, escorted by Japanese guards and a crowd of weeping villagers, the priests and the Sisters were loaded on the pinnaces. As if the sea itself were reluctant to bear away the missionaries from the people they had come to save, the pinnace that was to carry the priests and the Sisters was grounded firmly in the shoals. For two hours the Japanese worked frantically to get the craft afloat. Dusk was falling quickly and Manam was soon shrouded in night. Only the waving torches which the villagers swung about in farewell marked the shore of the volcano island.

At about eleven p.m. the pinnace, freed from the shoals, dropped anchor at Bogia. The missionaries were loaded into trucks, riding on top of boxes and suitcases, for the drive to the camp. No shelter had been built at the camp site, so the priest and the Sisters simply stretched out on the bare ground for the night. Rain cooled them in the dark, but the rain invited the mosquitoes, and the rats came uninvited, making sleep a serious challenge.

The next morning the Manam internees met the missionaries from the Bogia mission, and were allowed to speak to them for a few short minutes. Then, off to the camp outside the mission compound. A week later the personnel of the Bogia mission joined the Manam group in the camp. Though no news was supposed to reach the internees from Manam and Bogia, yet they knew that the Ulingan group would join them. So they set to work making a welcome placard.[11]

When the three groups were finally settled they got to work to make the camp somewhat habitable. The missionaries were housed in unfortified shacks which had been subject to American strafing. The shacks were an easy target for the American planes that constantly circled over the area seeking Japanese strongholds. Lying between the Japanese military supply dumps and the Japanese barracks huts in the hills, the shacks were in constant danger; but the Father in heaven guarded them.

Even though a shack had to serve as a chapel, the King of Glory was recompensed for his poor abode by the constant adoration of His own. The priests and Sisters kept up continuous prayer before the Blessed Sacrament in the tabernacle.

The prisoners' shacks were surrounded on all sides by extensive gardens where the missionaries toiled day in and day out under vigilant Japanese guards. However, the guards were careful to see that no crops were harvested save those for immediate use; they were urged to economize![12] "We'll not be here long," prophesized Sister Theophane when she saw how careful the soldiers were about the vegetables.

"Yes, and all this work in the garden will be for the benefit of the Japanese," commented one of the priests.

"Oh, no!" Sister Theophane shook her head vigorously. "The Americans are coming, I know they are! And I'm planting these sweet potatoes for the Yanks!"

There was little housework to do and absolutely no mission work. So once the laundry was done for the week, Sister Theophane was out in the garden. From early morning she was there, sweating in the tropical sun, but working vigorously. When a Sister asked her rather reprovingly why she worked so hard, she said, "Sister, it's almost killing me not to be able to go to my people! I've got to work for them, and I really think I can do more for them now by sacrifices, than I ever did by teaching. Yes, I MUST BE SAVING SOULS!"[13] If one had met her coming in from the field, hoe over the shoulder, singing joyously her "Deo gratias, Alleluia!" from the Easter liturgy, one would never have guessed that the morning had been one of continuous sacrifice. She was still guarding well the secrets of the King.

Almost every day the planes zoomed over the camp. Yet Sister Theophane was quite sure that the Allies knew of the whereabouts of the missionaries, and she was slow to heed the alarm. Moreover, she could not make herself fear the planes: Were they not messengers from the land she loved? She realized the dangerous position that the missionaries had been placed in, and was sure that though the Allies would be most careful to protect the priests and the Sisters, it would be a hazardous task. The Japanese soon noticed that Sister Theophane and Sister Ottonia remained at their work in the garden, kitchen, or church when the air raid alarm was sounded. The two Sisters were sharply rebuked and advised to run for shelter when the signal was given. Thereafter they dropped their work when the planes came, but they seldom ran as far as the shelter.

One night the community was assembled in the shack chapel for night prayer. They had just begun the prayer, "Holy Virgin Mary, Mother of Jesus and after Him my only hope," when the shrill siren screeched through the camp. The Sisters scrambled to their feet and dashed for the shelter. Sister Theophane remained kneeling. Then she turned to find that Sister Ottonia had also stayed.

Sister Theophane's face registered disgust. "After Him my only hope!" she exclaimed, "And then, out they rush!"[14]

The two Sisters were busy working near the house one day when a squadron of planes came droning up the coast, Sister Theophane snatched up a bucket and held it over her head, while Sister Ottonia crouched under a box. The minutes passed, the deafening noise continued, but nothing happened. It was too much for Sister Theophane. "Say," she exploded, tossing the bucket into the grass, "What are we ducking for anyway!" The two scrambled to their feet, and enjoyed a hearty laugh as they watched the planes circle over the camp.

The air raid alarm, it seemed, had no regard for the convenience of the internees. So one day just as they sat down to dinner it shrieked its ugly warning. The thing was becoming more annoying than frightening to Sister Theophane, and she sat down to table while the rest of the Sisters rushed to the shelter. Sister Ottonia came in from the kitchen. "Where is the . . ." she began.

"Out to the shelter," laughed Sister Theophane. "But you won't catch me ducking for shelter with a roasted duck on the table!" The two sat down to dinner. It was not often that the soldiers allowed the missionaries a treat like this, and neither had the intention of eating cold duck that day.

Sister Ottonia noted one day that the sewer had become clogged up and was giving off a strong odor. She got Sister Theophane and together they asked Sister Superior for permission to clean the sewer and lay it out with brick. Mosquitoes swarmed in the fetid water, but once the cleaning was done the hardest part of the job was over. Then the two Sisters got a wheelbarrow and began carting bricks. There were none in camp, so they had to cut through the palm fence; "our cloister wall" they called it, and a Japanese military police officer tagged along each time to see that the Sisters were taking nothing but bricks. A priest met them and protested that Sisters should not be doing that heavy work. "Two women to do one man's job," he teased.

"Nothing of the kind," retorted Sister Theophane. "It would take four husky men to do this!"

When Sister Theophane appeared at the workshop a few days later, looking for nails, the priest in charge asked in his same teasing tone, "And what kind of nails do you want?"

"Nails for women," replied Sister Theophane. She did not tell him she was making a kitchen table for fear he might come and inspect her work.[15]

Life in camp was not unbearable, but the monotony and the confinement were almost more than the active missionaries could endure. Sister Theophane, because of her ardent zeal, felt this confinement keenly, yet she was ever attempting to make it less trying for others. Her joyful spirit grew more jubilant and her song was ever cheering to those who met her.

There weren't many pets in camp, but the dog and the cats that were there could not complain of lack of attention. Sister Ottonia recalls what fun laundry day brought with it. After the clothes had been washed, the dog and the cats were given a good scrubbing. It was little things like this that broke the dull monotony. About every eighth day the Japanese allowed the missionaries to kill an animal for the joint benefit of the soldiers and missionaries. This also brought relief from the usual routine. The soldiers often tried to shoot animals for themselves, but more often than not they simply wounded the animal, and it ran off to perish in the surrounding jungle. Decaying carcasses in the bush caused an almost unbearable stench in the camp.

What news came to the camp came through the Japanese. It was not surprising that depressing communications about Allied concerns should often be circulated. At times Sister Ottonia grew very worried, but the reports had no effect on Sister Theophane's optimism. "Our boys will hold their own," she would affirm when Sister Ottonia confided her fears.

If the losses were evident, the great-souled Sister looked to heaven for reassurance. "Our boys all go to heaven," she consoled her Sisters, many of whom were from Europe. "But don't be afraid. America will come. You will see!"

On Sundays, Sister Theophane and Sister Ottonia would walk off to the far end of the enclosure and there they would sing, and sing, and sing. First came all the religious songs they knew—and they were many—then a salute to the Stars and Stripes. As the songs floated out beyond the palm cloister, the jungle rejoiced that Sister Theophane was still there.[16]

When evening came and the tired missionaries had gone to rest, silence fell over the camp. Then a silent figure crept softly to the altar, quite close to the tabernacle. And while the war tore across the jungle, a great missionary knelt in the shack that was a throne-room for the King of Kings, and she pleaded for the people.

Far from the Bogia prison camp, the American forces advanced steadily upon Alexishafen, so the Japanese decided to take the missionaries away from St. Michael's. The priests and the Brothers were told to build a refuge in the jungle. A site was chosen by the missionaries in the Gabaya Bush and the shacks that were built were placed under the protection of Our Lady of Perpetual Help. The Japanese were most anxious that the refuge should remain hidden and therefore forbade the missionaries to cut down any trees. The result was that with all sunlight shut out, the refuge was damp and unsanitary. When the heavy rains came the premises became a swamp.

Since the camp was not too far from St. Michael's the priests and the Sisters often went back for supplies, although the trek was attended with great danger. Several of the Brothers had been retained in Alexishafen by the Japanese so that they might care for the powerhouse and other machinery. Toward the end of August, 1943, a last solemn Requiem Mass was held in the cathedral. One of the Brothers at Alexishafen had succumbed to fever. A few days after his funeral, squadrons of allied planes raced over the jungle to Alexishafen. One after another, the mission buildings, now in possession of the Japanese army, disappeared in the flash and blast of exploding American bombs. On September 1, 1943, flames shot up from the cathedral, and when the fire died down the next day, nothing but the foundation was left. A newspaper reporter who surveyed the ruins declared that nothing remained. The destruction wrought by the planes was complete, but it was like a clean incision compared to the filth and foulness of the cathedral vaults that had been used by the Japanese soldiers as dugouts. With the destruction of the cathedral, it seemed as if the heart of the mission had been pierced.

About the middle of October, the Alexishafen missionaries had to evacuate once more. They hurriedly packed what was left of their possessions and set out from the refuge in the Gabaya Bush without the least notion of their destination. When the party reached the wharf, the baggage was first loaded on a ship. Then the missionaries were put down in the baggage room and the door was shut. After hours of sailing, the heavy door was flung open and the missionaries found themselves at Manam Island. A trek through the jungle brought them to the mission station which the priests and the Sisters, now in the Bogia prison camp, had been compelled to leave four months before.

The buildings of the mission were still standing, though they were stripped of all furnishings. The church building was intact on the outside; all within was destroyed and ruined beyond repair.

Everywhere foulness and indescribable filth met the new inhabitants. The Sisters got busy scrubbing.

Scarcely had they succeeded in getting off the first layer of filth when rumors reached them that a new detachment of missionaries was due. They guessed and wondered. The news of evacuation did not come as a surprise to the Bogia internees. The gardens were just filled with vegetables. It was time to move. Sister Theophane did not regret leaving the precious gardens where she had sweated; but her heart did break when once more the Blessed Sacrament was taken from the church and another tabernacle was empty. "We had come here thousands of miles from home to bring Christ to these good people," she said sadly, "and now one tabernacle after another is lost to Him!"

Once more the packing began, and on November 9, 1943, the Bogia camp was deserted. Down the bomb-shattered road jolted the trucks of the Japanese Imperial Army. Sister Theophane clung to the box on which she sat. A deep hole sent the truck into a grasshopper leap. "This is better than a roller-coaster ride," grinned Sister Theophane as she regained her precarious seat.

The two hours of a roller-coaster ride were not refreshing, and the priests and the Sisters were all quite sea-sick when they arrived at Hansa Bay, separating Bogia from Manam Island. While the soldiers stood by and watched, the priests and the stronger of the Sisters loaded the boxes on pinnaces. A sudden visit from the planes sent the soldiers scurrying for shelter. Some of the missionaries followed suit. In a few minutes the loading was resumed. At about three o'clock in the afternoon the pinnaces were ready to leave. Contrary to all of their own safety rules, the Japanese set sail in the broad daylight.

Seasick to start with, the missionaries hardly felt better when the pinnaces rocked on the waves, but they got to Manam shortly before midnight. Now the Japanese had concentrated all the missionaries of Ulingan, Alexishafen, Bogia, and Manam on the volcano island. Though the weary voyagers could hardly have desired any food on their arrival, they were somewhat surprised when no refreshment was offered them after the exhausting journey. Only the next morning did they learn that the cupboards were bare.

The Japanese had set out extensive gardens around the Manam mission compound, and though the missionaries were working in the gardens, they had no right to the vegetables. Since the priests did not know how long their internment would last, they were very careful about preserving some ordinary flour, rice, cornmeal, and manioc (tapioca). Friendly villagers smuggled in some fruits, especially bananas. However, great care had to be taken in bringing food to the internees, and it was not done extensively.

Since there was not enough tableware at Manam for so many people, the internees took turns using the cups and soup dishes. Sister Theophane solved her problem by using a coconut shell for all purposes. She wore her "tableware" on a string tied to her cincture. Always more or less indifferent to food, Sister Theophane became even more so in camp. When she noted that the supply of what she called "beautiful tea" (it was no more than colored water) was getting low, she managed to get passed by, so that others might have a little more. The peculiar broth, dignified by the name of soup, was the cause of much merriment. The Sisters enjoyed trying to discover a bean in the watery broth.

Built to accommodate six Sisters, the little convent was now housing forty-seven refugee Sisters! They slept on the verandah, under the stairs, and five or six on the floor of each little private room. Despite the discomfort, they enjoyed it. These privations and hardships answered the call for sacrifices that burned in each missionary heart, and, unable to get out to catechize, the Sisters were glad to have something else to offer to God for the souls of their people.

The strenuous labor in the garden, the lack of proper food, and the unsanitary conditions were telling on the missionaries, many of whom had spent fifteen to twenty years in the tropics. First the veterans' health gave out. Then one by one the others took to bed. Fever, tropical wounds, and diseases tortured the emaciated sufferers. Yet, whenever they could, they went to the chapel for prayer. Here at Manam the beautiful perpetual adoration was kept going. Six strong Sisters were left to do the hard work, and Sister Theophane was one of them. As one Sister after another had to go to bed, Sister Theophane took up their work, in the laundry, in the kitchen, and in the garden. One day she played carpenter again and built a cunning little shelter for the extra food that the villagers brought to the Sisters. The Japanese came so often for inspection of the pantry that it was not safe to keep it there. The concealed shelter escaped the notice of the inquisitive Japanese.

Sister Theophane went from one job to another, wherever help was needed. Many of the Sisters remonstrated with her for working so hard, but she pleaded in defense, "I must be about redeeming people!" The fact that Sister was spending all her strength was not surprising to the Sisters who had been with Sister Theophane for the past nine years. She had always given of herself entirely. However, loving eyes noticed a definite change in the devoted missionary. Her step was still quick and elastic. Her laugh was even more joyous than it had been; though her manners were losing something of their brusk, almost boyish nature. Her strong soul had become mellow under the anvil of suffering. The beautiful work of the Lord, which she had tried so hard and so successfully to hide, was shining through. Sister Theophane could no longer conceal the fact that she was constantly in communion with God. During one recreation she admitted that her thoughts were ever turning to the life of Christ, especially to His passion. "I watched her closely during the last months," wrote a Sister. "She seemed to be carried away by grace!"[17]

Not satisfied with the myriad privations that hedged in the lives of the war prisoners, Sister Theophane was looking for more. She still had two pairs of shoes: one pair worthy of the name, the other remnants of a one-time pair of sandals. One of the Sisters noticed the shabby sandals and offered Sister Theophane a better pair. "Oh," laughed Sister, "these are so comfortable. I don't need more!"

A few days later Sister Superior, seeing that several Sisters were badly in need of shoes, asked those who could do so to give a pair to the more needy. A motley assortment of shoes appeared on the verandah. After all had been picked over, Sister Ottonia spied Sister Theophane at the far end of the verandah, examining her same old sandals. "Sister Theophane, why didn't you get a pair of shoes? If anybody needs a pair . . ."

Sister Ottonia took one of the sandals from Sister Theophane. "How can you ever walk on this?" She rubbed her hand over the protruding nails which Sister Theophane had been trying to push in. Caught unaware, Sister Theophane smiled sheepishly and tried to recover her sandal. By the time the two reached the shoe display no pair was left that would fit Sister Theophane.

"A missionary must not want to have everything she sees," she told Sister Ottonia when the latter scolded her for not hurrying to get a decent pair of shoes.[18] Sister Theophane simply could not think of herself.

Camp life dragged on and Christmas came again. With all the solemnity possible, the internees celebrated the birth of the Christ. They hunted up the old crib and found that the camels were gone. "Well," suggested Sister Theophane, "since no new statues can be made, why not choose three Sisters by lot to take the place of the camels at the crib?" The plan was carried out with great glee and at Christmas the three camels enjoyed an extra hour of adoration.

On New Year's Day, 1944, Sister Matritia Haag celebrated the silver jubilee of her religious profession. The silver wreath was perhaps the only thing missing to make the occasion as solemn as it might have been. Even the Japanese came and congratulated Sister on her perseverance in the service of God.

Then the routine of the camp was broken, and the missionaries went into retreat. Never had priests and Sisters prayed so fervently. There were few meditation books to be had, but the retreatants had little need for them.

After the close of the spiritual exercises, Sister Theophane wrote a long letter to her mother. The same exuberant spirit pervaded the pages. Even as she wrote those lines, her family at home was trying by every means to get news to her of her mother's death. The report never reached her. She confided her letter to Sister Ottonia, begging her to keep it safe until they had a chance to mail it.

Since retreats in Alexishafen were followed by the joyful celebration of Family Feast, Sister Theophane asked if the community could observe the custom. Sister Superior consented and again Sister Theophane's free time went into a humorous program for the occasion. In quiet joy the priests and the Sisters renewed the bonds of charity.

When the internees were taken to Manam they were promised a quiet site for their camp. However, since the Japanese military had established a large base in Hansa Bay, just a short distance from Manam Island, quiet was out of the question. Allied planes daily zoomed over the volcano island as they attacked the base at Hansa Bay. Yet the missionaries were quite sure that the Allies knew of their presence. At one time rumor was that the Americans wanted to take the missionaries away from the danger zone. They planned to come up to the island in submarines. The prisoners learned of the plans only after a new detachment of Japanese soldiers arrived and set up watch houses all along the coast, keeping a vigilant eye on the sea.

Toward the end of January, 1944, definite news of another removal was received. The Bishop feared that this would mean disaster because travel on the sea was most dangerous now, and the missionaries would have to be transferred in Japanese vessels, sure targets for the Allied planes. The aging Bishop spent much time in prayer, and then wrote a letter to the Japanese headquarters in Hansa Bay requesting that the order for removal from Manam be recalled. He pointed out the danger of such a transfer. The Japanese authorities rejected his advice and reiterated the command, though no specific day was set for the departure.

Since removal was inevitable, the Bishop ordered all work in the gardens to cease. All who were able were to get to work packing what provisions were left, and getting things in order. The little chapel was beautifully decorated and the Blessed Sacrament exposed. Day and night adorers knelt in prayer before the altar, gaining strength and courage for the days before them. After four days and nights of adoration, the final order came. One group was to leave immediately, march to Tabelle—about two hours from the camp site—and from there take a pinnace to Avara on the coast. A second group would set out a few days later following the same procedure.

When Sister Theophane saw how ill many of the Sisters were, she quickly volunteered to carry some of the extra luggage to Tabelle. Loaded down with forty pounds of food stored in large tin cans, she trudged along for two hours. The sharp tin cut into her shoulders, then into her side as she shifted the unwieldy burden. Yet she returned to camp and took another load to Tabelle the next day. Finally, with the second group of Sisters, she reached Avara before midnight.

The Japanese had established themselves in the coastal town.

The beach was a scene of disorder. The Japanese had brought plentiful supplies of food to the town, but had been unable to ship them further because attacks from Allied planes were too heavy. Bags of rice in huge piles lined the shore, although the rice was soaked by the tropical rains and green shoots protruded from the bags. Stacks of canned goods, much of it riddled with bullet holes, stood about.

It was only when the missionaries pressed into the jungle that they discovered unburied corpses lying about. The stench was nauseating. The officers told the prisoners that the ship was due that night, and that it was not safe to wait on the shore. After steaming in the jungle for two hours, the missionaries were informed that the ship would not come that night. The ship had been bombed and would have to be repaired before it could be used.

Once more the priests and the Sisters were on the march, not back to the shore, but to a large shed, if it could be called that. The shed consisted of a roof; that was all. Many of the internees preferred to sleep in the open since the roof of the shed did not look very safe. The mosquitoes were jubilant over their new prey, and succeeded in making the missionaries miserable for the rest of the night.

The next morning the Sisters were surprised to see their companions, who had left for Avara some days before, standing a short distance away and looking at them in silence. Finally one of the Sisters called out, "We can't talk to you!" Even the guard laughed and let the two groups mingle. After all there could be little danger to the Japanese Empire in such conversation.

The morning was quiet. However, the Japanese insisted that all who were able should repair to the bush in case planes should come. In the afternoon the Sisters cooked an odd broth which served for all three meals that day. Toward evening the *Dorish Maru* dropped anchor at Avara. The missionaries were immediately ordered to the beach. They went, each carrying their little box or suitcase with clothes and some tins of food.

The *Dorish Maru* had brought a large supply of rice for the Japanese, and the entire detachment of soldiers got busy unloading. A drizzle changed to a downpour, but the unloading continued and the missionaries stood at attention in the rain. They stood and they stood. Twelve o'clock, one o'clock, two o'clock—the rain poured down and the missionaries still stood and waited. As the trying minutes slowly passed, a murmur of prayer arose from the group. Their habits and veils clung to the Sisters; their feet sank in the mud; and still their hearts could rejoice in the Lord. When someone called out, "All for the glory of God, even this rain," Sister Theophane rejoined with her usual enthusiasm, "You're right! Let's have some more!"

Toward morning the skies cleared, and then came the order, "March back to the shed! We will not sail in the daylight!" Their feet leaden from the hours of standing, their bags heavy with rain, the missionaries headed for the bush. There they tried to build small fires to dry their clothes and heat a bit of water, except that the soaked firewood gave off clouds of smoke. "All fires out!" barked the officer.

Sister Theophane was still stamping out the smoking wood when the planes zoomed low over the trees. "*Deus in adjutorium meum intende! Papa!*" she screamed, and then ran, she knew not where. Branches cracked and leaves swept down to the ground as the strafing plane grazed the tree tops. In fright, one of the Sisters simply leaned against a tree. A bullet imbedded itself in the trunk just above her head. Sister Barnaba, dear old missioner, could not be disturbed. Her veil had been badly soaked the night before and she calmly stood in the opening trying to get it back into shape. One of the Sisters grabbed her by the arm and pulled her along. After what seemed an hour, the planes flew down the coast and the shooting was over. None of the missionaries had been injured. Sister Barnaba found a seat on the log and finished doctoring up her veil.

Two of the younger Sisters, who had not yet made their final vows, now pronounced them in the bush. It was perhaps the most simple final profession ever made in the Congregation.[19]

Around three o'clock in the afternoon, the prisoners were once more lined up on the wharf. Sister Theophane and Sister Ottonia sat on the latter's suitcase, and together recited the Vespers and Compline of the Divine Office. Then they mused; and as ever, Sister Theophane's thoughts were back in Rivo, in Ilala, in Malmal, in Ulingan. "Wait till this old war is over," she exclaimed, "we'll get things going!"[20]

A group of soldiers from India, also prisoners of the Japanese, was cutting grass near the Japanese huts. The prisoners eyed the missionaries with sympathy, and when the guards were not looking, they cleverly hooked various articles to the ends of their long knives. Then they pretended to look over to the jungle, and at the same time they swung their knives over their heads so that the farewell gifts flew off and landed among the missionaries. A package of cigarettes fell in Sister Siglinde's arms. "He wants you to have a smoke," teased a priest as Sister hastened to relieve herself of the gift.[21]

Toward evening the prisoners began to board the ship. The *Dorish Maru* was slightly larger than the *Stella Maris*, though constructed much more crudely. The deck was slanted, rising in the middle. Along the rail ran an aisle some feet lower than the center deck. At either end of the deck, on elevated platforms, stood a 25mm anti-aircraft gun.

Up the plank marched the soldiers, the Protestant missionaries, the priests, the Sisters, and a great number of mestizos. When the plank was removed, two hundred and fifty persons were jammed on the deck, although about one hundred of the Japanese soldiers eventually moved down to the hold below the main deck. Sister Theophane had been carrying Sister Ottonia's suitcase, but when she turned to give it back to her she found they were separated. She swung the suitcase lightly over the heads of the intervening persons to its owner. The prisoners lapsed into silence when the officer issued orders: "No talking on the ship! No smoking! Sisters remove your white collars!"

CHAPTER 14

VOYAGE OF TEARS

IT WAS dark, late in the evening of Saturday, February 5, 1944, when the *Dorish Maru* put to sea. The ship had scarcely moved out of Hansa Bay when she slowed down and moved in close to shore. The Japanese did not reveal the reason, yet everyone knew why. The air was not clear of the Allied war planes that posed a continuous threat of disaster for any Japanese shipping.

It was an hour or more before the ship resumed its course. All noticed with great satisfaction and relief, that she was going fast. By the next day, at about 7 o'clock, it could be in the protection of the Kairiru Island.

The various groups on the ship tended to gather together with their own. The Japanese soldiers who stayed on the main deck were mostly toward the front. Sister Ottonia, Sister Theophane, and the other Sisters were clustered around the front hatch cover. Fr. John Tschauder, together with other SVD priests and Brothers, as well as Bishop Wolf, were near the bridge. The protestant group was situated more toward the rear of the ship.[1]

It was a fairly clear night, with only a thin veil of clouds to obscure the bright half-moon that clearly illuminated the ship, its superstructure, and its long silvery wake. Nothing could be seen of the promised escort of Japanese aircrafts, although there had been talk of as many as thirty planes. No help could be expected from those who had promised to do their utmost to "protect" the prisoners. No mercy could be hoped for from a patrolling plane once it had spied its victim. In the words of Fr. Tschauder:

> I said the Rosary. Five times the beads glided through my fingers. My ever-recurring prayer was: "Good Lord, please, let there be no attack on the ship, no bombs on her that carries so precious a cargo." I turned to the Little Flower, the patron saint of all missionaries. I remembered how she had once saved a group of China missionaries from certain death in a watery grave. I have never been a fervent devotee of hers, I regret to say, but this did not embarrass me just then when I found myself in so terrible a danger. I knew that Saint Thérèse would help even those who could not number themselves among her special devotees. Kindness always seems greatest when one least expects it. Moreover, the Little Flower did not make any conditions when she promised her help for the missionaries.[2]

At Midnight, and all was peaceful and quiet except for the rhythmic throbbing of the ship's engine and the slapping of the sea against the hull as she ploughed toward the island destination. The anxious prisoners prayed quietly that the small ship would move faster as it headed for Kairiru Island, hopefully to dock unobserved before daybreak.

Then it happened! Suddenly a siren screamed. Gone were the peace and the calm which had prevailed until a moment ago. A great commotion ensued. "What is it? Is it an air-raid?" Quickly the instruction came, "Lie down!"

The soldiers were ready for action. With rifles pointed skyward, they stood densely packed on the foredeck. Their response to the call of the siren was that of a soldier. They stood by their guns. For them it meant, "Be ready for action!" For the prisoners, who laid down on the deck, praying and wondering what would become of them, it meant, "Be ready for death!"

Suddenly the plane was visible as it came streaking toward the ship. The Japanese captain yelled the order through a megaphone from the bridge, his voice harsh and cruel: "Fire!" The ship almost reared out of the water when a bomb crashed down right near the bow. The anti-aircraft cannons bellowed; the machine-guns of the troops on deck chattered and spit a hail of bullets; and the rifles cracked at the monster which almost flattened everyone to the deck as it swooped low overhead and then quickly away.

That was only the first round of the duel. The big twin engined-plane would come back for another run over the victim, which frantically zig-zagged at full speed through the sea. And the plane did come back.

About ten minutes had elapsed when the same order came again: "Fire!" Again anti-aircraft guns bellowed, machine-guns chattered, and rifles rattled. Again the deafening detonation. This time the bomb exploded in the sea on the portside, amidships. The explosion was very close, as fragments of metal crashed against the hull, and another large explosion struck the bulwarks nearly decapitating Fr. Tschauder.

The attacking plane flew back towards the coast and then turned in for its third onslaught. Over ten minutes elapsed. Then the same command rasped out from the bridge. Again, cannons, machine-guns, and rifles went into furious action. Again, a bomb crashed down and missed the *Dorish Maru*. The plane stormed over at almost mast-top height; the prisoners sensed the pressure of its wings. But it was the last flight; one cannon fired a single shot after it and that struck home. There was great excitement and triumphant shouts from the Japanese, "*Senso banzai!*" (Long live war!) The American plane had been hit and down it went into the sea, blazing fiercely.

The American airmen of course, did not know, and could not know of the missionaries being aboard the ship. Nevertheless, if one of their bombs had hit squarely on the *Dorish Maru* would have taken them all into a watery grave.

The *Dorish Maru* and her extraordinary cargo proceeded on her journey. All were still safe and sound and very much alive; nay, more alive and excited after such an adventure. The atmosphere of tense expectation had vanished. "My word, this teaches one to pray!" someone said.

Excitement soon gave way to a mood of disappointment as daybreak of Sunday, February 6 came nearer. The *Dorish Maru* was too slow and could not make Wewak Harbor or the shelter of Kairiru Island before sunrise.

When the plane had attacked, the ship was perhaps off the mouth of the Sepik River. The attack had delayed her and put her off course. At daybreak Terebu appeared on the coast, and then Wewak. Kairiru was a long way off.

Spirits drooped. The missionaries knew what was coming. Time dragged by, and slowly the ship plodded on as the Japanese soldiers remained quiet and ready for combat.

Towards eight o'clock Kairiru loomed up closer and on the left the Wirui Mission of the Holy Cross was seen. The great residence of the SVD Regional still stood there on the mountain's crest. It was Holy Cross Mission. Now it was the way of the cross for the prisoners. The missionaries talked among themselves, wondering about their colleagues from Wewak and exchanging opinions concerning their whereabouts. Another ship near Kairiru was seen to be burning fiercely. Then sheer terror arose as at least ten planes were seen heading for the little *Dorish Maru*. The order came for the prisoners to lie down. A squadron of planes against one little ship! This would surely be the end.

Shells rained down and shook the vessel as plane after plane in quick succession came over the unfortunate *Dorish Maru*, each one releasing a hail storm of machine-gun bullets. Thousands splashed harmlessly into the sea; but all too many struck the ship and its innocent passengers. The anti-aircraft guns worked furiously, and the machine guns and rifles of the soldiers rattled in reply to the fire of each on-coming plane. Several of the anti-aircraft gun crews were wiped out, but there were always others to take over. While bullets whistled and whined, the air filled with smoke and dust and the acrid smell of burned cordite from the guns firing. Father Tschauder wrote:

> I was terrified. I think all of us were. Right at the beginning I felt a trickle of warm blood running down my face. I had the same feeling on my back and my legs, and something very hot stung me in my right hand. It was only then that I realized that I was hurt. I saw the blood running from a cut in the back of my hand. I prayed. There was nothing I could do but expect death. I remember that in my terror I called my mother several times. I thought of her far away. I had not heard of her for five years. Was she with me? Did she know?
>
> Whenever a plane had made its run over the stricken ship, there was a short spell, until the next was ready to follow in. I looked straight in the face of the first ones to come over, terrible and cruel things they were as they roared low over the *Dorish Maru*, with their wings almost touching the masthead. Instinctively, my head went down. Then came a terrific bang right at my ear, and again I felt the same warm trickle of blood. Only afterwards, when all was over, did I realize how narrow an escape I had. A bullet had grazed the back of my head, torn away a piece of skin, and pierced a neat hole clean through the steel plate against which I had been leaning.[3]

"*Deus in adjutorium meum intende! Papa!*" Sister Theophane lay on her back, her eyes fixed as more planes raced toward the ship. In a swift second, as the fliers approached within several hundred yards of the *Dorish Maru,* they opened fire. From each of the mighty planes, the machine guns blazed down upon prisoners lying unprotected on the open deck.

Shrieks of horror mingled with the deafening blast of the guns and the roar of aircraft engines while the menacing smell of burned gunpowder mixed with the fresh sea breeze. The wounded sprang to their feet. The little mestizo children rushed from one spot to another in bewildered terror. Finally the pilots sighted the habits of the Sisters. Shocked at the sight, the guns at once were still, and the bombers quickly veered from the ship.

Sister Theophane's hand moved slowly to her chest as if to check the blood that streamed through her habit. Once more she looked up: the skies were clear now and a wondrous blue. "My Lord and My God!" she murmured. Sister Frances Bott heard the murmur and as she turned toward Sister Theophane, that great self-giving missionary's heart ceased to beat. Sister Theophane died on the deck in a pool of her own blood.

Cautiously Sister Ottonia lowered the suitcase she had been holding over her face. She stood up, but paled, and grasped for support as her eyes swept the deck. Blood streamed over the bodies of the dead. The wounded stumbled to their feet and fell again, dizzy and stunned. The Bishop, mortally wounded but clinging to life, raised himself on his elbow and imparted general absolution to the dying.

New horror seized the survivors when flames shot up from the baggage room. Anyone who could possibly hold a bucket of water poured it below in an effort to quench the fire. Although there were no life boats on the *Dorish Maru,* the officers produced several large boards and dropped them into the sea. The ship was near Dallman Haber, close to Wewak, and the soldiers there set out in a ferry and a pinnace when they saw that the ship had been damaged in the attack. Slowly and painfully, the dead, the wounded, and the precious few who were not hurt were loaded on the ferry and the pinnace, and taken to the dock at Wewak. A gruesome day of horror followed the tragic morning.

CHAPTER 15

The Spirit Lives

THE DEAD were removed from their transports and arranged in rows along the beach. The wounded were laid on the ground nearby, some in tents set up by the Japanese. Five Sisters were not hurt. These spent the day ministering to the wounded, of whom there were about forty. American planes circled over Wewak several times that day, but no shots were fired. They had probably come back to see what had happened in the raid.

Toward evening orders came that the survivors would continue their journey during the night. They shuddered at the thought of boarding the *Dorish Maru* once more. As carefully as they could, the Sisters and the priests helped to bring the wounded back to the ship now moored at Wewak. The deck had been swept, but not washed. Blood still ran in the lower aisles like rain in the gullies after a heavy shower.

Before she left, Sister Ottonia, whose finger had been wounded, went down the beach for a last visit to the dead. More than fifty bodies, wrapped in blankets soaked with blood, lined the beach. Reverently Sister Ottonia walked from one corpse to another and, from her Sisters in religion, she carefully removed the rings and profession crosses. These would be cherished by loved ones at home. She counted them—twenty-seven Sisters had finished the work God had given them to do.

Under the cover of night the *Dorish Maru* pulled away from Wewak with its cargo of human suffering. The muffled moans of the wounded stole over the silent waters; while on the shores of Wewak all was still. From a cloudless sky the tropical brilliance of the stars mingled with the glow of the full moon and outlined the corpses on the beach. The sight was an agonizing one to the missionaries who looked back longingly at their beloved dead. Slowly the ship moved away and Wewak became a speck in the distance, then was swallowed in the night.

Bishop Wolf had asked that if the bodies could not be buried, they should be cremated rather than left to decay on the beach. In spite of the request, the smoke generated by the necessary fire would certainly be observed by American aircraft, and would most likely draw a direct and immediate attack. Consequently, cremation was not a viable option for the Japanese remaining in Wewak—nor was the option of digging individual graves, given the almost daily air attacks combined with the imminent threat of a landing by advancing Allied ground forces. The only practical solution for the disposal of a large number of dead bodies in this war zone was a mass grave. A large crater carved in the beach by an American bomb not far from the line of bodies was the obvious solution to the struggling Japanese. Thus the body of Sr. Theophane found its final resting place, together with those of all the others killed on the *Dorish Maru*, beneath the beach at Wewak, covered by a thick blanket of sandy soil.

Today the gravesite is not marked, and its precise location is unkown, although tradition has it that the site is near the Windjammer hotel, either between the hotel and the Post Office, or perhaps between the hotel and Wiriu Cathedral, possibly near the site of St. Mary's primary school.[1]

While it is tempting to imagine that a carefully marked gravesite would have been appropriate for Sister Theophane and for each of her Sisters in faith, based upon the way she lived her life, it seems clear that she would not have sought any special honor in death. In fact it is doubtful, if given the option, she would have objected to her mortal remains ending in the most humble grave possible, near the missions she loved, and beneath the feet of the people she served. But such speculation misses the truly significant point that while her mortal body had finished its work, her spirit lives on in the place where her life's work is being properly rewarded. Of course the memory of her life remains vividly alive in the missions and in these pages, hopefully serving as a force to inspire others to follow lives of heroic virtue as she did. And like St. Thérèse of Lisieux, one must assume that even now she continues her prayers for the redemption of lost souls.

Epilogue

IT WAS not until the following Wednesday, February 9, 1944, that the *Dorish Maru* finally reached its destination, and the prisoners were put off at Hotegan in Hollandia.

The weeks that followed were a nightmare of suffering. Scarcity of good food, lack of medical care, incessant danger from bombers, the oppression by their captors, all combined to make the prison term at Hollandia a time of unforgettable hardship. But the prisoners never forgot that hope on which they lived. Again and again Sister Ottonia recalled Sister Theophane's emphatic, "The Americans will come! You will see!"

The weeks dragged on, one after another, as tired missioners were laid to rest in jungle graves. The old Bishop held on for a time, and then his wounds became worse. The doctor gave up hope and the kindly old Bishop resigned himself to death.

When one of the priests staggered into the hut and declared that he could not go on but must die, his confreres could still grin. "You'll have to dig your own grave," they teased. "None of us can do it anymore!" They laughed, but they knew the fact was true.

The Japanese realized that they were losing the deadly game of war, and they tried desperately to save face. All prisoners, some scarcely able to move, were dragged farther into the bush.

When on April 22, 1944, the Japanese captain received definite reports from his scouts that the Americans had landed, he ordered all to be ready to leave the camp at Goya within an hour. All were to flee before the American army and try to reach Arso, about forty miles away in the bush.

Appalled, the emaciated prisoners listened to the order. The critically ill, who were unable to walk, were to be fed once more and then left alone in Goya. Sister Ottonia shrank in horror at this command. She knew, as did the Japanese officer, that Goya would be bombed by the Americans. Fearlessly the nun approached the officer and refused to obey his orders. She would never leave the sick, she declared. Her Superior was there among the bedridden.

The officer laughed coarsely, but allowed her to remain with the sick at her own risk. Tearfully Sister Ottonia watched the rest of the prisoners drag themselves out of the camp under Japanese guard. Overhead purred the American bombers, but the retreating prisoners and Japanese soldiers were hidden by the dense foliage of the jungle.

Toward evening the fleeing prisoners were allowed to encamp near a river for the night. When morning came the captain called several together for a conference, and then—to the surprise of the prisoners—he gave a grand final speech and declared that Japan could no longer protect the missionaries. They were free to return to Goya, but he warned them that dire punishment would be meted out to anyone who should attempt to contact the Americans. With this the captain bade farewell to the bewildered prisoners and continued with his soldiers on the way to Arso.

It was a day of jubilee for the free prisoners. Exhausted as they were, they dragged themselves back through the jungle to Goya. On the following day two of the priests and a Brother undertook the hazardous task of contacting the Americans. "That meeting was not without tears," wrote Father Hermann Hagen, one of the three who risked their lives to reach the American lines. As soon as the Americans heard of the imprisoned missionaries in the jungle, a detachment of two hundred soldiers volunteered to rescue them. They did not march into the bush—they ran!

To the surviving missionaries the scene of that day will ever remain a sacred memory. The Americans had come at last! Sister Theophane was not there to receive with open arms the countrymen for whom she had waited long months, but her spirit was there, saluting the stars and stripes that had not failed her, and exulting in the knowledge that the work for which she had given her life would be carried on. Today 3,161 professed Sisters are carrying out their charism to the missions in 5 continents in Africa, the Americas, Asia, Europe, and Oceania.

BIBLIOGRAPHY

PRIMARY

1. Letters from Sister Theophane Maier, S.Sp.S.

To William Maier from Greenville, Mississippi, 19 March 1929

To William Maier from Greenville, Mississippi, March 1929

To Louise Maier from Greenville, Mississippi, 7 April 1929

To William Maier from Greenville, Mississippi, 7 April 1929

To William Maier from Greenville, Mississippi, 28 April 1929

To Louise Maier from Greenville, Mississippi, 21 May 1929

To Louise Maier from Greenville, Mississippi, 14, June 1929

To Louise Maier from Waukegan, Illinois, 26, November 1933

To Louise Maier from Waukegan, Illinois, 18 June 1934

To Louise Maier from Waukegan, Illinois, 14, October 1934

To Louise Maier from Waukegan, Illinois, 4, November 1934

To Louise Maier aboard the Niagara, 10 December 1934

To Louise Maier from Epping, Australia, 30 December 1934

To Louise Maier from Brisbane, Australia, 2, February 1935

To Louise Maier from Alexishafen, Papua New Guinea, 16 March 1935

To Louise Maier from Alexishafen, Papua New Guinea, 28 July 1935

To Louise Maier from Alexishafen, Papua New Guinea, 11 November 1935

To Rosalie Maier from Alexishafen, Papua New Guinea, 26 January 1936

To Louise Maier from Alexishafen, Papua New Guinea 26 April 1936

To Louise Maier from Alexishafen, Papua New Guinea, 29 July 1936

To Rosalie Maier from Alexishafen, Papua New Guinea, 22 August 1937

To Louise Maier from Alexishafen, Papua New Guinea, 9 January 1938

To Louise Maier from Alexishafen, Papua New Guinea, 27 February 1938

To Louise Maier from Alexishafen, Papua New Guinea, 20 August 1938

To Louise Maier from Alexishafen, Papua New Guinea, 8 November 1938

To the Maier Family from Alexishafen, Papua New Guinea, 21 November 1938

To the Maier Family from Alexishafen, Papua New Guinea, 26 April 1939

To Rosalie Maier from Alexishafen, Papua New Guinea, 29 July 1939

To Louise Maier from Alexishafen, Papua New Guinea, 30 July 1939

To Ray Maier Alexishafen, Papua New Guinea, 6, August 1939

To Louise Maier from Alexishafen, Papua New Guinea, 26 November 1939

To Rosalie Maier from Alexishafen, Papua New Guinea, 17 December 1939

To Louise Maier from Ulingan, Papua New Guinea, 1 September 1940

To Rosalie Maier from Ulingan, Papua New Guinea, 3 March 1940

To Louise Maier from Ulingan, Papua New Guinea, 21 January 1941

To Louise Maier from Ulingan, Papua New Guinea, 20 April 1942

To Her Nephew from Ulingan, Papua New Guinea, 27 April 1941

To Ray Maier from Ulingan, Papua New Guinea, 27 April 1941

To Rosalie Maier from Alexishafen, Papua New Guinea, 29 May 1941

To Sr. Rose Gonzaga from Alexishafen, Papua New Guinea, 29 May 1941

To Louise Maier from Alexishafen, Papua New Guinea, 26 October 1941

To Rosalie Maier from Alexishafen, Papua New Guinea, 20 November 1941

Undated Letter (probably from Ulingan, Papua New Guinea) arrived in 1943 (censored)

To Louise Maier from Alexishafen, Papua New Guinea, 1 January (no year)

To Techny S.Sp.S from Alexishafen, Papua New Guinea, 2 February 1936

To Techny S.Sp.S from Alexishafen, Papua New Guinea, 21 June 1936

To Techny S.Sp.S from Alexishafen, Papua New Guinea, 18 October 1936

To Techny S.Sp.S from Alexishafen, Papua New Guinea, 16 May 1937

To Techny S.Sp.S from Alexishafen, Papua New Guinea, 24 October 1937

To Techny S.Sp.S from Alexishafen, Papua New Guinea, 1 May 1938

To Techny S.Sp.S from Alexishafen, Papua New Guinea, 8 October 1938

To Techny S.Sp.S from Alexishafen, Papua New Guinea, 20 August 1938

To Techny S.Sp.S from Alexishafen, Papua New Guinea (undated)

To Techny S.Sp.S from Ulingan, Papua New Guinea, April 1948

To Rev. G. Weimann from Alexishafen, Papua New Guinea, 13 February 1938

2. Letters from the Far East to the Author

Sister Ottonia Ruholl (Sister Mary Elise), S.Sp.S. from Queensland, Australia, 28 June 1944.

Sister Ottonia Ruholl (Sister Mary Elise), S.Sp.S. from Queensland, Australia, 30 July 1944.

Sister Ottonia Ruholl (Sister Mary Elise), S.Sp.S. from Queensland, Australia, 26 November 1944.

Sister Ottonia Ruholl (Sister Mary Elise), S.Sp.S. from Queensland, Australia, (treats of life in camp), 18 February 1945.

Sister Ottonia Ruholl (Sister Mary Elise), S.Sp.S. Reminiscences of Sister Theophane written in Queensland, Australia from 10 December 1944 to 23 January 1945.

Sister M. Tarcisia, O.S.F. from Cross Roads, Jamaica, 6 February 1945.

3. American Letters to the Author

Sister Makaria Iten, S.Sp.S. from Milwaukee, Wisconsin, November 1944.

Sister Genevieve Regal, S.Sp.S. from New Hampton, Iowa, December 1944.

Sister Inviolata Krueth, S.Sp.S. from Little Rock, Arkansas, December 1944.

Sister Bertholda Gruhn, S.Sp.S. from Greenville, Mississippi, December 1944.

Sister Ehrentruda Schuster, S.Sp.S. from Meridian, Mississippi, December 1944.

Sister Gaudiosa Moennig, S.Sp.S. from Meridian, Mississippi, December 1944.

Sister Alwine Rutterdam, S.Sp.S. from Techny, Illinois, December 1944.

Sister Meline Karasz, S.Sp.S. from Mauston, Wisconsin, December 1944.

Sister Florence Henry, S.Sp.S. from Bay St. Louis, Missouri, December 1944.

Sister Maristella Carr, S.Sp.S. from Meridian, Mississippi, December 1944.

Sister Uriele Issermann, S.Sp.S. from Meridian, Mississippi, December 1944.

Sister Lorraine Becker, S.Sp.S. from Sharpsville, Pennsylvania, December 1944.

Sister Gertrude, S.S.J. from Rochester, New York, 8 December 1944.

Sister Gabriela Hausdorf, S.Sp.S. from Waukegan, Illinois, December 1944.

Sister Angilberta Schellenberger, S.Sp.S. from Watertown, Wisconsin, December 1944.

Rev. M. Miller, S.J. from Buffalo, New York, 12 January 1945.

Dr. Leo Simpson from Rochester, New York, 5 January 1945.

Dr. Elmer O'Brien from Rochester, New York, 9 January 1945.

Sister Alice Berghoff, S.Sp.S. from Watertown, Wisconsin,15 January 1945.

Rev. W. Miller, S.J. from Woodstock, Maryland, 16 January 1945.

Mrs. E. McCaffrey from Rochester, New York, 21 January 1945.

Sister M. Gregory, S.S.N.D. from Notch Cliff, Maryland, 28 January 1945.

Sister M. Gemma, S.S.N.D. from Malden, Massachusetts, January, 1945.

Sister M. Lourdes, S.S.J. from Rochester, New York, 11 February 1945.

Sister M. Florence, S.S.J. from Geneva, New York, 18 February 1945.

Miss E. Mertz. from Columbus, Ohio, 23 February 1945.

Sister Joan of the Cross, D.C. from Wheeling, West Virginia, 2 March 1945.

Miss Helen Rauber. from Utica, New York, 7 May 1945.

Sister M. Martina, S.S.J. from Rochester, New York, 4 July 1945.

4. Manuscripts

Sister M. Rosalie, S.S.J. *Pre-Convent Days of Sister Theophane*, an unpublished manuscript prepared by Sister Rosalie to be of use in writing a full biography of her younger sister.

Sister M. Rosalie, S.S.J. Manuscript of Sister Theophane's Parents.

Mr. Rufus Maier. *Notes on the Early Life of Inez*, an unpublished manuscript prepared by Inez's older brother.

Sister Siglinde Poboss, S.Sp.S. *My Captivity Experiences*, a private manuscript written in Sidney, Australia. November, 1944.

5. Reports from the Far East to the Author

Rev. L. Mey, S.V.D. from Sidney, Australia, December 26, 1944.

Sister Elreda Ruiter, S.Sp.S. from "Somewhere in Australia", January 1945.

Sister Milreda Zeller, S.Sp.S. from "Somewhere in Australia," January 1945.

Sister Nazaria Albers, S.Sp.S. from "Somewhere in Australia" January 1945.

Sister Auxilium Reiser, S.Sp.S. from "Somewhere in Australia," January 1945.

Brother Emmerich, S.V.D. from Sidney, Australia, January 1945.

Rev. E. Van Barr, S.V.D. from Sidney, Australia, January 1945.

Unidentified. from "Somewhere in Australia," January 1945.

Unidentified. from "Somewhere in Australia," January 1945.

Brother Gerhoch, S.V.D. from Sidney, Australia, February 1945.

6. Interviews

Sister M. Rosalie, S.S.J. from 29 December 1944 to 5 January 1945 at Rochester, New York.

Mrs. I. Hennessy. Rochester, New York, 11 January 1945.

Rev. H. Geck. Rochester, New York, 21 January 1945.

Sister Crispina Rehnen, S.Sp.S. Techny, Illinois, January 1945.

Sister Lorraine Becker, S.Sp.S. Techny, Illinois, 21 June 1945.

Sister Othberta Wundrock, S.Sp.S. Techny, Illinois, 25 June 1945.

Mrs. M. H. Keough. Rochester, New York, 25 January 1945.

Mrs. Marie Spahn, R.N. Rochester, New York, 13 January 1945.

7. Diary

Sister Theophane's *Diary* is often referred to in the biography. It is cited in the text only when Sister specifically states that she is using it in compiling her letter. I was not able to use it directly since it was confiscated by the Japanese, later returned, and finally the prisoners reached Hollandia, New Guinea.

SECONDARY

Humphries, W. *Patrolling in Papua*. New York: Henry Holt and Co., 1923.

Lindt, J. *Picturesque New Guinea*. London: No publisher, 1887.

Miller, C. *Cannibal Caravan*. New York: L. Furnam, 1939.

Vandercook, J. *Dark Islands*. New York: Harper Brothers, 1937.

Romilly, H. *From My Verandah in New Guinea*. London: David Nutt, 1889.

Overell, L. *A Woman's Impressions of German New Guinea*. New York: Dodd, Mead & Co., 1923.

Monckton, C. *Taming New Guinea*. New York: John Lane Co., 1921.

Murray, J. *Papua; or British New Guinea*. New York: C. Scribner's Sons., 1912.

Crockett, C. *House in Rain Forest.* Boston: Houghton, Mifflin Co., 1942.

Haughland, V. *Letter from New Guinea.* New York: Farrar and Rinehart, 1943.

Hagspiel, B. *Mission Trail in New Guinea.* Techny, Illinois: Mission Press, 1926.

Fischer, H. *Arnold Janssen.* Techny, Illinois: Mission Press, 1925.

ADDITIONAL RESEARCH FOR THIS EDITION

Aerts, Theo (Ed). *The Martyrs of Papua New Guinea*, Port Moresby, University of Papua New Guinea Press, 1994.

Best, M. (Sister Bernard S.Sp.S.) *She Walked with Courage*, unpublished manuscript.

Hickey, L. J. and Levy, M. *Rampage of the Roarin' 20's*, Boulder Colorado, International Historical Research Associates, 2009.

Hickey, L. J. and Levy, M. *Harvest of The Grim Reapers,* Vol. II, Boulder Colorado, International Historical Research Associates, Manuscript dealing with Dorish Maru incident, 2011.

Lipscomb, A. McKinnon, R. Murray, J. *Papua New Guinea*, Papua New Guinea, Lonley Planet Press, 1998.

Maier, Rosalie (Ed). *New Guinea Adventures,* Rochester, N.Y., James Conolly, Co., 1945.

NOTES

Chapter 2

1 Sister M. Rosalie Maier, S.S.J., Interview, Rochester, N.Y. January 3, 1945, all factual material in Chapter I, unless otherwise designated, is taken from personal interviews with Sister Rosalie and from her unpublished manuscript, Pre-Convent Days of Sister Theophane.
2 "Inez" is the Spanish form of "Agnes."
3 Sister M Rosalie Maier, S.S.J., Personal Letter, Rochester, New York. April 1, 1945.
4 Ibid.
5 Sister M. Rosalie Maier, S.S.J., Interview, Rochester, New York. January 3, 1945.

Chapter 3

1 Sister M. Rosalie Maier, S.S.J., Interview. Rochester, New York. January 4, 1945.
2 Sister M. Rosalie Maier, S.S.J., Notes on the Early Life of Inez.
3 Records of St. Michael's School, Rochester, New York. 1912.
4 Sister M. Rosalie Maier, S.S.J., Notes on the Early Life of Inez.
5 Rufus Maier, Notes on Inez Childhood.
6 Sister M. Rosalie Maier, S.S.J., Notes on the Early Life of Inez. See also: Rufus Maier, Notes on Inez' Childhood.
7 Rev. Walter Miller, S.J., Personal Letter. January 16, 1945.
8 Rufus Maier, Notes on Inez' Childhood.

9 Sister M. Rosalie Maier, S.S.J., Notes on the Early Life of Inez.
10 Sister Uriele Isermann, S.Sp.S. Letter. Meridian, Mississippi. December 27, 1944
11 Sister Gregory, SS.N.D., Letter. Notch Cliff, Maryland. January 28, 1945.
12 Sister Theophane Maier, S.Sp.S., Letter to Mrs. M. Maier. Alexis, New Guinea. January 16 (no year).
13 Sister M. Rosalie Maier, S.S.J., Notes on the Early Life of Inez.
14 Ibid.
15 Ibid.
16 Ibid.
17 Ibid.
18 Ibid.
19 Ibid.
20 Ibid.
21 Sister M. Gemma, SS.N.D., Report.
22 Ibid.
23 Sister M. Rosalie Maier, S.S.J., Notes on the Early Life of Inez.
24 Sister Florence Henry, S.Sp.S., Letter. Bay St. Louis, Mississippi. December 1944.

Chapter 4

1 Sister M. Rosalie Maier, S.S.J., Notes on the Early Life of Inez.
2 Ibid.
3 Sister M. Annunciata, S.S.J., Interview. Rochester, New York, January 1, 1945.
4 Mrs. I Hennessy (Inez Poericca), Interview, Rochester, New York. January 11, 1945.
5 Sister M. Rosalie Maier, S.S.J., op. cit.
6 Sister M. Agnes Patricia, S.S.J., Interview, Rochester, New York, January 4, 1945.
7 Ibid.
8 Mrs. I. Hennessy. Interview, Rochester, New York, January 11, 1945.
9 Nazareth Academy Yearbook, 1921.
10 Sister M. Rosalie Maier. S.S.J., Personal Letter, January 12, 1945.

11 Sister M. Teresa Marie, S.S.J., Dean of Nazareth College, Interview, Rochester, New York. January 4, 1945.
12 Ibid.
13 Mrs. F. McGaffery (Beatrice McGrath), Personal Letter, January 21, 1945.
14 Ibid.
15 Sister M. Rosalie Maier, S.S.J., op. cit.
16 Sister M. Rosalie Maier, S.S.J., Interview, Rochester, New York, January 4, 1945.
17 Sister Joan of the Cross, D.C., Personal Letter, Wheeling, West Virginia, March 11, 1945.
18 Maier Family, Interview, Rochester, New York, December 31 1944.
19 Miss E. Mertz, Personal Letter, Columbus, Ohio, February 23, 1945.
20 Rev. G. Weimann, Interview, Rochester, New York, December 30, 1944.
21 Sister Joan of the Cross, Personal Letter, Wheeling, West Virginia, March 11, 1945.
22 Sister Makaria Iten, S.Sp.S., Personal Letter, Milwaukee, Wisconsin, November 1944.

Chapter 5

1 Sister M. Teresa Marie, S.S.J., Interview, Rochester, New York, January 4, 1945.
2 Sister M. Rosalie Maier, S.S.J., Interview, Rochester, New York, January 5, 1945.
3 Sister M. Rosalie Maier, S.S.J., op. cit.
4 Sister M. Gemma, SS.N.D., Personal Letter, Malden, Massachusetts, January 1945.
5 Rev. G Weimann, Interview, Rochester, New York, December 30, 1944.
6 Statistics of Annunciation Parish, Rochester, New York.
7 Ibid.
8 Sister M. Rosalie Maier, S.S.J., Interview, Rochester, New York, January 4, 1945.

9 Rev. G. Weimann, Interview, Rochester, New York, December 30, 1944.
10 Sister M. Rosalie Maier, S.S.J., Personal Letter, Rochester, New York, July 13, 1945.
11 Sister M. Rosalie Maier, S.S.J., Interview. Rochester, New York, January 1945. (Used with the permission of Doctor Simpson.)
12 Sister M. Rosalie Maier, S.S.J., Interview, Rochester, New York, January 5, 1945. (Used with the permission of Dr. Elmer O'Brien.)
13 Sister M. Rosalie Maier, S.S.J., Early Life of Inez.

Chapter 6

1 Sister M. Agnes Patricia, S.S.J., Interview, Rochester, New York, January 4, 1945.
2 Ibid.
3 Sister Joan of the Cross, D.C., Letter, Wheeling, West Virginia, March 11, 1945.
4 Mrs. E. McCaffrey (Beatrice McGrath), Personal Letter, Rochester, New York, January 21, 1945.
5 Ibid.
6 Ibid.
7 Sister Joan of the Cross, D.C., op. cit.
8 Sister Alice Berghoff, S.Sp.S., Personal Letter, Watertown, Wisconsin, January 15, 1945.
9 Herman Fischer, S.V.D., Arnold Janssen. Techny, Illinois: Techny Mission Press, 1925, 132-147.
10 Statistics, approximate for 2012.
11 Herman Fischer, S.V.D., op. cit. Pp. 427-36.
12 Sister Florence Henry, S.Sp.S., Personal Letter, Bay St. Louis, Mississippi, December 1944.
13 Ibid.
14 Ibid.
15 Ibid.
16 Ibid.
17 Sister Maristella Carr, S.Sp.S., Personal Letter, Meridian, Mississippi, December 1944.
18 Ibid.

19 Ibid.
20 Sister M. Rosalie Maier, S.S.J., Interview, Rochester, New York, January 4, 1945.
21 Sister Meline Karasz, S.Sp.S., Personal Letter, Mauston, Wisconsin, December 1944.
22 Theophane Venard, a French priest of the Foreign Mission Society of Paris, was martyred in Tonkin, Vietnam on February 2, 1861, J. Walsh. Modern Martyr, Catholic Foreign Mission Society: Maryknoll, New York, 1913, 199.
23 Archives, Holy Spirit Convent, Techny, Illinois.
24 Sister Florence Henry, S.Sp.S., Personal Letter, Bay St. Louis, Mississippi, December 1944.
25 Ibid.
26 Sister Alice Berghoff, S.Sp.S., Personal Letter, Watertown, Wisconsin, January 1945.
27 Sister Meline Karasz, S.Sp.S., Personal Letter, Mauston, Wisconsin, December 1944.
28 Ibid.
29 Sister Maristella Carr, S.SpS., op. cit.
30 Sister Florence Henry, S.Sp.S., op. cit.
31 Ibid.
32 Ibid.
33 Sister Lorraine Becker, S.Sp.S., Personal Letter, Sharpsville, Pennsylvania, December 1944.
34 Sister Genevieve Regal, S.Sp.S. Personal Letter, New Hampton, Iowa, December 1944.

Chapter 7

1 Sister Makaria Iten, S.Sp.S., Personal Letter, Milwaukee, Wisconsin, November 1944.
2 Sister Florence Henry, S.Sp.S., Personal Letter, Bay St. Louis, Mississippi, February 1945.
3 Ibid.
4 Sister Lorraine Becker, S.Sp.S., Personal Letter, Sharpsville, Pennsylvania, December 1944.

5 Sister Alwine Rutterdam, S.Sp.S., Personal Letter, Techny, Illinois, December 17, 1944.
6 Sister Florence Henry, S.Sp.S., Personal Letter, Bay St. Louis, Mississippi, February 1945.
7 Sister Ehrentruda Schuster, S.Sp.S., Personal Letter, Meridian, Mississippi, December 1944.
8 Sister Florence Henry, S.Sp.S., op. cit.
9 Sister Alwine Rutterdam, S.Sp.S., op. cit.
10 Sister Theophane Maier, S.Sp.S., Letter to Her Father from Greenville, Mississippi, April 28, 1929.
11 Sister Theophane Maier, S.Sp.S., Letter to Her Mother from Greenville, Mississippi, April 7, 1929.
12 Sister Florence Henry, S.Sp.S., op. cit.
13 Sister Rosalie Maier, S.S.J., Interview, Rochester, New York, January 4, 1945.
14 Sister Theophane Maier, S.Sp.S., Letter to Her Father, from Greenville, Mississippi. March 19, 1929.
15 Ibid.
16 Sister Theophane Maier, S.Sp.S., Letter to her Father, from Greenville, Mississippi, Holy Thursday, 1929.
17 Sister Theophane Maier. S.Sp.S., Letter to Her Father, from Greenville, Mississippi, March 19, 1929.
18 Sister Theophane Maier, S.Sp.S., Letter to Her Mother, from Greenville, Mississippi, May 21, 1929.
19 Sister Theophane Maier, S.Sp.S., Letter to Her Mother, from Greenville, Mississippi, June 14, 1929.
20 Sister Florence Henry, S.Sp.S., Personal Letter, Bay St. Louis, Mississippi, February 1945.
21 Sister Florence Henry, S.Sp.S., Report, December 1944.
22 Sister Genevieve Regal, S.Sp.S., op cit.
23 Sister Lorraine Becker, S.Sp.S., op. cit.
24 Sister Lorraine Becker, S.Sp.S., Personal Letter, Sharpsville, Pennsylvania, December 1944.
25 Sister Inviolata Krueth, S.Sp.S., Personal Letter, Little Rock, Arkansas, December 1944.
26 Sister Bertholda Gruhn, S.Sp.S., Personal Letter, Greenville, Mississippi, December 1944.

27 Ibid.
28 Ibid.
29 Sister Lorraine Becker, S.Sp.S., Personal Letter, Sharpsville, Pennsylvania, December 1944.
30 Sister Bertholda Gruhn, S.Sp.S., op. cit.
31 Sister Ottonia Ruholl, S.Sp.S., Personal Letter, Queensland, Australia, February 18, 1945.
32 Sister Lorraine Becker, S.Sp.S., op. cit.
33 Sister Crispina Rehnen, S.Sp.S., Interview, Techny, Illinois, January 1945.
34 Sister Genevieve Regal, S.Sp.S., op. cit.
35 Sister Lorraine Becker, S.Sp.S., Interview, Techny, Illinois, June 21, 1945.
36 Sister Gabriela Hausdorf, S.Sp.S., Report, Waukegan, Illinois, December 1944.
37 Ibid.
38 Ibid.
39 Ibid.
40 Ibid.
41 Sister Genevieve Regal, S.Sp.S., op cit.
42 Sister Angilberta Landgraf, S.Sp.S., Personal Letter, Watertown, Wisconsin, January 1945.

Chapter 8

1 Sister Ottonia Ruholl (Sister Mary Elise), S.Sp.S., In Memory of Sister Theophane. This is a forty-page manuscript prepared by a fellow missionary in Papua New Guinea. It was sent by installments from Australia. The present quotation is taken from Part I, written December 10, 1944.
2 Sister Genevieve Regal, S.Sp.S., Personal Letter, New Hampton, Iowa, December 1944.
3 Sister Theophane Maier, S.Sp.S., Letter to her Mother, St. Therese's Hospital, Waukegan, Illinois, June 18, 1934.
4 Sister Othberta Wundrock, S.Sp.S., Interview, Techny, Illinois, June 25 1945.

5 Sister Crispina Rehnen, S.Sp.S., Interview, Techny, Illinois, December, 1944.
6 Archives of Holy Spirit Convent, Techny, Illinois, 1934.
7 Formula of Profession, Missionary Congregation of the Servants of the Holy Spirit.
8 Ibid.
9 Sister Makaria Iten, S.Sp.S., op. cit.
10 Sister Theophane Maier, S.Sp.S., Letter to Her Mother, Waukegan, Illinois, October 14 1934.
11 Ibid.
12 Sister Gabriela Hausdorf, S.Sp.S., op. cit.
13 Sister Theophane Maier, S.Sp.S., Letter to her Mother, "RM.S. Niagara," December 10 1934.
14 Brother Gerhoch , S.V.D., Report, Australia, February 1945.
15 Sister Theophane Maier, S.Sp,S., Letter to her Mother, Epping, Australia, December 30, 1934.
16 Ibid.
17 Ibid.
18 Sister Theophane Maier, S.Sp.S., Personal Letter to Her Mother, Brisbane, Australia, February 2, 1935.
19 Sister Theophane Maier, S.Sp.S., Personal Letter to Her Mother, Alexishafen, Papua New Guinea, March 16, 1935.
20 Ibid.
21 Sister Ottonia Ruholl (Sister Mary Elise), S.Sp.S., op. cit.
22 Sister Theophane Maier, S.Sp.S., Personal Letter to Her Mother, Alexishafen, New Guinea, March 16, 1935.
23 Ibid.
24 Sister Ottonia Ruholl (Sister Mary Elise), S.Sp.S., op. cit.
25 Sister Theophane Maier, S.Sp.S., Personal Letter to Her Mother, Alexishafen, New Guinea, March 16, 1935.
26 Alexisharbor is variously called Alexis, Alexishafen, or Alexisharbor in Sister Theophane's letters.
27 Bruno Hagspiel, S.V.D., Along the Mission Trail, Techny, Illinois: Mission Press, 1926, 115-18.
28 The Sisters' house was cloistered, and therefore the natives were not allowed to take their lessons in domestic science there.

29 Sister Theophane Maier, S.Sp.S., Personal Letter to Her Mother, Alexishafen, New Guinea. March 16, 1935.

Chapter 9

1 Sister Theophane Maier, S.Sp.S., Personal Letter to Her Mother, Alexis, New Guinea March 16, 1935.
2 According to returned missionaries, in 1946 Pidgin English was slowly disappearing from the schools in Papua New Guinea. After the war, more pure English was taught.
3 William Ross, S.V.D., "There Were Giants in New Guinea," Christian Family and Our Missions, XL (March 1945), 83.
4 Sister Ottonia Ruholl (Sister Mary Elise), S.Sp.S., op cit.
5 Rev. William Ross, S.V.D., op. cit.
6 Sister Theophane Maier, S.Sp.S., Personal Letter to Her Mother, Alexishafen, Papua New Guinea, July 28, 1935.
7 Ibid.
8 Sister Ottonia Ruholl (Sister Mary Elise), S.Sp.S., op. cit.
9 Sister Theophane Maier, S.Sp.S. Personal Letter to Her Mother, Alexishafen, Papua New Guinea, July 28,1935.
10 Sister Ottonia Ruholl (Sister Mary Elise, S.Sp.S., op. cit.
11 Sister Theophane Maier (Sister Mary Elise), S.Sp.S., Personal Letter to Her Mother, Alexishafen, New Guinea, July 28, 1935.
12 Ibid.
13 Ibid.
14 Ibid.
15 Ibid.
16 Sister Theophane Maier, S.Sp.S., Personal Letter to Her Mother, Alexishafen, Papua New Guinea, September 11, 1935.
17 Ibid.
18 Sister Theophane Maier, S.Sp.S., Personal Letter to Her Mother, Alexishafen, Papua New Guinea, July 28, 1935.
19 Sister Theophane Maier, S.Sp.S., Personal Letter to Her Mother, Alexishafen, Papua New Guinea, July 28, 1935.
20 Sister Theophane Maier, S.Sp.S., Personal Letter to Her Mother, Alexishafen, Papua New Guinea, September 11, 1935.
21 Ibid.

22 Ibid.
23 Sister Theophane Maier, S.Sp.S., Personal Letter to Her Mother, Alexishafen, Papua New Guinea, November 26, 1939.
24 The Missionary Communication Association (Missions-Verkehrs-Arbeitsgemeinschaft) was begun in Cologne in 1927.
25 Sister Theophane Maier, S.Sp.S., Personal Letter to Her Mother, Alexishafen, Papua New Guinea, November 11, 1936.

Chapter 10

1 Sister Theophane Maier, S.Sp.S., Personal Letter to Her Mother, Alexishafen, Papua New Guinea, April 26, 1936.
2 Sister Theophane Maier, S.Sp.S., Personal Letter to Techny, Alexishafen, Papua New Guinea, February 2, 1936.
3 Sister Theophane Maier, S.Sp.S., Personal Letter to Techny, Alexishafen, Papua New Guinea, June 21, 1936.
4 Allusion is here made to St. Paul's beloved converts at Philippi.
5 Sister Theophane Maier, S.Sp.S., Personal letter to Techny, Alexishafen, Papua New Guinea, June 21, 1936.
6 Ibid.
7 Sister Theophane Maier, S.Sp.S., Personal letter to the Family, Alexishafen, Papua New Guinea, April 26, 1939.
8 Sister Theophane Maier, S.Sp.S., Personal Letter to Techny, Alexishafen, Papua New Guinea, October 18, 1936.
9 Sister Theophane Maier, S.Sp.S., Personal Letter to the Family, Alexishafen, Papua New Guinea, November 21, 1938.
10 Sister Theophane Maier, S.Sp.S., Personal Letter to Her Mother, Alexishafen, Papua New Guinea, November 8, 1938.
11 Sister Theophane Maier, S.Sp.S., Personal Letter to Her Mother, Alexishafen, Papua New Guinea, November 26, 1939.
12 Sister Theophane Maier, S.Sp.S., Personal Letter to Techny, Alexishafen, Papua New Guinea, May 16, 1937.
13 Unidentified manuscript from one of the surviving missionaries in Papua New Guinea.
14 Ibid.
15 Sister Theophane Maier, S.Sp.S., Personal Letter to Techny, Alexishafen, Papua New Guinea. Pentecost, 1937.

16 Ibid.
17 Ibid.
18 Ibid.
19 Ibid.
20 Ibid.
21 Sister Nazaria Albers, S.Sp.S., Report, Brisbane, Australia, January, 1945.
22 Sister Theophane Maier, S.Sp.S., Personal Letter to the Family, Alexis, New Guinea, November 21, 1938.
23 Ibid.
24 Ibid.
25 Ibid.
26 Ibid.
27 Unidentified manuscript from one of the surviving missionaries in Papua New Guinea.
28 Ibid.
29 Ibid.
30 Sister Theophane Maier, S.Sp.S., Personal Letter to Her Mother, Alexishafen, Papua New Guinea, July 29, 1936.

Chapter 11

1 Sister Theophane Maier, S.Sp.S., Personal Letter to Her Mother, Ulingan, Papua New Guinea, September 1, 1940.
2 Ibid.
3 Ibid.
4 Sister Theophane Maier, S.Sp.S., Personal Letter to Her Mother. Alexishafen, Papua New Guinea, February 27, 1938.
5 Sister Theophane Maier, S.Sp.S., Personal Letter to the Family. Alexishafen, Papua New Guinea, April 26, 1939.
6 Sister Theophane Maier, S.Sp.S., Personal Letter to Her Mother. Ulingan, Papua New Guinea, September 1, 1940.
7 Ibid.
8 Ibid.
9 Ibid.
10 Sister Theophane Maier, S.Sp.S., Personal Letter to Her Mother. Alexishafen, Papua New Guinea, October 26, 1941.

11 Sister Theophane Maier, S.Sp.S., Personal Letter to Her Mother. Ulingan, Papua New Guinea, September 1, 1940.
12 Sister Theophane Maier, S.Sp.S., Personal Letter to Her Mother. Ulingan, Papua New Guinea, April 20, 1941.
13 Sister Theophane Maier, S.Sp.S., Personal Letter to Rosalie. Ulingan, Papua New Guinea, March 3, 1940.
14 Ibid.
15 Sister Theophane Maier, S.Sp.S., Personal Letter to Her Mother. Ulingan, Papua New Guinea, September 1, 1940.
16 This incident is reconstructed from the combined report of Sister Theophane in a letter from Ulingan, September 1, 1940, and a report from Rev. Lawrence Mey, S.V.D., assistant missionary at Ulingan. His report came from Epping, Australia, December 26, 1944.
17 Sister Elreda Ruiter, S.Sp.S. Report. Epping, Australia. December, 1944. (Sister Elreda is one of the survivors from the Ulingan station.)
18 Sister Theophane Maier, S.Sp.S., Personal Letter to Rosalie. Ulingan, Papua New Guinea, March 3, 1940.
19 Sister Theophane Maier, S.Sp.S., Personal Letter to Her Mother. Ulingan, Papua New Guinea, January 21, 1941.
20 Ibid.
21 Ibid.
22 Ibid.
23 Ibid.
24 Ibid.
25 Ibid.
26 Sister Theophane Maier, S.Sp.S., Personal Letter to Techny. Ulingan, Papua New Guinea, April, 1941.
27 Sister Theophane Maier, S.Sp.S., Personal Letter to Her Mother. Ulingan, Papua New Guinea, April 20, 1941.
28 Rev. Lawrence Mey, S.V.D., op. cit.
29 Ibid.

Chapter 12

1 Sister Theophane Maier, S.Sp.S., Personal Letter to Her Mother, Alexishafen, New Guinea, October 26, 1941.
2 Ibid.
3 Sister Theophane Maier, S.Sp.S., Personal Letter to Techny, Alexishafen, Papua New Guinea, May 1, 1938.
4 This account is reconstructed from the following reports: Sister Theophane Maier, S.Sp.S., Personal Letter to Her Mother, Alexishafen, Papua New Guinea, February 27, 1938. Sister Theophane Maier, S.Sp.S., Personal Letter to Techny, Alexishafen, Papua New Guinea, May 1, 1938. Sister Elreda Ruiter, S.Sp.S., Report, Sidney, Australia, December, 1944.
5 Sister Theophane Maier, S.Sp.S., Personal Letter to Techny, Alexishafen, Papua New Guinea, June 21, 1936.
6 Ibid.
7 Brother Gerhoch, S.V.D. Report, Sidney, Australia, February, 1945 and Sister Theophane Maier, S.Sp.S., Personal Letter to Techny, Alexishafen, Papua New Guinea, January 9, 1938.
8 Sister Theophane Maier, S.Sp.S., Personal Letter to Rosalie, Alexis, Papua New Guinea, May 29, 1941.
9 Sister Theophane Maier, S.Sp.S., Personal Letter to Techny, Alexcishafen, Papua New Guinea, October 24, 1937.
10 Sister Theophane Maier, S.Sp.S., Letter to Techny, Alexishafen, Papua New Guinea, May 1, 1938.
11 Ibid.
12 Sister Theophane Maier, S.Sp.S., Personal Letter to Her Mother, Alexishafen, Papua New Guinea, July 29, 1936.
13 Sister Theophane Maier, S.Sp.S., Personal Letter to Rosalie, Alexis, Papua New Guinea, December 17, 1939.
14 Sister Theophane Maier, S.Sp.S., Personal Letter to Techny, Alexishafen, Papua New Guinea, August 20, 1939.
15 Sister Theophane Maier, S.Sp.S., Personal Letter to Her Mother, Alexishafen, Papua New Guinea, April 26, 1936.
16 Sister Theophane Maier, S.Sp.S., Personal Letter to Her Mother, Alexishafen, Papua New Guinea, January 9, 1938.
17 Sister Theophane Maier, S.Sp.S., Personal Letter to Techny,

Alexishafen, Papua New Guinea, October 18, 1936.

18 Sister Theophane Maier, S.Sp.S., Personal Letter to the Family, Alexishafen, New Guinea, November 21, 1938.

19 Sister Theophane Maier, S.Sp.S., Personal Letter to Her Mother, Alexishafen, Papua New Guinea, April 26, 1936.

20 Sister Theophane Maier, S.Sp.S., Personal Letter to Her Mother, Alexishafen, Papua New Guinea, July 30, 1939.

21 The rest of this chapter, unless otherwise specified, is taken from Sister Ottonia's (Sister Mary Elise) Report from Australia, 1945.

22 Sister Theophane Maier, S.Sp.S., Personal Letter to Techny, Alexishafen, Papua New Guinea, May 16, 1937.

23 Sister Nazaria Albers, S.Sp.S., Report, Brisbane, Australia, December 1944.

Chapter 13

1 Sister Elreda Ruiter, S.Sp.S., Report, Brisbane, Australia, December 1944.

2 Ibid.

3 Sister Siglinde Poboss, S.Sp.S., "My Captivity Experiences 1943-1944," a detailed report prepared "Somewhere in Australia" for the Mother General of the Congregation, November 18, 1944.

4 Rev. Lawrence Mey, S.V.D., Report, Sidney, Australia, December 1944.

5 Sister Ottonia Ruholl (Sister Mary Elise), S.Sp.S. Personal Letter, Queensland, Australia, July 30, 1944.

6 Rev. Ewald Van Barr, S.V.D., Report, Sidney, Australia, January 1945.

7 Ibid.

8 Sister Ottonia Ruholl (Sister Mary Elise), S.Sp.S., op. cit.

9 Sister Ottonia Ruholl (Sister Mary Elise), S.Sp.S., Report on Manam, Queensland, Australia, February 18, 1945.

10 Rev. Lawrence Mey, S.V.D., op cit.

11 In the middle of August, 1943 the Japanese had transferred all the missionaries from Manam Island, Ulingan, and Bogia to the internment camp just outside the Mission Compound at Bogia.

12 Sister Ottonia Ruholl (Sister Mary Elise), S.Sp.S., Report, Queensland, Australia, July 30, 1944.
13 Sister Elreda Ruiter, S.Sp.S., op, cit.
14 Sister Ottonia Ruholl (Sister Mary Elise), S.Sp.S., Report on Manam, Queensland, Australia, February 18, 1945.
15 Ibid.
16 Ibid.
17 Sister Siglinde Poboss, S.Sp.S., Note on Manam, Sidney, Australia, June 1945.
18 Sister Ottonia Ruholl (Sister Mary Elise), S.Sp.S., Personal Letter, Queensland, Australia, February 18, 1945.
19 Sister Siglinde Poboss, S.Sp.S. op cit.
20 Sister Ottonia Ruholl (Sister Mary Elise), S.Sp.S., Personal Letter, Queensland, Australia, June 30, 1944.
21 Sister Siglinde Poboss, S.Sp.S., op. cit.

Chapter 14

1 This account of the voyage is reconstructed from the eyewitness accounts of Sister Ottonia SSpS, Sister Theophane's close friend; a Catholic priest, Father John Tschauder SVD; and Reverend Dr. Gerhard Reitz, a Lutheran missionary.
2 From eyewitness account of Father John Tschauder, SVD.
3 Ibid.

Chapter 15

1 The exact location of the mass grave remains unknown to this day. Sister Katherine Mair S.Sp.S., presently located in Wewak, has suggested the location as between the hotel and the Post Office based on her research. Fr. Joseph Maciolek, S.V.D., located in Port Moresby, has suggested the location at or near St. Mary's primary school, based on his research.

ACKNOWLEDGMENTS

Although I have shepherded this work into print, the entire effort would have been simply impossible had it not been for the input and support of so many.

I must first thank the Missionary Sisters Servants of the Holy Spirit for so many gifts and kindnesses. The order initially gave Sr. Theophane a home in Papua New Guinea, the perfect place for her to practice her natural skills, and to allow her zeal for the Catholic missions to explode into full bloom. This in turn inspired her fellow nun, Sr. Immolata Reida, to invest years in researching and writing her life story, the heart of the present work. Finally, the present Leader of the U.S. Province, Sr. Carol Welp, and her archivist, Sr. Anita Marie Gutierrez have been fully supportive of my efforts to bring this work to publication, providing priceless photographs as well as textual advice and guidance.

Special thanks also to my faithful secretary, Susie Hockaday, who worked tirelessly and with great enthusiasm to support my editorial efforts, and especially to place the original hard copy of the work into a modern electronic format.

My dear wife Sue Maier deserves great credit for her continual encouragement and support as I struggled at times to complete a final edited draft of the work. She merits special thanks for conceiving the one-word title of the work, which so eloquently captures the full spirit of the biography in a single word.

Finally, I thank my children and grandchildren for motivating me to pass on to them this powerful story so steeped in the Catholic faith. Thanks to Erin and Jeff Dausch and their children Zach, John Paul, Mary Kate, Charlie and Timmy; Beth and Tim Maier and their children Matthew and Megan; and Jeanine and Chris Maier and their son Jack. My most sincere hope is that all of them will be inspired by this powerful biography, and keep it alive as a part of our family tradition.

I also remember my deceased parents, Alma and Raymond, as well as my brothers Steve (now deceased) and JB (who took Theophane as his confirmation name) and my late aunt, Sr. Rosalie, SSJ (who collected Sr. Theophane's letters from Papua New Guinea, and had them published), all of whom revered Sr. Theophane and made sure that the remarkable story of her life was passed on to me.